The
𝕎illis 𝔉amily

OF THE
NORTHERN NECK
IN
VIRGINIA

1669-1737

Peggy Frances Rush

HERITAGE BOOKS
2007

HERITAGE BOOKS

AN IMPRINT OF HERITAGE BOOKS, INC.

Books, CDs, and more—Worldwide

For our listing of thousands of titles see our website
at
www.HeritageBooks.com

Published 2007 by
HERITAGE BOOKS, INC.
Publishing Division
65 East Main Street
Westminster, Maryland 21157-5026

International Standard Book Number: 978-0-7884-0832-8

Contents

Acknowledgments

This family history represents fourteen years of research and would not have been accomplished except for the assistance and support of several people.

In 1983 Margaret Schroeder, a friend and genealogist in Bardstown, Kentucky, now deceased, gave me the name of George B. Loeffler of Phoenix, Arizona, also now deceased. With Mr. Loeffler's guidance and his articles about the Willis family, I began to explore the records. As of this writing I have reviewed approximately eighty rolls of microfilm at the local LDS Family History Center and many books and articles in an effort to learn more about this family's roots on the Northern Neck.

Merrill Hill Mosher, C.G., of Coos Bay, Oregon, patiently led me through the complexities of land patents and grants, headrights, the law of primogeniture, and early changes in county and parish lines in the Northern Neck. She also helped me read and interpret some of the original patents, grants, and deeds which are cited below. Without her help and advice, this story would never have developed to its present depth and breadth.

In addition, I want to express my appreciation to Ruth and Sam Sparacio of The Antient Press and to John Frederick Dorman for their excellent transcriptions and abstracts of the old county record books. Their work, as well as that of George H. S. King, greatly facilitated my research.

In October 1993 I began corresponding with another family researcher, Newman Arnold Hall. Because he has added so much to my knowledge of the Hudson, Arnold, and allied families on the Northern Neck and shares my passionate interest in a grandmother named *Sarah*, this book is dedicated to him.

Finally, my gratitude to Patricia J. Hurst of Rapidan and Ann L. Miller of Madison for their marvelous tour in 1990 of the Rapidan River area where many of John Willis Sr.'s descendants lived after their migration from King George County; to Mrs. Elizabeth Womeldorf, the present owner of "Locust Grove," the Willis family home on the Rapidan River, for her gracious hospitality; and to my aunt Leona Willis Stage and my cousin Keith Byrd Willis and his wife, Helen, for their encouragement.

Without the contributions of all these people and other friends, my history of the Willis family would never have been written. They not only helped to make it possible, but each in his or her own way made my quest a journey to be remembered and cherished.

Reference chart for Willis families reviewed in this manuscript
(Direct descendants given in boldface.)

John Willis Sr.
d. 1715 Richmond Co.

: (1) John Willis Jr. d. 1728 King George Co. (Chapter V)
:   m. Mary Coghill who m. 2nd John Jennings;
:   d. 1748 King George Co.
:   No surviving issue

: (2) **William Willis** d. 1716 Richmond Co. (Chapters VI and IX)*
:   m. Sarah (—) who m. 2nd Henry Wood, 3rd Rush Hudson,
:   4th Edward Turberville;
:   d. 1760–1761 Orange Co.
:   Sons **John Willis** and William Willis
:   Daughter Sarah Willis (see note)

: (3) Charles Willis d. by 1725 King George Co. (Chapter VII)
:   m. Matilda (Thacker?)
:   Known son John Willis

: (4) Mary Willis d. by 1742 (Chapter VIII)
:   m. Thomas James
:   Known sons David James and William James

: (5) Susannah Willis d. after 1715; no further record

Others (relationship to the family of John Willis Sr. unknown)

James Willis d. 1655 Northumberland County
    m. Rachell (Chapter XI)

John Willis b. *circa* 1617, d. 1682 Westmoreland County
    (Chapter X)

William Willis d. 1713–1714 Westmoreland County
    m. Bridgett (Robinson?) who d. 1717 Westmoreland County
    (Chapter X)

William Willis d. 1720 Westmoreland County
    m. Mary (—) Offile, the widow of William Offile
    (Chapter X)

Col. Francis Willis d. 1689–1691 England
    m. Jane (—)
    (Chapter XII)

Col. Henry Willis d. 1740 Spotsylvania County
    m. three times
    (Chapter XIII)

*See page 222 for the descendants of William Willis (d. 1716) and Sarah (—?—).

Introduction

Traditionally, there have been important similarities and differences between a genealogist and a family historian. While both searched records and gathered information, the primary goal of the genealogist was to prove a person's lineage or descendants. The goal of the historian was to tell the story of a particular family in order to preserve that family's history. In recent times, however, the differences have narrowed, and the final product has become more than a lineage chart on the one hand or an anthology of personal recollections on the other hand. The rewards of sharing the strengths of each approach have resulted in personal, yet credible, accounts which go beyond dates to portray the everyday lives of people.

The resources which genealogists and family historians use include both public and private information. Public records range from court records and censuses to land records, estate files, vital statistics, cemetery records, and other documents which are generally available for public examination. Private records include family bibles, diaries, letters, personal interviews, family stories passed on from one generation to the next, and pictures. Distinctions between the two types of records vary and are not as important as the validity of the record itself. Either type may provide new insights about the family which the researcher or historian is attempting to trace or to describe.

This is neither a novel nor a compilation of family group sheets for the descendants of John Willis Sr. My original goal was to create a factual, historical account of his life and his known family based on extant documents, and I hope that element has been preserved.

However, during the twelve years in which I have been researching the Willis family, I made an important discovery. In order for the records to become living documents which tell a story about real people, I had to learn how to interact with the facts, because without that interaction the records were merely a collection of impersonal names and numbers. Novelist Wallace Stegner defines this process eloquently by saying that it is only with the reader's participation that history becomes what he calls "a usable human memory." He describes this phenomenon as follows:

> *Like any other part of the human tradition, history is an artifact. It does not exist until it is remembered and written down; and it is not truly remembered or written down until it has been vividly imagined. We become our past, and it becomes part of us, by our reliving of our beginnings.* [1]

So, for me, what began as a search to find one family evolved into a quest to understand more about my ancestors as part of a community which no longer exists except in the records and the past. Questions began to spring from a sentence or paragraph or name in a document, taking me beyond the bare facts and luring me in

---

[1] Wallace Stegner, foreword to *The Big Sky* by A. B. Guthrie Jr. (New York: Bantam Books, 1976).

new directions. While some answers were found, many were not. But the magic is still there because I learned how to imagine.

The theme of community is obvious throughout this manuscript. The Introduction has been expanded to discuss living conditions on the Northern Neck during the colonial period. Several sketches of neighboring families have been incorporated into the text. While some of this information may seem superfluous at first reading, it may be valuable to future researchers. Personally, I decided that I could not omit those friends and neighbors from my story because they were a living part of my family's history.

When I started to review records which were nearly three hundred and fifty years old, I was immediately faced with several problems. First was the poor readability of some of the records because of condition, archaic language, and obsolete spelling. Second, my lack of understanding of the prevailing legal system (especially as it related to patents, deeds, and primogeniture) and social customs made it difficult for me to analyze the documents after deciphering them. Third, although the records suggest that the Willis family originated in the British Isles, I knew very little about conditions in England in the 1600s which might have motivated my ancestors to migrate to the colonies. A final hurdle was understanding the calendar which was used at that time when the new year began on March 25th so that I could compile the records chronologically. Because I assume that others may be faced with similar problems when they try to make sense out of these old documents, I will share some of the insights which were acquired during my research in order to make this story more understandable and enjoyable—or, in current parlance, more reader-friendly. Both my comments on these topics and my interpretation of the records in this manuscript are always open for correction.

Nothing can be done about the condition of old documents, but we can certainly be thankful that they exist at all as they are basically our only recorded link to the past. The language or vocabulary problems were only partially resolved during my research, and I still do not understand the purpose of many items in estate inventories which were filled with clues to our ancestors' daily lives.

Although the records were in English, it was a form which was closer in both spelling and usage to Shakespeare than to our current language. Many of the words were not only spelled differently, but they had meanings which differed from the way in which we use those words today. While I modernized the spelling and added punctuation in later records, I left the will of John Willis Sr. and some of his deeds as they were in the originals so that the reader could get a flavor of the documents as they were written.

Many of the early names for rivers and streams are unknown or forgotten, and the records can be painfully slow in revealing their secrets. Poultridges Creek was found with many different spellings, but the records prove that it was the same stream or watershed regardless of the way it was spelled by different people at different times. Some were first called by their now extinct Indian Names (*cf.* Comistank and Weequionedike in Indian Ned's 1665 patent below). To my knowledge historians still have not found the first name for Jett's Creek or Bristol Mines Run. Often it was only by cross-referencing the data from one document to another that a correlation could be verified.

Another problem relating to names was the fact that several men of the same name could be living in a given county at a given time. It was a common practice for families to name children for their parents, grandparents, and other family members, and the Willis family was no exception. In 1715 there were four males in Richmond County by the name of John Willis. John Sr. died in 1715. His son John Jr. was an adult in 1715 and died in 1728, and two of John Sr.'s grandsons were still minors in 1715. This problem increases with each generation, and the researcher must carefully examine each record and clue to properly identify the person.

The second hurdle involved trying to understand some of the laws and customs by which our ancestors lived on a daily basis. While I do not claim to be an authority on the laws of colonial Virginia, my research has made me aware of certain concepts and legal practices which were very important when interpreting the documents and which I offer in this brief overview. I learned how the County Court, under the aegis of the established church, set the bounds for acceptable social behavior and the nature of penalties which were designed to keep the church–state "harmless," or not liable for damages which might have to be paid from its coffers.

The headright system was instituted to encourage settlement. Men (or widows in the right of their deceased husbands and orphans in the right of their deceased fathers) were entitled to fifty acres of land for each person whom they transported at their own expense to the colonies. In the Northern Neck the land certificates which they received (called "patents" until 1690, then "grants") were negotiable instruments and could be sold or assigned to another person, making it difficult to trace some of the tracts, especially if county records have been lost. The system was designed to be beneficial to both the immigrants and to the Crown. Without it many landowners who had patented hundreds of acres would not have been able to fulfill the seating requirements. Lacking money to pay for their passage, others would not have been able to immigrate. And England would not have had the settlers to defend the Crown's claims in the New World which would have significantly changed the country's development.

The appearance of a person's name as a headright does not prove that he or she was an indenture because many of the headright lists included names of extended families who immigrated together. Researchers frequently use immigration records and the names of headrights on early patents to search for ancestors. In the case of the Willis family I did not find this approach particularly helpful. Many people with the surname *Willis* were found in the early records, but I could not prove any direct relationship between them and John Willis Sr. However, I have cited some of the most promising entries in Chapter XI because circumstantial evidence suggests that one of those men may have been his father.

Few parish records exist from the 1600s on the Northern Neck. Consequently, most of my time was spent reading county records such as County Court orders or minutes, wills and estate administrations, and deeds. I had the most success reviewing land records, original patents or grants, and later deeds and wills.

The promise of land was obviously a powerful factor in immigration. The best land lay on a stream which provided water for the family and its livestock, in a watershed which contained good soil and moisture for growing crops, and had ample timber which was used to build houses and boats. Many wills and leases contain references to timber and might admonish the legatee or lessee not to "embezzel" (waste or sell) the valuable trees beyond what was "needfel."[2] Later timber became very important in the smelting of ore.

Land acquisition also had its cost. Patentees assumed both dangers and conditions when they "took up" new land. They had to protect their families and survive with the bare essentials while they were in the process of clearing and seating their tracts which could take years of back-breaking work. Food crops had to be raised, and reliable commercial links had to be established with outside markets for their products as well as for resupply of things which they could not yet produce. Owners of land or indentured servants (and later, slaves) were assessed for the support of the County Court, the church glebe (farmland provided to the clergymen), and other state-provided services such as ferries. These assessments or levies were called *tithes*. In 1664 there were 609 (or 614) tithables in Westmoreland County.[3]

Livestock were another form of taxable wealth, but acquisition of good breeding stock was a slow and costly process. Often a man would give a cow or calf to a nephew, niece, or grandchild when he or she was born, and the deed was recorded with the Clerk of Court. Stock marks were also registered. Settlers were supposed to keep the ears of an animal when it was butchered to prove that the animal was, in fact, theirs and not their neighbor's livestock running loose in the woods — an occurrence which resulted in several law suits. Horse racing was a popular sport; betting was allowed, and the loser could be taken to court if he failed to pay off his wager.

For most people, travel by horse, foot, or boat was the only means of transportation on the Northern Neck in the 1600s. Roads are seldom mentioned in early deeds, and wagons were not listed in estate inventories for many years. Eventually settlements, churches, and courthouses were built near rivers or streams which were the interstate highways of the time. No bridges existed, and because the Neck was long and narrow, contained many creeks and streams, and was bounded by two great rivers, its inhabitants were somewhat isolated. Consequently, ferries became so important to developing communities commercially, politically, and socially that they were funded by the County Court. As settlement increased and crude roads were built, inns called *ordinaries* sprang up every five or six miles along well-traveled routes as the forerunners of today's bed and breakfast establishments.

One misconception which I personally had to change related to the demographics of

---

[2] See John Willis Sr.'s will in Chapter I.

[3] John Frederick Dorman, *Westmoreland County, Virginia, Records 1661–1664* (Washington, D. C.: author, 1972).

the early colonists. Rather than congregating together in towns, the settlers were initially rural dwellers, each (with a few related families) establishing his own settlement on his own land. By contrast, the native Indians were urban dwellers who lived together in villages and considered the surrounding land as open territory to be hunted freely by everyone. The differences between the two groups regarding the concept of land ownership significantly affected the entire westering movement. For purposes of this manuscript the fact that communities were often a matter of kinship and were located in rural areas is very important in understanding the decisions people made, their opportunities for socializing, and their choices of marriage partners—the last often being a matter of age and proximity.

Each landowner, perhaps with help from a neighbor or relative, was his own blacksmith, cooper, carpenter, and boatbuilder. (A canoe was as important to the colonist as a vehicle is to us.) As the plantation system arose, larger landowners might employ a craftsman or use indentured servants to provide those services. In fact, skilled craftsmen in England were often sought by plantation owners who for the cost of the indenture's passage provided the owner with another fifty acres of land through the headright system and a skilled worker for several years. Upon fulfilling their indentures, many of these craftsmen would become what we now call *entrepreneurs* their communities.

The Northern Neck was criss-crossed by many streams, and Court records contain petitions of men who wanted to build mills on their land. If a family later leased or sold a mill, it was often with the stipulation that it would continue to get its grain processed either free or at a reduced cost. Mining was also practiced, first by individual landholders and later by companies, some of which were local and others which were foreign. Items such as nails were quite valuable because they were a scarce commodity, and the records show that more than one man was taken to Court because he was accused of stealing them. One of the items which John Willis Sr. bequeathed to his son Charles in 1715 was "three thousand nayles [*sic*] or thereabouts being all the nayles that I have in my house."

The merchant class rose quickly in the colonies because the settlers needed supplies from England and an outside market for their goods. Small general stores were scattered around the countryside. Daniel Hutt, a merchant on Herring Creek in Westmoreland County, was fined for selling firearms to the natives. John Foxhall, an early neighbor to the Willises, was a local merchant, and the Washingtons and Popes, also neighbors, were active in trans-Atlantic trade. As can be expected, there was a significant amount of risk, however, because ships frequently sank with loss of life and cargo.

If a man was fortunate and lived to be sixty, he was relieved of his levy by the Court due to age. He was expected to serve on juries and, during Indian uprisings, provide a man (either himself, a hireling, or a servant) and arms to protect the settlers and, much later, to help build "rolling roads" which were little more than trails through the brush over which people would literally roll their hogsheads of tobacco to a warehouse where the crop was inspected and counted. The planter would then be given a receipt which he used as cash. For many years tobacco was the medium of exchange, whether it was for purchasing land or merchandise, paying tithes and levies, or making bequests in wills. Hard cash was rare.

Titles used in the records such as *Planter* and *Mr.* had different meanings in different areas or times. In general, the term *Planter* identified the man as a landowner, and *Mr.* was an honorific title which signified a certain standing in the community. Likewise, the use of the term *Mrs.* was often used to indicate that a woman (whether single, married, or widowed) had social status.

Once established, parishes covered vast, sparsely populated areas. There were few licensed ministers who were designated in documents as a clerk (*i.e.*, clergyman)—not to be confused with the Clerk of the County Court. Church attendance at least once a month was obligatory (when enforced), and the County Order Books frequently note fines for non-attendance. Considering the distances families often had to travel to attend services, it is surprising that more fines were not mentioned. Only later were dissident groups like the Quakers exempted from fines for non-attendance and legally allowed to hold services in their own meeting houses on the Northern Neck. Some of the Quakers, like William Duff of King George County (who began as a tailor), became very wealthy men and large landowners.

Often a husband or wife died young, leaving a spouse and small children. Again both the laws and customs were designed to keep the Crown, church, and community from expense. There was little need for welfare reform in the colonies although there was an abundance of what we would see as poverty. This helps to explain the fact that both men and women who lost their spouses tended to remarry quickly. It also gives us a better understanding of the practice of "binding out orphans" which will be discussed below.

If a man died testate, his will was supposed to be produced in the next Court session following his decease, and witnesses to the will were required to appear in Court to prove the testator's signature. When a man died intestate (without leaving a will), his widow or another close relative would petition the Court for permission to administer his estate. A will was executed by an executor (or co-executors if more than one) who was named by the deceased in his or her will. If a designated executor refused to serve, the Court could appoint an administrator and attach the will to the Letters of Administration. An intestate estate was administered by an administrator who was appointed by the Court. In both cases a performance bond was required from the executor(s) or administrator(s) as security and was often provided by a close relative or someone who had an interest in the estate.

The Court would then appoint three or four men, usually neighbors, to inventory and appraise the deceased's estate. Some inventories were only a few lines long; others covered several pages. Few estate settlements are found in the early records. As will be seen below, estates could become embedded in previous, unsettled estates, and probate might continue for many years.

A man could dispose of any property which he owned in fee simple by either deed or will prior to his death, but under the prevailing practice of primogeniture he could not totally disinherit his eldest son who was his legal heir-at-law. (John Willis Sr. had already deeded land to his two eldest sons, so neither was given land in his will.) The eldest son or heir-at-law might also never be mentioned in the will, but he was entitled to his share of the personal estate and any real property which his father did not mention in his will or which the father owned *entail*.[4]

Confusion in interpreting early deeds involving *entail* and *fee tail* (or fee simple) can be a result of not knowing what language to look for. According to personal correspondence with Merrill Hill Mosher, C. G. (and to whom I owe so much for her advice), the words "to—and the heirs of his body lawfully begotten" entailed land to that devisee, making it impossible for the devisee to sell or deed during his lifetime without legislative action. The words "to his heirs and assigns forever" denoted a transfer of title in fee simple, and the devisee could sell or will it to anyone he chose. The practice of primogeniture and entail varied from region to region in colonial America, and it was abolished in 1776. It played an important part in proving that John Willis of Orange County was the grandson of John Willis Sr. who died in 1715 in Richmond/King George County.

John Willis Sr. owned all of his land in fee simple and therefore could dispose of it as he wished. When he deeded to his sons John Jr. and William before his death, he entailed the land and gave their future wives lifetime occupancy rights. This provision was quite unusual because John did not stipulate that their wives would lose their occupancy rights should they be widowed and remarry. John Sr.'s second eldest son, William, died intestate in 1716 at which time William's eldest son, John, became his (William's) legal heir-at-law. When John Willis Jr. died in 1728 without surviving issue (commonly seen as *d.s.p.*[5] in the records), the entailed land which his father had deeded to him in 1694 automatically became the property of his nephew John Willis (his brother William's son) because he was the eldest son of John Sr.'s second eldest son. However, both Mary Coghill Willis (the widow of John Willis Jr.) and Sarah (the widow of William Willis and the wife of Rush Hudson in 1728) still held life occupancy rights to his grandfather's first patent. Those rights were addressed in the deeds from John to the Church Wardens and his mother's release in 1737.

Women had few legal rights, could not vote, and did not serve on juries. They could be witnesses to deeds and wills, as could minors. If married, they could not own land or make wills (although rare exceptions were found to the latter and usually denoted a certain social position and involved property from a former husband's estate which was to be passed to his children). Consequently, it is not surprising that we know so little about the women who lived in the colonies in the 1600s, and the loss of the mother's family name results in the loss of one-half of a family's history from that

---

[4]John Frederick Dorman, *Colonial Laws of Primogeniture* (paper read at the World Conference on Records and Genealogical Seminar at Salt Lake City, Utah, August, 1969).

[5]Latin for *decessit sine prole*, or died without issue (not necessarily a single person, although that may have been the case).

moment backwards. A review of the indexes of the old county record books quickly shows the frequency in which a man's name is found in the documents as compared with his mother's, wife's, or daughters' names.

A classic example of the status which some women held is found in a 1676 Westmoreland County will which Oliver Griffin wrote when he was about to take a trip to England.[6] He left everything to his wife, Elizabeth, and *her* son, Francis Griffin, but with explicit conditions. Elizabeth was not to "misdemean herself" contrary to Oliver's will and was not to "absent herself from my house day or night." Oliver set aside a tract on the river which would go to any informant who could prove that Elizabeth had broken any of the articles of the will. Oliver further stipulated that (in case of his death) if Elizabeth should marry "any persons that hath not the value of 10,000 pounds of tobacco or any scandolous [*sic*] rogue," his estate would be given to the Upper Church of Copeley [Cople] Parish except for the 100 acres and "my part of earthen waire" which was to go to the captain of the sloope on which Oliver was traveling (perhaps as security for his passage). If Elizabeth complied with the terms of the will and Oliver died at sea, she would receive all of his estate until Francis was of age when Elizabeth would receive her thirds and Francis would receive his land and the rest of his estate. Sometimes the records speak volumes about family relationships on the frontier.

Girls traditionally married young and faced hardships, but even after marriage they usually lived close to other family members for support during critical times. Dower might be paid by the girl's father in the form of land or livestock when she married if her family was able to pay. Frequently a daughter who had received her dower at the time of her marriage would not be named later in her father's will, or he would leave her only a share of his personal estate and say that she had already received her share. Infrequently documents are found in the old files showing that a couple had agreed to live separately, but divorce was virtually nonexistent and granted only by the Colonial Assembly.

Although officially discouraged by the established church, marriages between cousins in the colonies were acceptable, especially if they were of second or greater degree, and many such cases are found in the records. These intermarriages were due in part to the small number of people on the frontier and the lack of social interaction with other groups because of isolation. On Mattox Creek, for example, many landowners were related to each other in several ways and by varying degrees.

Because of early deaths, it was not unusual for a man or a woman to have three or four different spouses during his or her lifetime. Two instances were found showing that a woman had married five times. In such cases the task of unraveling and sorting the families can be formidable.

Adding to the confusion was the fact that degrees of kinship were frequently called

---

[6]John Frederick Dorman, *Westmoreland County, Virginia, Deeds, Patents, etc. 1665–1677*, Part three (Washington, D. C.: author, 1974), p. 68. Hereafter called Dorman.

something quite different from our current system. For example, *son* might mean son or stepson. *Brother* could mean brother, stepbrother, half-brother, or a stepmother's or stepfather's son who was not related biologically, but through the extended family. The same applied to daughters and sisters. The term *in–law* can be particularly confusing because it often meant a *step* relationship (*cf. mother–in–law* for stepmother or *son–in–law* for stepson). The terms *niece* and *nephew* usually referred to younger relatives (even grandchildren). The word *cousin* commonly denoted a nephew and niece, first cousin, second cousin, etc., and again might be unrelated lineally. Usage depended largely upon the particular family and accepted practices in that community. This difference in usage can be very important when interpreting the records, and a good example is given in Chapter IV involving the Underwood and Combs families.

Life in the settlements was demanding, and options, limited. Occasionally a woman who had left position and family in England would eventually return home—perhaps overtly to visit relatives, but never to return. Based upon some things I have read, I suspect that this happened with men, too.[7] It is not illogical to suspect that occasionally a man who was very unhappy with his situation, whether it be due to marital incompatibility or financial problems, might find a ship's captain who would attest to his death en route and so that he could create a new life in some distant place.

Except for some of the wealthier landowners, the concept of aristocracy was not a part of the immigrant's daily life, and refinements were few. For most, the frontier was the great leveler. Even the Washingtons, who owned much land and served in the militia and county offices, were not considered as part of the ruling class because they weren't aggressive enough according to one biographer. Thomas Pope, son of the immigrant Nathaniel Pope Sr. and brother-in-law of John Washington (the President's great-grandfather), was one of the Mattox Creek landowners who returned to England where he married and settled down in Bristol as a merchant. Mildred Warner Washington, the widow of Lawrence Washington who died in 1698 and grandmother of the President, remarried and took her children back to England where she died.[8]

As the settlements grew, conditions improved generally. If women belonged to the middle or upper class, they might have servants to help them with household chores. Their homes could contain a few, cherished articles which they or their ancestors had brought from Europe or which their husbands had purchased from one of the ships which supplied the settlements, but most homes were meagerly stocked compared to contemporary standards. Homespun cloth was generally of the coarser variety, and in 1693 an Act was passed which awarded prizes for the manufacture of good linen. John Willis Sr.'s estate inventory listed an unusually large amount of sheeting, linen, cambridge (cambric), dimity, and flannel. It may be that John held these items for resale, but that is another question which remains unanswered.

A wife's name rarely appeared on a deed when her husband purchased land, the

---

[7] For an example see Ruth and Sam Sparacio, *Deed Abstracts of (Old) Rappahannock County, Virginia, 1668–1670* (McLean, VA: Antient Press, 1989), p. 35. Hereafter called Sparacio.

[8] See Chapter IV.

exception being if the grantor was her father, grandfather, or uncle. When her husband sold land, she might cosign the deed. By law she was supposed to be "examined" separately from her husband at which time she would acknowledge her release of dower rights, but that practice was not always followed. It seems the Court did not always place high priority on obtaining women's releases. Sometimes people would give a man (not a woman unless she was unmarried or a widow, and even that was a rare occurrence) their Power of Attorney to acknowledge a deed in Court. Occasionally a woman would witness a will, but it was unusual for a woman's name to be found as a witness on a deed until the late 1600s or early 1700s.

Frequently both women and men signed documents with their "mark," suggesting that they did not read or write. On the other hand, several inventories listed books and reading glasses.

Although a single woman or a widow could receive land by will or deed, her property became her husband's upon her marriage or remarriage, including any legacy from a prior husband's estate unless circumvented by a prenuptial agreement. Examples will be found in Chapter XI when James Willis left all of his land to his wife Rachel in 1655, in Chapter IV when William Freake left his land to his wife Martha in 1684/85, and in Chapter I when John Willis Sr. signed a prenuptial deed of gift to his last wife, Matilda Thacker, before their marriage in 1693.

A woman could contest her husband's will if he gave her less than her statutory dower rights, but she had no claim on her husband's land if he had a surviving son unless the husband specifically willed it to her. More commonly, the husband gave his wife occupancy rights until she remarried or until her death at which time the land reverted to his heirs.

Minor children without inheritances and orphaned by the death of their fathers were often "bound out" or apprenticed to learn a trade until they became adult—a method of keeping children from becoming dependents of the County Court and the established church. If orphans were heirs to estates, they were furnished with a legal guardian or trustee to administer the estate until he or she became an adult. The Court normally appointed a guardian if the child was under the age of fourteen. Above that age the orphan could petition the Court to have a specific person named as his or her guardian. As noted in Chapter VII, John Willis, orphan of Charles and grandson of John Willis Sr., was at least fourteen when his father died, and he petitioned the Court to appoint his uncle (John Willis Jr.) as his guardian. After John Willis Jr. died, his nephew again petitioned the Court for Thomas Goffe to be his guardian. So in spite of the loss of parish records, it can be assumed that John Willis, son of Charles, was born sometime between 1707/08 and 1710—a birthdate previously ascribed by family historians to his first cousin John (son of William) who migrated to Orange County.

In some cases a mother was very astute in protecting her children's inheritances. In 1675 Mary (Lisson?) Pope Bridges, the widow of Nathaniel Pope Jr., deeded her personal property to her underage son Nathaniel Pope *alias Bridges* in Washington County and appointed a local clergyman as his trustee before she remarried. When

Mary was widowed a third time in 1677, she deeded to her two sons, Nathaniel Pope alias Bridges and Lewis Nicholas, and named her kinsman David Whitlife as trustee. Whitlife (or Wickliffe) in turn assumed the trusteeship, agreed to teach the boys to read and write, and gave Mary permission "at her owne pleasure to remove the children to the care of whome shee pleaseth" at her discretion, adding a note in the record that there was no intention of marriage between Mary and himself—which, of course, would have been the first thing that neighbors would assume under the circumstances. (In fact, it appears that Whitlife/Wickliffe did later marry the widow as will be noted in Chapter IV.)

A family's life revolved within approved boundaries—the land, rituals of birth, marriage, and death, the family, County Court sessions, and church. Deviations from those boundaries were dealt with, sometimes severely. The more serious offenses handled locally involved land disputes, cattle theft, slander, trespass, and runaway servants or slaves.

If a child was born out of wedlock (which, according to the records, happened frequently), the Court tried to learn the name of the father so that he could be fined—500 pounds of tobacco being the customary rate—again to keep the Court harmless. If the woman was an indentured servant, her time of indenture to her master was extended for the inconvenience and loss of labor caused by her pregnancy. In addition, the child could be bound out, presumably after he or she was weaned, until the child reached legal age.

When someone died of unknown causes, a jury of twelve local men was impaneled to determine the cause of death, much like a coroner's jury today. However, if the jury found that the person had died by suicide, he or she was buried at a busy crossroads with a stake through the body because suicide was considered to be a sin and a felony.[9] If the jury found that death was the result of an accident or "an act of the Devil," proper burial was allowed.

Various County Court records also provide a few insights into relations with the Indians. In 1677 the Westmoreland County Court took lengthy affidavits regarding both the murder of five Indians at the "Susquehannock fortt [sic]" in Maryland and about prisoners who had been taken in "Backen's" [Bacon's] Rebellion.[10] Norris's history of Westmoreland County also describes Indian settlements on the Northern Neck.[11]

Alcoholic spirits were made and used in the colonies, and they were apparently expected at wakes and estate sales. Conversely, a man could be fined for making or

---

[9] Dorman, *Westmoreland County, Virginia, Records 1658–1661* (Washington, D. C.: author, 1970), p. 85.

[10] Dorman, *Westmoreland County, Virginia, Deeds, Patents, etc., 1665–1677*, Part three (1974), pp. 35 and 72.

[11] Walter Biscoe Norris Jr., *Westmoreland County, Virginia, 1653–1983* (Montross, VA: Westmoreland County Board of Supervisors, 1983).

selling spirits on Sunday, and the Court recorded the names of those who were fined for imbibing too heavily.

When the Northern Neck was first settled, there were many indentured servants who bought their passage to the colonies by paying for it with several years of labor. The length of the indenture varied depending upon the agreement which they made with the person who paid for their passage. Much has been written about deported convicts and men from debtors' prisons being shipped from England to the colonies, and that undoubtedly occurred. Probably a majority of the immigrants, however, were political or religious dissidents, landless sons and daughters, and men who were described as "adventurers."

Most indentured males performed general labor in the fields, and females became domestics in the home. Some men were placed on patented tracts to clear timber, plant a crop, and build a small house so that the patentee would not lose his land to escheat. Others were hired out by the owner and were called "hirelings" in estate inventories, or they were used as laborers on ferries. As mining developed, servants were also used in mining and processing of ore. Indentures were counted as tithables, so the men who held their papers had to pay an annual levy on them. If a man concealed the name of a tithable and was found out or reported by a neighbor, he was fined by the County Court (see Chapter VI).

Although the law was not uniformly enforced, indentured servants had certain basic protections. If mistreated, they could appeal to the Court without fee or monetary reward. If the master was found guilty of inhumane treatment, the servant could be taken from him and placed with a new master. At the end of the indenture period, the servant became a free and full citizen.

Servants who had specific talents such as (black)smithery or carpentry were valuable additions to plantations and after their term of indenture might open their own businesses or remain on the same plantation with pay or other compensation. Some learned the principles of land acquisition from their masters and eventually became substantial landowners themselves. Occasionally an Indian would indenture himself to a settler or a merchant in order to learn a trade or to travel to England on the merchant's ship. Sometimes a settler would voluntarily bind a son to a ship captain or shipwright to learn the profession in hopes that the son might become a captain or shipbuilder when he was an adult.

Slaves were noted in a few of the early patents in the 1650s and the records of the Northern Neck in the 1660s, but slavery was not common until the turn of the century. It was interesting to note that slaves could be counted as headrights for the purpose of obtaining patents even though there was no contract as there was with indentures, and they certainly had nothing to gain from their importation. Indentures were identified on headright lists by their full names. Slaves were shown by their first names (*i.e.*, "Evan" or "Evan Negro") or they might be nameless and merely included in a group of several slaves.

Two distinctly different legal codes were applied to indentured servants and to slaves. If indentured servants attempted to run away, they were punished and their time of servitude was extended; but after their servitude they were freemen with equal access to the law. Based upon accounts in the records, punishment of runaway slaves was more stringent and often brutal by contemporary standards. They had no legal status, individual rights, or recourse, and their lives were totally in the power of their masters and a legal system which viewed them as chattel. In 1727 the Virginia Assembly passed an Act which allowed slaves to be annexed to lands which were held in fee simple so that they could be devised *entail* by deed or will which helped to perpetuate the system for another 135 years.

According to their estate inventories, neither John Willis Sr. who died in 1715 nor his son William who died in 1716 owned slaves, but both had indentured servants. The fact that John Willis Jr. owned two slaves when he died in 1728 and that his wife Mary owned seven in 1745 reflects some of the changes which took place regarding indentures and slavery in the first half of the 1700s on the Northern Neck.

The third barrier I faced in interpreting the records was my lack of knowledge of the political and social climate in England just preceding our family's emigration. The following information may be found in most history books but bears noting. Jamestown was founded in 1607, but settlement in outlying areas did not escalate until around 1640. In 1645 the Chickocoan Indian District was established, and either that year (or in 1648, the records being unclear) the first county in the Northern Neck, Northumberland, was created. The western boundary of Northumberland was undefined, patents were not yet being issued in the Neck, and officially no settlement was allowed there although some people (especially a group which had fled from Kent Island) were moving into areas along the Potomac River.

England did not take any drastic steps to stop the settlers from moving onto the Neck because she had greater problems at home. King Charles I was captured by Parliamentary forces in 1645 and executed in 1649. This was followed by the emigration of many Royalists to the colonies. Oliver Cromwell ruled as Lord Protector from 1653 until 1658 when his son Richard succeeded him. In 1660 Charles II was restored to the throne, and during his reign two memorable catastrophes occurred—the plague and the Great Fire of London. Thus, within a few years several events in England gave many people cause to migrate for a variety of reasons.

During Cromwell's Protectorate three new counties were created in that part of Virginia where the subjects of this manuscript lived. In 1652 Lancaster County was created from Northumberland along the Rappahannock watershed, and residents there were required to take an Oath of Allegiance to the new Commonwealth. The following year Westmoreland County was formed in the western part of Northumberland County on the Potomac watershed. In 1656 Old Rappahannock County was created from the western part of Lancaster County and included land on both sides of the Rappahannock River. On the north side of the Rappahannock River the dividing line between Old Rappahannock and Westmoreland counties was a ridge which ran generally from southeast to northwest. The settlers on Mattox Creek (first known as Hallowes' Creek, then Appomattox, then Mattox) lived on the Westmoreland County side of the dividing line. Settlers living south of the ridge were in Old Rappahannock County which was dissolved in 1692.

Because the exact location of John Washington's 1664 patent and John Willis's adjoining 1669 patent cannot be traced without an understanding of some of the changes in both county and parish lines, the formation of those counties and parishes will be outlined briefly. The records show that John Washington lived in Washington Parish, Westmoreland County, although he owned land on both sides of the ridge line.[12] John Willis lived in that part of Old Rappahannock which later became Richmond County and in 1721 became King George County. In 1692 Old Rappahannock County was dissolved with that part of the county on the north side of the Rappahannock River becoming Richmond County and the part on the south side of the river becoming Essex County. According to deeds, John's land was then in St. Mary's Parish, Richmond County. After the formation of King George County from the upper part of Richmond County in 1721, John's land was described as being in Hanover Parish, King George County, as it was in 1737 when his grandson sold it to the Church Wardens. A final adjustment was made in the King George and Westmoreland line in 1777 at which time King George County received land abutting the Potomac River and Westmoreland County received land on the Rappahannock River. At that time the lower boundary of King George County on the Rappahannock River was also moved from Charles Beaver Dams to Bristol Mines Run.

For family researchers this means that the records for early Northumberland, Lancaster, and Westmoreland counties, as well as Old Rappahannock, Richmond, and King George counties, are important in searching for the parents, siblings, and wife or wives of John Willis Sr.

Unfortunately, many of the early parish records have been lost and with them dates and boundaries for the creation or consolidation of parishes. Information from Charles Francis Cocke's book, *Parish Lines, Diocese of Virginia*,[13] helped me to understand some of those changes as they related to John Willis Sr. His 1669 patent did not mention the parish where he lived, but in 1694 and 1701 it was given as St. Mary's Parish and in 1715 it was described as being in Hanover Parish. This data suggests that his 1669 patent was west of present Bristol Mines Run which prior to 1732 was the dividing line between Hanover Parish in the upper part of King George County and Sittenburne Parish in the lower part of King George County.[14]

As many of the descendants of John Willis Sr. eventually moved to Orange, Culpeper, and Madison counties, a few comments should also be made regarding the formation of those counties. In 1721 Spotsylvania County was created from parts of Essex, King William, and King and Queen counties. Orange County was created from Spotsylvania

---

[12] See Chapters II and IV.

[13] Charles Francis Cocke, *Parish Lines, Diocese of Virginia* (Richmond: Virginia State Library, 1967, Repr. 1978).

[14] See Chapter II.

in 1734, Culpeper was created from Orange in 1749, and Madison was created from Culpeper in 1792–93.

Finally, prior to 1752 the Old Style Julian calendar was used with the new year beginning on March 25th. With that calendar the 8th month was not August, but October, the 10th month was December, and so on. In 1752 the New Style Gregorian calendar was adopted, although it was being used in different areas before then depending primarily upon the County Clerk. The Gregorian calendar corrected an eleven-day discrepancy and placed the new year on January 1st. As a result, dates between January 1st and March 25th in documents prior to 1752 may be "off" by one year and eleven days compared to our current calendar (although some records before then do show both dates). As this sometimes causes a problem in interpreting data in wills and deeds, for the reader's convenience dates will be consistently given in this manuscript to reflect both old and new style years (*cf.* 12 February 1715/16). The eleven-day correction has not been calculated.

So many clues have emerged in my research that it has been difficult to decide exactly what should and what should not be included in this manuscript and also what directions my research should take from this point. With the recent popular interest in dinosaurs, I read the following in *Digging Dinosaurs* by John R. Horner and James Gorman:

> *...In some ways, scientific research is like taking a tangled ball of twine and trying to unravel it. You look for loose ends. When you find one, you tug on it to see if it leads to the heart of the tangle. Sometimes the loose end leads nowhere; sometimes it leads you deeper into the ball, to unexpected and intriguing knots ...*[15]

While differing in methods and materials, genealogical research can also be described as a tangled ball of twine with loose ends. However, the family historian must interact with each document both objectively and subjectively if that evidence is to lead him or her deeper into the unknown. When and why was a particular document written, and what was it really all about? Who was named in the record, and how were they related or connected? No document was written in a social vacuum, so what conditions or events in the community may have influenced those involved? And perhaps most important, how did the document change their everyday lives and the lives of their descendants? Without personal interaction with the data and vivid imagining, we, too, are digging for dinosaurs rather than for living ancestors to whom we owe our heritage.

My hope is that the material I have selected for this history is both valid and clearly presented. May it and your own research lead you to imagine the facts and explore those "unexpected and intriguing" knots so that your family's history will become a "usable human memory" in your own personal journey.

---

[15] John R. Horner and James Gorman, *Digging Dinosaurs* (New York: Harper & Row, 1988), p. 23.

Plat of John Washington's 1,700-acre patent and John Willis Sr.'s 261-acre adjoining patent.

John Washington's 1,700-acre patent (1) dated 1 June 1664 which included 300 acres (3) which Washington assigned to William Freake in 1674. Freake willed this 300 acres to his wife Martha Freake. Martha married Robert Vincent, and they sold the tract to Thomas Tippett and John Hauxford. In 1675 John Washington willed the remainder of this patent (plus another patent of 1,200 acres not shown here) to his daughter Ann Washington, later the wife of Maj. Francis Wright. In 1705 Francis Wright and John Wright, husband and son of Ann Washington Wright, sold 1,000 acres of this tract to Francis Thornton Sr. In 1716 Thornton bought an additional 171.5 acres (4) directly north of John Willis's patent; the deed said that it was partly in Westmoreland County and partly in Richmond County (*i.e.*, on the ridge which was the boundary between the two counties). In 1726 Thornton willed the lower half of his 1,000 acres on Crowes Swamp to his son Rowland and the upper half plus the 171.5 acres to George Riding, his stepson. Rowland Thornton willed his interest to his son Francis (d. 1766–67). It then descended to his son Francis (d. 1780), then to his nephew Francis, and finally to this nephew Francis's daughters, Mary (Taylor), Sarah (Woodford), and Elizabeth (Chevis), who sold it to Nathaniel H. Hooe in 1818.

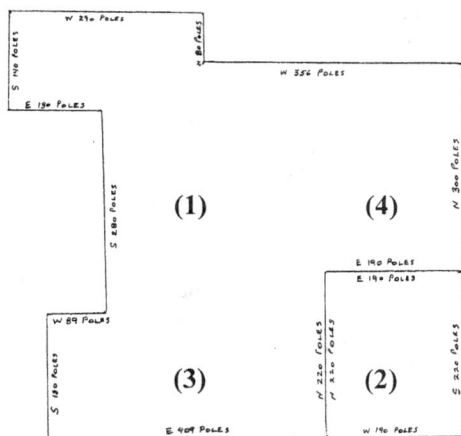

John Willis Sr.'s 261-acre patent (2) dated 21 October 1669. John deeded 100 acres of his patent to his son John Jr. in 1694 and the remaining 161 acres to his son William in 1701. In 1709 John Hauxford and Thomas Tippett exchanged land (acreage not given, but part of the 300 acres which Freake had purchased from Washington); William Willis sold 12 acres of his father's patent to Hauxford; and Hauxford sold 12 acres of Washington's patent to John Willis, Jr. (although it was called an "exchange" in John Willis Jr.'s will in 1728). John Willis Sr. died testate in 1715. William Willis died intestate in 1716. John Willis Jr. *d.s.p.* testate in 1728, and his interest in the patent reverted to his nephew John, the eldest son of William. In 1737 John Willis (son of William and grandson of John Sr.) sold the patent to the Church Wardens of Hanover Parish to be used as the church glebe. In 1767 the Church Wardens sold the tract to William Thornton.

Chapter I

John Willis Sr.

The first reunion of what would become the Willis–Gordon–Garnett and Allied Families Association was held on 11 August 1935 at "Locust Grove," the Willis family home on the north side of the Rapidan River in Culpeper County.[1] The original section of "Locust Grove" was built in the 1730s and is probably the oldest existing home in Culpeper County.[2] The Association was founded by the descendants of Capt. Isaac Willis of Culpeper County and his wife, Ann Garnett. Prior to World War II the Association met every year. Since 1950 it has met every two years in August, usually in Culpeper, Orange, or Spotsylvania County.

In 1962 the Association began publishing a *Journal* which recorded family stories, tradition, and research. Probably the most meticulous and prolific researcher who contributed to the *Journal* was the late George B. Loeffler.[3]

Capt. Isaac Willis was the great-great-grandson of John Willis Sr. (who died testate in what was then Richmond County, Virginia, in 1715), the great-grandson of William Willis (who died intestate in 1716 in Richmond County), the grandson of John Willis (who died testate in 1761–1762 in Orange County), and the son of William Willis Sr. and his wife, Elizabeth Garnett (who died in 1833 and 1835 respectively in Boone County, Kentucky). As later generations have been extensively reviewed in the *Journal* and elsewhere, this account will focus upon John Willis Sr. who died in 1715 in that part of Richmond County which became King George County.

During his research, Mr. Loeffler did not find any documents which identified the parents of John Willis Sr. and consequently concluded that he was the earliest known ancestor.[4] The recovery of King George County Will Book A-1 and other documents which are noted at the end of this chapter, however, provide new areas of consideration, especially as they relate to John Willis Sr.'s neighbors and known maternal lines, because Mr. Loeffler did not extend his research to those particular areas. This manuscript will take a more global view toward analyzing the records from a "community" viewpoint and with greater emphasis on the extended family.

The family of John Willis Sr. of Old Rappahannock, Richmond, and King George counties in Virginia left so many records between 1669 and 1737 that finding a way

---

[1] Willis–Gordon–Garnett and Allied Families Association *Journal*, vol. 1, no. 1, August 1962–August 1964 (pub. by the family association), hereafter referred to as *Journal*.

[2] Mary Stevens Jones, *An 18th Century Perspective: Culpeper County, VA* (Culpeper, VA: Culpeper Historical Society, 1976), p.114. Also see United States Department of the Interior, National Park Service, National Register of Historic Places File #23–49.

[3] *Journal*, vol. 1, no. 6 (1974); vol. 1, no. 9 (1980); vol. 1, no. 10 (1982); vol. 1, no. 12 (1986).

[4] *Journal*, vol. 1, no. 10, p. 10.

to summarize them in a comprehensive, understandable manner was a challenge. After experimenting with various methods, I decided to group the records chronologically within a topical format.

The first chapter of this manuscript will focus upon the documents which directly prove the relationship between John Willis Sr. and his grandson John Willis who died in 1761–1762 in Orange County, Virginia, and whose descendants founded the Willis–Gordon–Garnett and Allied Families Association. Because those records are so important, many will be given in their entirety.

Additional land patents and supporting data, including efforts to locate John's land in present King George County, will be discussed in succeeding chapters, followed by sketches of his known neighbors and information on his children. Later chapters explore other Willis families whose possible connections to John Willis Sr. are still undetermined.

The documents which are given in this chapter were transcribed from microfilmed copies of the originals and include the following:

1. John Willis Sr.'s 1669 patent for 261 acres adjoining a patent to John Washington.
2. His deeds to sons John Willis Jr. and William Willis in 1694 and 1701.
3. His will and estate inventories in 1715 and 1716.
4. His prenuptial deed of gift to Matilda Thacker in 1693.
5. John Willis's (son of William) deeds to the Church Wardens of Hanover Parish in King George County in 1737.
6. The Hanover Parish Vestry's deed to William Thornton in 1767 for the tract which was John Willis Sr.'s 1669 patent.

The earliest record which I found for John Willis Sr. that can be traced directly to subsequent generations was a patent for 261 acres signed by Governor William Berkeley on 21 October 1669. It is given here with its original spelling and punctuation.[5]

> *To all &c whereas &c now know yee that I the said Sr Wm Berkeley knt Govr &c Give grant unto Mr. Jno Willis two hundred sixty one acres of Land being in Westmoreland County upon the falling branches of Appomatox Creeke in the forrest betweene potomack and Rappa Rivers beginning at a red oake being a corner tree of Lt Coll John Washingtons extending into the maine woods S: 220 po: to a red oake from thence W: 190 po to the Lyne of the land yt the said Mr Washington from thence N: along the said Mr Washingtons lyne 220: po: to a marked oake finally E: 190 po along another lyne of the sd quantity The said land being due p(er) transp six p(er)sons and held &c to be held&c p(rovided) and due this 21st day of October 1669.*
>
> | | | |
> |---|---|---|
> | *John Temple* | *Tho Parrott* | *ffran King* |
> | *Simon Bird* | *Jane Davys* | *Oliver Thomas* |

---

[5] Virginia Land Patents 6:285 from microfilm.

An abstract of this patent is also found in Nugent's *Cavaliers and Pioneers*.[6]

> *Mr. John Willis, 261 acs. W'moreland Co., upon brs. of Appomattox Cr., bet. Potomack & Rappa. Rivs., adj. Lt. Col. John Washington; 21 October 1669, p. 283. Trans. of 6 pers: Jno. Temple, Simon Bird, Tho. Parrott, Jane Davys, Fra. King, Oliver Thomas*

John deeded 100 acres of this patent plus his interest in another tract to his eldest son, John Willis Jr., on 1 December 1694.[7]

> *To all Christian people to whom this present writing shall come I John Willis do send greeting to our Lord God Everlasting know he that I the said John Willis Senr. of the County of Richmond in St. Mary's Parish in Virginia Planter for divers good causes and considerations me hereunto moving especially for the natural love and affection I bear unto my loving son John Willis Junr. of the County & Parish aforesaid do give and grant and make over unto the said John Willis Junr. all the whole parcel or messuage of land belonging to and now in my possession that was taken up between myself and John Persons (i.e., Parsons) Senr. late of this County deceased and (by) patent will appear bearing date the 27th day of February 1690/1 under the hand of Philip Ludwell Deputy to the Proprietors in England and likewise one hundred acres of land more to be laid out next and adjoining to the land abovementioned being part of a patent of land containing two hundred sixty and one acres granted to the said Willis Senr. (by) Sr. Wm. Berkley as (by) a patent will appear bearing date the 21st day of October 1669 and abovesaid land I the said John Willis Senr. do give grant make over () off and confirm unto the said John Willis Junr. with all appurtenances fences houses orchards gardens woods and underwoods timber trees with all mines minerals whatsoever from (ane) my heirs and assigns or any claiming by or under me unto the said John Willis Junr. and his heirs lawfully begotten of his body And if in case that the said John Willis Junr. should die without issue lawfully begotten of his body that then the said parcells of land to return to me and my Heirs and Assigns But if in case the said John Willis Junr. should marry and die without issue that then the said John Willis Wife to have occupy and enjoy the said parcells of land during her natural life and no longer but to return as aforesaid But if in case when the hundred acres of land be laid out which is last given (by) this Instrument of writing that (said) House and Land should fall within the said John Willis line as it is supposed it will that the said Willis Senr. is to have occupy and enjoy the said old plantation as far as the branch that runs between that and the plantation called the Indian Field and the said John Willis Junr. doth promise and agree if he should have occasion to make*

---

[6] Nell Marion Nugent, *Cavaliers and Pioneers, Abstracts of Virginia Land Patents and Grants*, vol. II :72 (Baltimore: Genealogical Pub. Co, Richmond: VA State Library, 1977).

[7] Richmond County Deed Book 2:81–83 from microfilm. Abstracted by Ruth and Sam Sparacio, *Deed Abstracts of Richmond County, Virginia 1692–1695*, pp. 86–87.

*any fencing upon the north east side of the main road which comes through
the Indian Field to make a (land) for free passage for the said John Willis
Senr's stock to the plantation where the said John Willis Senr. did formerly
live In Witness my Hand and Seal this 1ˢᵗ day of 10ber [Dec.] 1694.*

Signed: John (mark) Willis

Signed sealed & delivered in presence of
  Nathl [Nathaniel] Pope
  Wm (mark "W") Willis

*Know all men by these presents that I Matilda Willis true and lawfull wife of
John Willis Senr. do assign over all my Right of my Thirds and Dower of the
abovementioned land unto John Willis Junr. as abovesaid Witness my hand
(and) seal this 1ˢᵗ day of December 1694.*

Signed: Matilda (mark "M") Willis

Signed sealed & delivered in presence of
  Nathll [Nathaniel] Pope
  Willm. [William] Willis
*Rec. in Cur. Ct. Richmond 5 Dei 10ber Ano 1694 and record(ed) 14
(Dei)...Wm. Colston, C; Cur*

*Know all men by these presents we John Willis & Matilda Willis do authorize
& appoint Nathanl Pope our Attorney to acknowledge in Court a parcell of
Land unto John Willis Junr. as (per) Instrument of Writing will appear
bearing date with these presents Witness our hands this 1ˢᵗ day of 10ber 1694.*

Signed: John Willis (his mark)
Matilda Willis (her mark)

Teste Wm. Willis (his mark)
  John Willis Junr. (his mark)
Record Teste William Colston Cl Cur

On 26 April 1701 John Willis Sr. deeded the remaining 161 acres of the above 261
acre patent to his son William.[8]

*To all Christian people to whom this presents writing shall come I John Willis
of St. Mary's Parish in Richmond County in Virginia Planter send Greeting
now know ye that I the said John Willis for divers good causes and
considerations me hereunto moving but more espetially for the naturall love
& affection I beare unto my loving son William Willis of the same place
Planter do hereby give & grant unto my said son and his heirs legally
begotten or to be begotten of his body for ever all the remaining part of the
within patent of land except one hundred acres formerly given to my
["eldest" inserted] son John as by record of Richmond County will appeare
and if the said Wm. Willis should marry & die without (issue) then the said
land to remaine to my son John Willis & his heirs forever after the death of
her the said Wm. Willis should intermarry with, who shall enjoy the same*

---

[8] Richmond County Deed Book 3:135 from microfilm.

during her life, the said John Willis only reserving to himself the liberty of timber of the said land during his life. Witness my hand & seal this 26th of April 1701.

Signed: John Willis (his mark)

Sealed & delivered in presence of
Xpher [Christopher] Butler
Nathll [Nathaniel] Pope
Recognitr. In Cur. Court Richmond 7:d die Maii Ano Dom 1701. Et recordr 28th die. Wm. Colston, Cl Cur

I the subscriber do by these presents authorize & appoint & depute my friend Nathanll Pope of Richmond County my Attorney to acknowledge the above deed of land to my son Wm Willis & for so doing this shall be his warrant 26th of April 1701.

Signed: John Willis (his mark)

Teste James Compll [Campbell]
Xpher [Christopher] Butler
Recordatr: in Cur: Court Richmond 28:d die Maii Ano Dom 1701. Wm. Colston, Cl Cur

While John's will in 1715 does not mention the 261 acre tract or the deeds to his sons, it provides important supporting proofs. His will, as copied from microfilm, is given with the original spelling and punctuation retained.

In the name of God, Amen the seventh day of June 1715 I John Willis Senr. of the County of Richmond & Parish of Hanover in Virginia being in health of body and of good and perfect sence and memory thanks be to God Do make this my last Will & Testament in manner & forme following that is to say first I bequeath my soul and spirit into the hands of the Almighty God my heavenly Father by whom of his Mercy and only Grace I intrust to be saved and redeemed into Eternal Rest through the death of my Savior and Redeemer Jesus Christ in whose presious Blood I sett the whole and only hope of my Salvation in hope of a joyful Resurrection; my Body I commit to the Earth to bee Buried with such Charge as Itt shall please my Exekutors hereinafter named.

I give and bequeath to my son in law Thomas James and Mary James his now wife all that plantation and parcell of land whereon they the said Thomas and Mary now liveth for and during his and her natural lives and after his decease and the death of the surviver and longest liver of them the said land & premises to belong wholly to David James son of the said Thomas James to him & his heirs evermore, which land joyns upon land of Mr. John Wormley & upon the land of Isaac Arnold and running from the land of the said Isaac easterly with the fence of the said Thomas James the fence being the bounds on that side of the said land and from the said fence easterly as aforesaid not touching any part of my cleared ground to a line of marked

5

trees being the bounds of the said land hereby given unto the said Thomas James aforesaid running to the line of John Wormley aforesaid thence along the said Wormley's line to the land of Isaac Arnold aforesaid thence with the said Arnolds line to the place where it began; I doe also give unto Thomas James aforesaid one young cow called Browney with all her fewter increase.

I doe give and bequeath unto Mary Cullins which now Liveth with mee all that Plantation or parcel of land whereon William Pullin now liveth together also with some part of my cleared ground according to the trew bounds and distances which I have latly given (to make round) the said Mary Cullins her land hereby given which said land joyns upon the land of John Combes and also being some part of my Plantation as aforesaid the said land I doe give to the said Mary Cullins and her heirs lawfully begotton of her body for evermore; but if in case Ye said Mary should dye without ishew lawfully begotten as aforesaid that then and in such case the said land wholly to return to my Son Charles Willis and his heirs for Evermore. I do also give unto Mary Cullins aforesaid one fether bedd and one rugg which is now in my house and one pare of new blankitts and one small iron pott one bell mettle spice morter and pestle and one dozen of pewter spoons which are new and one new pewter basson and Bright Bay Mare with a Starr in the forehead and spring taile and also one ewe and lambe and one pide heffer about two years ould with all and every of their fewter increase to her and her heirs for Evermore butt if in case the said Mary should dye without ishew then all and whatsoever I have hereby given to the said Mary of personall estate to returne and be devided amongst all and every one of my children Sons and Daughters. And I doe also Give unto the said Mary Cullins one oaken chest and one trunk which chest and trunk are to return as aforesaid if in case Mary should dye without ishew as aforesaid.

I doe give and bequeath unto my Son Charles Willis the Plantation and Land I now live on and also that Plantation whereon the said Charles now Liveth together with all the land contained and held by Pattent or Grant for this tract and two Plantations hereby given to the said Charles excepting that part which I have hereby given to Thomas James and Mary Cullins aforesaid My will is that the whole remaining part of this tract or divident with the two Plantations aforesaid doe belong wholley to my Son Charles & Mattildoe his now wife for and dewring his and her naturall lives and from and after the death of the said Charles & Mattildoe the said land and premises to belong wholley to John Willis Son of the said Charles to him and his heirs for Evermore. My will is that my Son Charles doe not sell or imbezell no timber from all the said land but to make use of what hee hath needfel ocation of making no waste.

It being the Will of my Late wife Mattildoe Willis that my Son Charles Willis aforesaid and Mattildoe his wife & their heirs should have of my estate the fether bedd which I now lye on and furniture curtains and Vallins rugg and Blankitts and Boulster and Pillows theirto belonging and four young cows and a young mare, my Will is that my wife's desier bee fullfilled and that for the said Charles and Mattildoe the said Bedd and Cows and Mare doe wholley belong to them and their heirs for Evermore together with the increase of said cows.

And for the remaining part of my cattle and also my whole stock of hoggs sheep excepting one ewe and lambe hearby given to Mary Cullins I doe give to my Son Charles and his heirs for Evermore I doe also give to my Son Charles one small iron pott and my least or smallest brass kettle and all the insewing cropp of Indian Corne and the insewing crop of tobacco I doe give to my Son Charles and my Son William to be equally devided between them the said Charles and William paying out of the said cropp to my Daughter Sewsannah five hundred pounds of tobacco, and paying also out of the said cropp to Mary Gardener five hundred pounds of tobacco.

I doe give to my Son Charles three thousand Nayles or thereabouts being all the Nayles that I have in my house and also all my powder and Stroll which is in my house My Will is that for that part of my Plantations which I have hearby given to Mary Cullins my son Charles Willis aforesaid have Liberty of Pasture Ground therein; I doe give unto Mary Cullins aforesaid all the Rents of the Plantation which William Pullin now liveth on being five hundred pounds of tobacco to bee paid dewly and yearly dewring the term of his lease which is nine years from ye date hearof and one years rent which is not yett paid but remains due being five hundred pounds of tobacco which tenn years rent I doe give to Mary Cullins aforesaid and her heirs for Evermore butt in case she should Dye without ishew the rents or tobacco to return to all my children and to bee equally devided amongst them all Sons and Daughters.

My will is that Isaac Arnold and William Willis as guardians of the said Mary Cullins doe look after and are hearby impowered to look after and see that William Pullin aforesaid his heirs & () doe take into his costede and his or their care all the tobacco stock goods and moveables whatsoever hearby given unto Mary Cullins and that hee or they doe trewly pay and deliver all such tobacco and goods and stock the vallew of such goods and stock in tobacco unto the said Mary Cullins when she shall arrive at the age of sixteen or att the first day of marriage if married before sixteen and further if in case the said William Pullin his heirs & () shall neglect or delay the payment of such tobacco stock and goods when the same shall become dew that the same bee taken out of his hands by the Guardians, and they to see that shee the said Mary hath the same trewly and honestly paid her.

My Will is that what Goods and Moveables soe ever and all other things that apertains to my Estate and is not yett disposed of by this my Last Will and Testament goods pewter brass and iron and all other things theirto belonging bee equally divided amongst all and Everyone of my children Sons and Daughters each to have an equall part thereof.

I doe make and appoint my Loving Son John Willis and Isaac Arnold my Exekutors of this my Last Will and Testament and in confirmation whereof I have hereunto sett my hand and fixt my Seale the day month and year first above wrighten.

Signed: John (mark) Willis

Signed sealed and delivered in the presence of us:
Tho. Parker
Augustine (mark) Blake
Elliner (mark) Welsh

Proved in Richmond County the sixth day of July 1715 by the oaths of Thomas Parker, Augustine Blake and Elliner Welsh, witnesses thereto, and admitted to record. Teste: M: Beckwith, Clerk (of) Court

An appraisal of John Willis's estate was recorded in court on 7 September 1715.[9] The microfilm is in poor condition, but data which can be read is as follows:

Whereas in obedience to an Order of Richmond County Court bearing date the sixth day of July 1715 we(e) Francis Slaughter and Richard Tutt and John Combs being () the said Order to Appraise the estate of John Willis, Sr., deceased did on the 15th day of July 1715 meet at the house of said John Willis, deceased, and (appraised) all and every part of his estate brought by the executors to our view.

The lengthy inventory includes such items as livestock, furniture, household utensils (including pewterware), Indian corn, tobacco, two pairs of spectacles, a parcel of old books, looking glass, pictures, a Vallins rug, spinning wheel, grindstone, two bushels of salt, several ells of cloth (including serge, sheeting, linen, cambridge, dimity, and flannel), scissors, nine dozen pipes, and many items relating to iron, brass, and pewter. The unusually large quantity of fabrics and metalware suggests that John may have been involved in merchandising in a limited way, although he was never identified as a merchant in the records. The appraisers listed specific items which were inventoried and given to Charles Willis, Mary Cullins, and Thomas James according to specific provisions in John's will.

To Charles Willis as a legatee: 1 old cow, 2 yearlings and 2 young calves, 1 young steer and 2 heifers, 4 sheep, 16 hogs, 12 small pigs, and 1 young cow to Thomas James.

To Mary Cullins as a legatee: 1 ewe and 1 lamb, 1 old chest, 1 iron pot and a dozen pewter spoons, 1 spice mortar and pestle and 1 pewter basin, 1 rug and 1 pair blankets, 1 feather bed and 1 trunk, 1 heifer, and 1 Bright Bay mare with a star in her forehead.

An additional, short inventory in the amount of 33 pounds 9 shillings 9 pence was

---

[9] Richmond County Will Book 3:219–222 from microfilm.

presented in Court by the same men on 27 April 1716 and recorded on 2 May 1716.[10] While much of it is unreadable because of the deterioration of the record, it appears to include tobacco and a bull. Neither inventory was reported in previous research, and no estate settlement has been found.

According to George B. Loeffler and George H. S. King, John's last wife was Matilda Thacker, widow of Henry Thacker who died testate in Richmond County by 2 August 1693 when his will was presented in court by Matilda Thacker, his executor, and proved by Joshua Davis who was undoubtedly one of the witnesses.[11] Richmond County Will Book 1 is missing, but the recording of Henry Thacker's will is proved in Order Book 1.[12] The relationship, if any, between Henry Thacker and the Thackers of Gloucester, Middlesex, and Lancaster counties has not been established as yet. However, in 1671 Henry was living in Abbington Parish, Gloucester County, and owned land on the south side of the Rappahannock River. By 1686 Henry and Matilda Thacker were living in Rappahannock County when they sold 600 acres on the south side of the Rappahannock River to John Powell and John Battaile with Matilda giving her Power of Attorney to Joshua Davis to acknowledge it in Court.[13]

On 22 July 1693 John Willis made the following prenuptial deed of gift to Matilda.[14]

> *Be it known unto all persons to whom these presents shall come I John Willis of the aforesaid County for Love & Affection I have unto Matilda Thacker whom I desire to make my Wife, do give & bequeath unto the aforesd. Matilda Thacker her heirs Executrs: Admistrs: or assignes forever one bed & furniture which she shall make choice of & foure breeding cattle not under three years nor above six years old, & one young mare not under three years old & not above six years old, and all her cloathes, And in case I the said John Willis should out live my said Intended Wife, Matilda Thacker, shee to dispose of the aforesaid goods & cattle according as she pleases. And in case I should die before her then these goods & cattle to be first taken out of my Estate & delivered (to) my Wife and she to have her proporcon of my Estate according to Law over & above the goods & cattle aforemenconed. As Witness my hand & seale this 22 day of July 1693.*
>
> Signed: John (mark) Willis
>
> *Signed sealed & delivered in the presence of us*
>   *Joshua Davis*
>   *Charles Minthorne*

[10]Richmond County Will Book 3:260 from microfilm.

[11]See George H. S. King, *Marriages of Richmond County, Virginia 1668–1853* (Easley, SC: Southern Historical Press, 1964), pp. 232–233 and 219.

[12]Robert K. Headley Jr., *Wills of Richmond County, Virginia 1699–1800* (Baltimore: Genealogical Pub. Co., 1983), p. 1.

[13]Sparacio, *Deed Abstracts of Old Rappahannock County, Virginia 1670–1672*, pp. 87–88, and *Deed Abstracts of Old Rappahannock County, Virginia 1686–1688*, pp. 39–40.

[14]Richmond County Deed Book 2:166–167; Sparacio, *Deed Abstracts of Richmond County, Virginia, 1692–1695*, p. 45.

Recognitr. In Cur C() Richmond 3 die August 1693
Rich:ss: I the Subscriber do here authorize & impower Joshua Davis my
Attorney to acknowledge a Deed of Gift unto Matilda Thacker in the aforesaid
County bearing date the 22ⁿᵈ day of July 1692 [sic] and this shall be his
warrant for so doing as witness my hand & seale this 23ʳᵈ day of July 1693.

Signed: John (mark) Willis

Signed sealed & delivered in the presence of us
  Rebecca Lowrey
  James Tayler
Recordatr: Teste Wm. Colston, Cle[rk]

Returning to John's 1669 patent of 261 acres, the above records show that he deeded part of it (100 acres) to his son John, Jr., in 1694 and the balance (161 acres) to his son William in 1701. Both tracts were entailed and gave the widows of his sons lifetime occupancy rights if his sons married.

William Willis died intestate in 1716 leaving a widow named Sarah, sons John and William, and probably a daughter Sarah (who later married Benjamin Hawkins).[15] As John was William's eldest son, he became heir to his father's entailed portion of his grandfather's patent.

John Willis Sr.'s eldest son, John Jr., died testate and without surviving issue in 1728.[16] The 100 acres which John Jr. received from his father in 1694 then reverted to his nephew, John Willis, eldest son and heir of his brother William. Consequently, Williams's son John could sell the 100 acres which he held in fee simple from his uncle John Jr.'s estate (because it was not entailed to John Sr.'s reversionary heirs), but he could not sell the entailed 161 acres which he inherited from his father without petitioning the legislature.

In 1734 the Virginia Assembly passed an Act allowing entailed lands of less than 200 pounds in value, and which were not part of or adjoining to other entailed lands, to be sold if a writ of *ad quod damnum* was filed with the sheriff. This Act cleared the way for John, who then moved to Orange County, to sell the entire 261 acres, but the procedure involved three deeds and his stepfather's (Edward Turberville) release. Those documents, which conclusively prove the lineage of John Willis of King George and Orange counties (son of William Willis and grandson of John Willis Sr.), are very lengthy, so many repetitions found in the originals have been deleted here for brevity.[17]

The first deed from John Willis of Hanover Parish to William Robinson was dated 31 May 1737 and pertained to the entailed 161 acres.

  ...Whereas John Willis, deceased, grandfather of the above John Willis party

---

[15] See Chapter VI.

[16] See Chapter V.

[17] King George County Deed Books 2:123–134 and 2:137–138 from microfilm; abstracted by Sparacio, *Deed Abstracts of King George County, Virginia 1735-1752*, pp. 13–14..

to these presents, was in his lifetime seized in fee of 261 acres of land...lying or being in the aforesaid Parish of Hanover in the said County of King George granted unto him by Letters Pattent bearing date the 21ˢᵗ day of October 1669 and being so seized by deed or assignment endorsed on the back of the said Letters Pattent bearing date the 26ᵗʰ day of April 1701 did give and grant unto his son William Willis, now deceased, and his heirs lawfully begotten of his body 161 acres of land, part of the said 261 acres, (by) the same of all the remaining of the within Pattent of land except 100 acres formerly given to his eldest son John as by the said Letters Patent and assignment recorded in the County Court of Richmond...and whereas the said William Willis is dead and the said 161 acres of land are descended and come to the said John Willis, party to these presents, the eldest son and heir of the body of the said William Willis, whereby the said John Willis is seized of the said premises in fee tail, and whereas by an inquisition taken before Benjamin Berryman, Gent., Sheriff of the said County of King George, the 11ᵗʰ day of March last past by virtue of a Writ in the nature of an ad quod damnum to him directed persuant to the Act of Assembly in such cases made or proved it is found that the said 161 acres of the value of 60 pounds sterling and no more and that the same are a separate parcel and not parcel of or contiguous to other in(tailed) lands in the possession and seizen of the said John Willis...Now this indenture witnesseth that for and in consideration of the sum of 70 [sic] pounds current money of Virginia to the said John Willis in hand paid by the said William Robinson at or before the sealing and delivery of these premises the receipt whereof he doth hereby acknowledge and thereof dot release acquit and discharge the said William Robinson his heirs exrs and admrs forever by these presents, he the said John Willis hath granted bargained sold aliened released and confirmed ...unto the said William Robinson...the aforesaid 161 acres...

Signed: John Willis

Wit. Wm. Mackay and Harry Turner.

Received the day and year first within written of the within named William Robinson the sum of 70 pounds being the consideration money within mentioned to be paid to me.

Signed: John Willis

At a Court continued and held for King George County the 4ᵗʰ day of June 1737. Then came John Willis and acknowledged this Deed of bargain and sale together with the receipt for the consideration and money thereon endorsed to William Robinson Gent. which on the motion of the said William was admitted to record. Signed: Thomas Turner [Clerk of King George County Court]

The second document, dated 1 June 1737, was the first part of the typical lease/release of that time whereby John Willis and William Robinson leased the entire 261 acres for one year to Joseph Strother and Maximilian Robinson, Gent., Church Wardens of Hanover Parish.

This indenture made the 1ˢᵗ day of June 1737 between John Willis...and William Robinson...of the one part and Joseph Strother and Maximilian Robinson, Gentlemen, Church wardens of the said Parish of Hanover of the other part, witnesseth that the said John Willis and William Robinson for and in consideration of the sum of 5 shillings current money to them in hand paid before the sealing and delivery hereof, the receipt whereof they the said John Willis and William Robinson...by these presents have granted bargained and sold unto the said Joseph Strother and Maximilian Robinson...all that tract or parcel of land containing by estimation 261 acres be the same more or less situate lying and being the aforementioned Parish of Hanover in the County of King George formerly granted unto John Willis, grandfather of the said John Willis party to these presents, by Letters Pattent bearing date the 21ˢᵗ day of October 1669, one hundred acres part whereof were given by the said John Willis the grandfather to his son John Willis deceased in fee tail by deed bearing the () day of December in the year 1694 and by the death of the said John Willis his son without issue reverted and came to the said John Willis party to these presents as heir at law of the said John Willis the grandfather and the residue of the said premises were given by the said John Willis the grandfather to his son William Willis, father of the said John Willis party to these presents...in fee tail by deed or assignment endorsed on the back of the Letters Patent aforesaid bearing date the 26ᵗʰ day of April 1701 and by the death of the said William Willis are descended and came to the said John Willis party to these presents as his eldest son and heir...to have and to hold the said tract or parcel of land...unto the said Joseph Strother and Maximilian Robinson...for and during and unto the full end and term of one whole year from thence...

> *Signed: John Willis*
> *William Robinson*

Wit. Wm. Mackay and Harry Turner
Acknowledged in court by John Willis and William Robinson on 4 June 1737.
Attest T. Turner.

On the following day John Willis, his wife Elizabeth (nee Plunkett), and William Robinson released (deeded in fee simple) the entire 261 acres to the Church Wardens for the use of the church as a glebe in Hanover Parish.

This indenture made 2 June 1737 between John Willis of the Parish of Hanover in the County of King George, Planter, and Elizabeth his wife and William Robinson of the same Parish and County Gentleman of the one part and Joseph Strother and Maximilian Robinson Gentlemen Churchwardens of the said Parish of Hanover of the other part, Whereas the Vestry of the said Parish have contracted and agreed with the said John Willis for the absolute purchase of 261 acres of land lying in the Parish and County aforesaid being the premises herein aftermentioned in order to assign and set apart the same for a glebe for the use of the minister of the said Parish for the time being and his successors forever and Whereas the said John Willis being seized in fee tail of 161 acres part of the said 261 acres of land hath lately sued out a Writ in the manner of an ad quod damnum to the Sheriff of the said County directed to inquire of the value of the said 161 acres of land in order to dock the intail of the same pursuant to the Act of Assembly in that case and provided and by an inquisition taken by virtue of the said Writ before the said Sheriff the 11th day of March last past it is found that the said 161 acres are of the value of 60 pounds sterling and no more and that the same are a separate parcel and not parcel of or contiguous to other intailed lands in the possession and seizen of the said John Willis and thereupon the said John Willis by Deed of Bargain and sale bearing date the 31st day of May last past for the consideration therein contained hath granted bargained and sold unto the said William Robinson the aforesaid 161 acres of land to hold to him his heirs and assigns forever...Now this Indenture witnesseth that for and in consideration of the sum of 120 pounds current money of Virginia to the said John Willis in hand paid by the said Joseph Strother and Maximilian Robinson by the direction or appointment of the Vestry of the Parish aforesaid the receipt of which money the said John Willis doth hereby acknowledge and thereof doth release and discharge the said Joseph Strother and Maximilian...by these presents they the said John Willis and Elizabeth his wife and the said William Robinson have...granted bargained sold aliened released and confirmed...unto the said Joseph Strother and Maximilian Robinson their actual possession now being by virtue of a bargain and sale to them thereof made for one whole year by Indenture bearing date the day next before the day of the date of these presents...all that tract or parcel of land hereinbefore mentioned containing by estimation 261 acres...situate lying and being in the Parish of Hanover...formerly granted unto John Willis grandfather of the said John Willis party to these presents by Letters Patent bearing date 21 day of October 1669, one hundred acres part thereof were given by the said John Willis the grandfather to his son John Willis deceased in fee tail by deed bearing date the 10th day of December 1694 and by the death of the said John Willis the son without issue are reverted and came to the said John Willis party to these presents as heir at law of the said John Willis the grandfather and the residue of the said premises were given by the said John Willis the grandfather to his son William Willis (father of the said John Willis party to these presents now deceased) in fee tail by deed or assignment indorsed on the back of the Letters Patent aforesaid bearing date the 26th April 1701 and by the death of the said William Willis descended and came to the said John Willis party to these presents as his eldest son and heir and all houses, outhouses, buildings...and also all the estate right title interest use...possession benefit property claim and demand forever...of them the said John Willis and Elizabeth his wife and William Robinson...to have and to hold the said tract or parcel of land...unto the said Joseph Strother and Maximilian Robinson...in trust nevertheless and to the intent and purpose that the said tract or parcel of land and premises shall be and are hereby declared to be remain and continue forever hereafter as and for the glebe of the said Parish of Hanover for the use of the minister of the said Parish...and for no other use intent or () whatsoever...the estate for life of Mary Jennings widdow of and in 108 acres of land part of the said premises () escepted and fore()ed...

Signed: John Willis
Elizabeth Willis
William Robinson

Wit. Wm. Mackay
Harry Turner

Following this deed was a receipt for 120 pounds which was signed by John Willis and witnessed by the same men. The deed was recorded by T. Turner, Clerk of King George Court, on 4 June 1737 with Elizabeth Willis's release and consent, and John Willis acknowledged his bond in the amount of 200 pounds for good title. Those details indicate that John and Elizabeth were in King George in June 1737 and suggest that they had not yet migrated to Orange County. It is noted that the lifetime occupancy rights of Mary Coghill Willis Jennings, the widow of John Willis Jr., were protected. The difference in the acreage will be discussed in Chapter V.

On the same day that John and Elizabeth (Plunkett) Willis and William Robinson released the tract to the Church Wardens, Edward Turberville gave his Power of Attorney to Joseph Berry to relinquish any interest which he had in his wife's dower rights. Sarah (—) Willis Wood HudsonTurberville, the wife of Edmund Turberville, was the widow of William Willis and mother of John Willis of the above deeds.

I Edward Turberville do hereby authorize and impower Capt. Joseph Berry my Attorney in the Court of the County of King George to relinquish all the right of dower and thirds at the Common Law which I have in a certain plantation and tract of land by virtue of my marriage with Sarah the late widdow and relict of William Willis her former husband deceased and now sold and lawfully conveyed by her son John Willis to the Churchwardens of the Parish of Hanover and their successors for a glebe by deed of release bearing equal date with these presents In Witness whereof I have hereunto set my hand and seal this 2ⁿᵈ day of June in the year of our Lord 1737.

Signed: E. Turberville

Wit. Thomas Catlett
William Bartlett
Archibald McPherson

At a Court held for sd King George County this 2ⁿᵈ day of September 1737 Joseph Berry by virtue of this power of attorney (under the hand and seale of Edward Turberville proved by the oaths of Thomas Catlett Gent. And Archibald McPherson) acknowledged his Right of Dower and thirds at the Common Law in and to a certain tract of land sold by John Willis to the Vestry of Hanover Parish for the use of a glebe for the said Parish which on the motion of Joseph Strother Gent. Churchwarden of the said Parish was admitted to record. Teste T. Turner, Clerk

County Orders show that on 4 June 1737 John Willis appeared in Court and acknowledged his Deed of Bargain and Sale to William Robinson on behalf of the Parish of Hanover which on his motion was admitted to record. John, his wife Elizabeth, and William Robinson also acknowledged the above deeds to the Church Wardens of Hanover Parish.[18] John acknowledged his bond to the Church Wardens, and it was admitted to record. Sarah Turberville, his mother, also came into Court and acknowledged her release of dower rights.[19]

Having disposed of their lands in King George County, John and Elizabeth (Plunkett) Willis, Edward and Sarah (Willis Wood Hudson) Turberville, and members of their families moved to Orange County where Edward Turberville died intestate by 6 October 1750.[20] Sarah Turberville died testate between 18 June 1760 and 28 May 1761.[21] Her son John Willis died testate in Orange County between 25 November 1761 and 25 March 1762.[22] These families will be discussed in the chapters on William Willis and the family's transition to Orange County.

John Willis Sr.'s 261-acre patent was the glebe for Hanover Parish for thirty years. In 1767 the Vestry of Hanover Parish sold it to William Thornton for 200 pounds.[23]

> *This indenture made the sixth day of August in the year of our Lord 1767 between Charles Carter, William Robinson, John Triplett, Thomas Jett, Thomas Hodge, Max. Robinson, Jos. Murdock, Richard Payne, Thomas Berry, Horatio Dade, and John Skinker, Vestrymen of the Parish of Hanover and County of King George of the one part and William Thornton Gent. of the said county of the other part, Witnesseth that whereas by an Act of the Assembly made in the year of His Majesty's reign (empowering) the Vestry of the said Parish to sell and dispose of the Glebe Land of the said Parish containing 261 acres, the said Vestry have bargained with the said William Thornton for the same for the sum of Two Hundred pounds agreeable to the purport of the said Act, Now this indenture witnesseth that the said Gent. Of the Vestry for and in consideration of the said sum of money to them in hand paid the receipt whereof they do hereby acknowledge have granted bargained and sold and by these presents do grant bargain and sell unto the said William Thornton his Heirs and Assigns the said 261 acres of land (which) was purchased by the Vestry of the said Parish of Hanover of John Willis and Elizabeth his wife as by a deed recording among the records of King George County Court may more fully appear, to Have and to Hold the said 261 acres*

---

[18] King George County Order Book 2:113–114.

[19] King George County Order Book 2:115.

[20] Orange County Order Book 5:284.

[21] Orange County Will Book 2:310 and 2:319 from microfilm; also abstracted by Sparacio, *Digest of Orange County, Virginia, Will Books 1734–1838*, p. 114.

[22] Orange County Will Book 2:323 and Book 13:484.

[23] King George County Deed Book 5:684–685.

of land unto the said William Thornton his Heirs and Assigns... [signed by all ten Vesterymen and acknowledged in Court on 6 August 1767].

While not directly related to this research, it is noted that on the same date the Vestry replaced this glebe tract with 339 acres which they purchased for 624 pounds 10 shillings from the estate of Richard Tutt.[24] The deed for the new glebe mentions that Tutt's tract joined a parcel which had been purchased by Joseph Murdock, Gent., from John Jett, to a swamp, down the meanders of the swamp to the Rappahannock River, down the river to the sand hole branch, and to the beginning. Richard Tutt's will, which was written in January 1766 and proved in March 1767, referred to a bargain he had made with the Church Wardens for the land.[25]

A few comments regarding additions or corrections to earlier research reports will be offered at this point. As stated above, a considerable amount of research on the descendants of John Willis Sr. was done by George B. Loeffler, now deceased. After reviewing the records, my findings agree with his conclusions with few exceptions.

I concur with Loeffler that John Willis's will specifically proves only five children: John Willis Jr.; William Willis; Charles Willis (who in 1715 had a wife Matilda and a son John); Mary (the wife of Thomas James and who in 1715 had a son named David); and Susannah. However, there may have been other children who were unnamed but included in the statement, "all and every one of my children Sons and Daughters," which was given three times in John's will. Mary Cullins was the daughter of Catherine Cullins Pullen, but Catherine was not the daughter of John Willis.[26] I found no evidence that either Mary Gardener or Mary Cullins was a granddaughter. Although John's will names only one son of his daughter Mary and son-in-law Thomas James, a later deed given in Chapter VIII proves that they also had a son named William. Mary Willis James, Thomas James, and their eldest son, David James, were deceased by 1742.[27] It is likely that John Willis Sr.'s daughters Mary [James] and Susannah also left other children, although they have not been identified as of this date.

Earlier undocumented claims by Maud Potter and others that Isaac Arnold was John's son-in-law are incorrect.[28] Isaac Arnold married Margaret Goff(e), daughter of Thomas Goffe.[29] Proofs for Potters's claims that John Willis Sr. was the son of William Willis (brother of Col. Francis Willis) of Crany (or Craney) Creek and the brother of Thomas and William Willis have not been found, but inconclusive evidence is given in Chapter XII.

---

[24] King George County Deed Book 5:685–687.

[25] Spotsylvania County Will Book D.

[26] See Chapter VI.

[27] King George County Deed Book 2:398.

[28] Maud Potter, *The Willises of Virginia* (Mars Hills, NC, 1964); also see Chapter IV.

[29] Ibid. and Richmond County Deed Book 1:126–127a.

The estate inventories for John Willis Sr. and his son William and the names of their appraisers are new information not previously reported. According to Richmond County Court Orders, William Willis died by December 5, 1716, not in 1717 as given in prior accounts (see Chapter VI).

When Loeffler wrote his article on John Willis Sr., he did not include the information from King George County Will Book A-1.[30] This will book disappeared during the Civil War, was recovered in 1976, transcribed by George H. S. King, and published in 1978. Because it contains the wills of John Willis Jr. and his wife, Mary Coghill Willis Jennings, it has added greatly to our knowledge of the Willis family in Richmond and King George counties.

Family researchers have repeatedly assumed that Charles' wife Matilda was the daughter of Henry Thacker and Matilda (—) Thacker (who became the last wife of John Willis Sr.), but I did not find any evidence to prove that she was. Contrary to earlier reports, there is no mention of either Charles or Matilda in John's prenuptial deed of gift to his last wife, Matilda Thacker, which is given above. While Charles' wife may have been the daughter of Henry Thacker, other possibilities should not be dismissed.

There has been much confusion between John Willis Sr.'s grandsons John Willis (son of William) and John Willis (son of Charles). Charles Willis was deceased by 1725 when his son John petitioned the Court for his uncle, John Willis Jr., to be named as his guardian.[31] After John Willis Jr. died in 1728, Charles' son John again petitioned the Court for Thomas Goffe to be named as his guardian, indicating that this John, who was a first cousin of our direct ancestor also named John, was born between 1707 and 1711, a birthdate formerly assigned to John, son of William.[32] In order to minimize the ambiguity between the various men named John Willis in this manuscript, John Willis *Sr.* will refer to the eldest man who died in 1715, John Willis *Jr.* will refer to his son who died in 1728, and the two grandsons named John will be identified in the text as either the son of William or the son of Charles. Another John Willis who died in 1682 in Westmoreland County (and who may have been the father of John Willis Sr.) is given in Chapter X.

No other previous histories have comprehensively reviewed John Willis Sr.'s land records or have given his 1669 patent from the original patent book. To my knowledge no other researchers have attempted to trace this patent or reported the sale of the tract by the Hanover Parish Vestry to William Thornton in 1767. Information from these and related land documents provide Willis family researchers with new data not included by Loeffler. Also no one has attempted to trace John Willis's ancestors by examining his immediate community which almost assuredly included unknown relatives.

---

[30]George B. Loeffler, "Ancestry of the Willises of Locust Grove, Culpeper County, Virginia," Willis–Gordon–Garnett and Allied Families *Journal*, vol. 1, no. 10 (1982).

[31]King George County Order Book, 6 August 1725.

[32]See Chapter VII.

John Willis's land holdings were greater than as reported by Loeffler. Between 1669 and 1696/97 John acquired four tracts by patent, grant, or deed for a total of approximately 684 acres depending upon his share of a joint purchase with Thomas Goff and Thomas Kendall in 1687/88. The history of John's 1669 grant will be discussed in Chapter II, and his other land records will be given in Chapter III.

The co-owner of John's 1690/91 grant who was named in the above deed to his son John Jr. in 1694 was John Persons [*sic*], not John *Powers* as reported elsewhere. According to subsequent records, his name was actually John Parsons which will be used in this manuscript. The acreage of that parcel was 158 acres in the original grant, not 154 as stated in Gray and not 185 as given in Loeffler's article, the first probably a transcription error and the last undoubtedly due to a transposition of numbers.

Chapter IV will present an overview of the community where John Willis's family lived on the Northern Neck. This is followed by records for his children in Richmond/King George County and a brief discussion of their migration to Orange County.

Finally, in his articles Loeffler did not include the Willis families of early Westmoreland County who are reviewed in Chapters X and XI, Col. Francis Willis (Chapter XII), or Col. Henry Willis (Chapter XIII).

Chapter II

Tracing John Willis Sr.'s 1669 Patent

The primary goal of my research was to learn more about John Willis Sr. and to find the names of his parents. The evidence given in Chapter I proves that John Willis who died in 1761–1762 in Orange County, Virginia, was the grandson of John Willis Sr. and identifies some of their neighbors in King George County. However, it does not provide any insights about the parents of John Sr.

As I progressed through the old documents, I became increasingly aware of the importance of land records as being one way to trace events in John's life. Consequently, this chapter will focus on his first patent and finding the specific location of the tract because that knowledge might hold the key to identifying his family. In what part of King George County was it located? Was in above or below present Bristol Mines Run? On which side of the ridge or fall line was it? Did any part of his patent lie within what was then Westmoreland County, but which later became King George County? Who were his neighbors, and was John related to any of them?

My focus in this chapter is to provide some basic data about the men who either owned or lived on land which adjoined John Willis's 1669 patent so that the reader has a general framework for the other data which is given below. John's later grants and deeds will be given in Chapter III, and a summary of his neighbors will be found in Chapter IV.

Attempting to trace land which was obtained by early patents or grants in the Northern Neck is challenging, and finding the location of specific tracts is often impossible. Boundaries were described in metes, bounds, current landholders, and streams whose names changed, sometimes several times. Counties were being created and re-created, or, as in the case of Old Rappahannock County, discontinued. Parishes were formed and later re-created or dissolved.

It is assumed that John Willis Sr. was at least twenty-one when he received his first patent and was therefore born by 1648. During his lifetime dramatic changes occurred on the Northern Neck, and many of those changes involved land ownership. In 1648 an Act which prohibited settlement north of the York River was repealed. Immigrants who had been pressing for the opening of lands responded immediately, especially in the unsettled, upper regions between the Potomac and Rappahannock rivers. By 1650 some had received patents for tracts in that part of Northumberland County which in 1653 became Westmoreland County. One group of immigrants chose land in the Potomac watershed which was drained by Hallowes Creek, first named for John Hallowes and later called Appomattox Creek, then simply Mattox Creek. (As shown above, John Willis's patent was described as being on the falling branches of Appomattox Creek between the Potomac and Rappahannock rivers.) An early list of landowners in this area dating sometime between 1648 and 1652 included Nathaniel Pope, William Freake, John Hollis (Hallowes), and a James Willis.[1] The first three settled on Mattox Creek, while James Willis lived on Yeocomoco Neck where he died in 1655.[2]

In April 1652 settlers were required to take an Oath of Loyalty to the Cromwell government. Names on that list include John Hallowes and James Willis.[3]

John Hallowes received two patents in 1650/51—one for 600 acres for transporting twelve people to the colonies, including an unknown Richard Willis and William Freake, and the other for 1,600 acres for thirty-two headrights, again including William Freake. That year William Freake and Nathaniel Pope began patenting land on Mattox Creek.[4]

John Washington, great-grandfather of the President, and his brother Lawrence arrived on the Northern Neck around 1657. John married Nathaniel Pope Sr.'s daughter, Ann. Nathaniel Pope Sr. died in 1660 in Westmoreland County, his daughter Ann Pope Washington died before 1675, and John Washington died in 1677.[5] The reader must be careful not to confuse Ann Pope, who married John Washington the immigrant, with their daughter Ann Washington, who married Francis Wright. As cited in Chapter I, John Washington owned land adjoining John Willis' 1669 patent, and the heirs or assignees of John Washington, Nathaniel Pope, and William Freake were neighbors to John Willis Sr.

One aspect which I found interesting was that John Willis was probably the first immigrant to till the land which was included in his 1669 patent. No record has been found to indicate that someone had lived on the tract before John or that he got the patent by assignment.

Many patentees received their land through the headright system by which they were given 50 acres for each person they transported or for whom they paid passage to the colonies (see Introduction). According to Nugent, the patentee was supposed to pay a quitrent of one shilling for each 50 acres beginning seven years after the first grant or seating and not before.[6] However, if the patentee or his assignee did not seat his land or plant on the tract within three years, the land was subject to escheat and could be patented by someone else. As a result, the records include first patents, second or

---

[1] Walter Biscoe Norris Jr. *Westmoreland County, Virginia, 1653–1983* (Montross: Westmoreland County Board of Supervisors, 1983), pp. 1–9; hereafter referred to as Norris in footnotes. Also see Chapter XI.

[2] James Willis is discussed in Chapter XI.

[3] Norris, op. cit., pp. 11–13.

[4] Nell Marion Nugent, *Cavaliers and Pioneers. Abstracts of Virginia Land Patents and Grants 1623–1666*, vol. I (Baltimore: Genealogical Publishing Co., 1963), hereafter referred to as Nugent in footnotes.

[5] See Chapter IV.

[6] Nugent, op. cit., I:321

third patents (of all or part of the original patent or incorporating the first patent with new land), assignments, wills devising patented lands or parts thereof (with new patents being issued to the heirs), and a web of intermingled claims.

In May 1662 the following proclamation was issued:

> *Whereas the remoteness of Westmoreland makes one unable effectually to settle the revenue due to the King from his tenants in those parts as also would be troublesome to the inhabitants to bring their patents to one, I, Peter Jennings, Deputy Treasurer, have appointed Mr. William Horton to take an account of what lands is held in the said county to be entered in the Treasurer's Office as also to receive what monies or tobacco is due as well for rent as entries for my use and the last year's rent.*[7]

Clues suggest that John Willis was one of the youngest patentholders in this area. His known neighboring landowners in October 1669 were John Washington, Robert Nurse, Phillip Browne, John Piper, John Foxhall, Nathaniel Pope (Jr.), John Watts, John Wilsford, and some nonresidents. Of these, three men died around 1670—Nathaniel Pope (Jr.), Phillip Browne (who did not seat his land with the tract escheating), and John Piper. Robert Nurse died by 1673, John Washington died in 1677, John Foxhall died in 1678, and John Watts died by 1679.[8] It is likely that John Willis Sr. was somehow related to one of these men or that his family had a previous connection to one of them.

My search for John Willis's 1669 tract began with his patent in Virginia Land Patents.[9] I did not find any connection between John Willis and the people who were listed as headrights in his patent, and their names did not appear in other documents which I reviewed, so John may have purchased the headrights from someone which was a common practice. John Willis was the only man named "Willis" in this specific area in 1669, although others with that surname were found in early Northumberland and Westmoreland counties.[10]

Results of my review of immigrant and headright lists were inconclusive because several men and women named "Willis" were given. However, the most promising entries which were found in Nugent and on microfilm will be noted. George Read was given a patent in 1648 which was renewed in 1650. Among the headrights were John Willis (as given in the original record with Nugent reporting it as John *Wilks*) and John Fryer. In 1651 a patent was given to James Willis of Northumberland County for 50 acres for the transportation of Jack(?) Willis (which is a common nickname for John), and James assigned it to John Earle according to Northumberland County Orders. In 1653 John Willis and Anne Willis were among the headrights on a patent for John Gillett. Robert Newman, as assignee of Robert Branch, received a patent in 1654 in

---

[7] Dorman, *Westmoreland County, Virginia, Records 1661–1664*, p. 7.

[8] All dates taken from Westmoreland County records; see Chapter IV.

[9] Book 6, p. 283. Nugent, op. cit., II:72; see Chapter I.

[10] See Chapters X and XI.

which John Willis was listed as a headright according to Northumberland County Orders. In 1656 Richard Gibble's patent, which joined Newman's tract, named John Willis as a headright with several others who had been listed in Newman's patent. (It was not unusual for more than one person to claim the same list of headrights. The person paying the passage was entitled to headrights, and often the ship captain or another man involved in transporting the immigrant would also apply.) In 1658 a John Willis was listed as a headright on a patent issued to Capt. Augustine Warner.

No records were found to definitely prove that any of these men were John Willis Sr. As he was born by 1648 and died in 1715, it is doubtful that he was any of the above headrights. From data cited in Chapters X and XI, I suspect that one of these headrights was John Willis who died in 1682 in Westmoreland County although the evidence is circumstantial.

During the time these patents were issued, the boundary between the counties of Westmoreland (created from Northumberland in 1653) and Old Rappahannock (created from Lancaster in 1656) was the irregular and poorly defined ridge or fall line between the Potomac and Rappahannock watersheds.[11] Descriptions in the patents were often so vague that the land had to be traced through later deeds to determine where it was. Deeds were usually, but not always, recorded in the county where the land was located. If the tract lay on the ridge line, it might have been recorded in both counties or only one county. The fact that John's patent was for 261 acres, an unusual and odd number, made it much easier to trace than if it had been for an even number of acres, such as 200 or 300 acres.

In 1692 Old Rappahannock County was dissolved and divided into two counties with that portion of Rappahannock which lay on the north side of the river becoming Richmond County and the portion on the south side of the river becoming Essex County. Between 1692 and 1721 John Willis's tracts lay in that part of Richmond which eventually became King George County in 1721. Between 1721 and 1777 the dividing line between King George and Richmond counties was Brockenbrough Creek, and Westmoreland County did not abut the Rappahannock River. In 1777 the eastern border of King George was moved to Bristol Mines Run, and the land between Bristol Mines Run and Brockenbrough Creek was added to Westmoreland County, giving that county direct access to the Rappahannock River. Only by comparing the changes in county lines with the changes in parish lines was it possible to identify the location of John's land, and for that information and guidance I am greatly indebted to Merrill Hill Mosher.

When analyzing the old patents and deeds, it is important to know that Mattox (or Appomattox) Creek was in the Potomac watershed. The tracts which were described as being on Mattox were usually in Westmoreland County, although it appears that

---

[11] Merrill Hill Mosher, "Corrections to Published Maps of County Boundaries of the Northern Neck," *Virginia Genealogist*, vol. 37, no. 4, 1994. This article is highly recommended to anyone who is researching the early records in this area.

some of its headbranches lay on the south side of the ridge.[12] Likewise, when documents gave the location as being on the branches of the Rappahannock (on the north side of the river), those tracts were south of the ridge and in Old Rappahannock County. The terms "headbranches of Mattox and Rappa" or "falling branches" in the patents may have referred to streams whose meanders actually crossed the ridge or county line. Poultridges (Portridges, Portrages, etc.) Creek was frequently mentioned and was in the Rappahannock watershed south of the fall line even though a few early records imply that it was in Westmoreland County.

Because the following patents may be important in tracing John Willis' immigration and discovering any relationships between John Willis and his first known neighbors, they will be reported here as transcribed from the original patent books. It may be helpful for readers who are unfamiliar with those records to know that on the Northern Neck land certificates which were issued before 1690 were called *patents* because they originated from the Crown. After 1690 they were issued by the Proprietors and called *grants*.

Nugent's abstracts, which were taken from the patent books, do not include all of the data given in the original patent books which are available on microfilm. Both sources will be noted when used. The second page number given in parentheses refers to an earlier, now extinct, folio or patent book in which the patent had been recorded.

John Willis's patent was given in Chapter I. John Washington's patent which adjoined John Willis in 1669 is found in Virginia Patent Book 5, p. 168 (50) and is given here as transcribed from the original document:[13]

> *To all...the said William Berkeley Knight Governor, etc., give and grant unto Major John Washington seventeen hundred acres of land lying between the headbranches of Porotridge and Appomattox Creeks the one falling into the Rappahannock River and the other into Potomack River and Beginning at an oak by Wariscreek path being the corner tree that lyeth next to a tract of land belonging to Nathaniel Pope, from which oak (is extended) north three hundred perches over certain branches that fall into Appomattox Creek to an oak, thence west to and by a branch of Porotridge Creek (three) hundred and fifty six poles to a white oak, then over the said branch north eighty poles to a Pohickory, then west two hundred and ninety poles then south one hundred and forty poles then east one hundred and thirty poles then south two hundred and eighty poles to () oak by a branch of Porotridge Creek then west eighty nine(?) poles thence south one hundred and eighty poles then east four hundred and nine poles then north two hundred and twenty poles to an oak in (line of?) The ground now cleared by William Freake aforesaid and finally east one hundred and ninety perches to the first mentioned corner tree. The said land six hundred acres part thereof formerly granted unto William*

---

[12] Appomattox was also the name of an early parish in Westmoreland County; see Cocke, *Parish Lines*, pp. 166–167.

[13] Also abstracted by Nugent, op. cit., I:448.

Freake by patent dated the eighteenth of March one thousand six hundred and sixty two and by the said Freake assigned unto the aforesaid Major John Washington the twenty sixth of March one thousand six hundred and sixty four and eleven hundred acres () by and for the transportation of twenty two persons (etc.), dated the first day of June one thousand six hundred and sixty four.

Part of Washington's patent was first granted to William Freake in 1657 and repatented by Freake in 1662/63.

Wm. Freake patent of 600 acres 18 March 1662 on south side and head of Appomattox Creek behind a dividend of land of Lt. Col. Nathaniel Pope, beginning at a marked corner () by Warisquick path, the said land formerly granted to said Freake by patent 14 October 1657.[14]

Freake assigned all 600 acres to John Washington on 26 March 1664.[15] In 1674 Washington sold back his interest in 300 acres in the southernmost part of this tract to Freake, the record stating that Freake's portion lay next to Portridge Creek in Rappahannock County.[16]

The importance of this data is that Freake was the original patentee of part of the tract, but he held no interest in it on 21 October 1669 when John Willis received his patent and therefore was not mentioned—perhaps a seemingly minor detail, but evidence that Freake owned land there before Willis received his patent (although Freake may not have actually been living on it at the time). In 1674 Freake bought part of Washington's patent back and was John Willis's immediate neighbor until Freake's death in 1684/85.

In 1661 John Washington and Thomas Pope (*i.e.,* Jr., Washington's brother-in-law) had received another patent for 1,200 acres.

To all...Sir William Berkeley Knight Governor give and grant unto Major John Washington and Thomas Pope twelve hundred acres of land situated on the south side of Potomack River upon the branches of Appomattox in the County of Westmoreland beginning at a corner marked Pohickory standing on the north side of (arm) belonging to the said creek and at the northermost corner of a tract of land belonging to Mr. Nathaniel Pope extending west across a small runn [sic] unto a marked chestnut tree standing on the eastermost side of arm of water that falls into Rappahannock River four hundred poles, thence north to another marked Pohickory four hundred and eighty poles, thence east to a marked white oak standing on a point on the

---

[14]Westmoreland County Deeds & Wills 1:226 from microfilm.

[15]Dorman, *Westmoreland County, Virginia, Records 1661–1664*, pp. 88–89. Deeds and Wills 1:226–227.

[16]Dorman, *Westmoreland County, Virginia, Deeds, Patents, etc. 1665–1677*, Part three, p. 29.

westermost side of a swamp four hundred poles finally south along by and crossing the branches of the Beaver Dams of Appomattox unto the first station. The said land being () unto the said Washington and Pope by and for the transportation of twenty four persons...dated the fourth day of September one thousand six hundred and sixty one.[17]

This patent is an example of land described as being in Westmoreland County when in reality it was partly in the Rappahannock watershed and therefore on both sides of the ridge line.

In September 1668 Governor Berkeley granted the same 1,200 acres to Col. Nicholas Spencer, the tract "being formerly granted to John Washington and Thomas Pope on 4 September 1661 and by them deserted for want of seating." Spencer's patent was recorded on 29 October 1668, and on the same day he assigned his interest in the tract back to Washington.[18]

Consequently, when John Willis received his patent in 1669, John Washington held title to both of the above tracts—one containing 1,700 acres and the other being 1,200 acres. It is not clear if these two parcels were contiguous, but when Washington wrote his will in 1675, he devised these tracts to his daughter, Ann, who later married Major Francis Wright.[19] In 1705 Francis and John Wright (husband and son of Ann Washington Wright) sold 1,000 acres of the 1,700-acre patent to Francis Thornton Sr. From that time until the Willis patent was sold to the Church Wardens in 1737, the Thorntons were neighbors to John Willis Sr. and his family.

The other important patents for land which either joined John Willis or were close to his land in 1669 will be given in chronological order as abstracted from the original books with assistance of Merrill Hill Mosher, C.G. The patent books are difficult to read and contain obsolete spellings (i.e., lyne for line, oake for oak, and forrest for forest), so spelling has been modernized and I have highlighted the name of the patentees for the reader's convenience.

*Sir Wm. Berkeley, etc...unto **John Piper** 400 acres of land in Westmoreland County upon the falling branches of Appomattox Creek in the forest beginning at a marked black oak standing in the line of Mr. Jno. Washington and Mr. Robert Nurse extending along the said line 200 poles to a red oak west from thence 320 poles to a small Spanish oak S from thence E 200 poles to a marked red oak standing in the line of land of Mr. Jno. Watts finally N 320 poles along the said Mr. Watts line to the first station...2 July 1669.[20]*

*Sir Wm. Berkeley, etc...to **Jno. Foxhall** 314 acres of land in Westmoreland*

---

[17] Virginia Patent Book 5:171 (54) from microfilm. Nugent, op. cit., I:449.

[18] Dorman, *Westmoreland County, Virginia, Deeds, Patents, etc., 1665–1677,* Part one, p. 53. (Deeds & Wills 1:352–353.)

[19] See Chapter IV.

[20] Virginia Patent Book 6:236 and Nugent, op. cit., II:60.

County in the body of the main forest betwixt the headbranches of Potomack and Rappa beginning at the line of Lt. Col. Jno. Washingtons land extending E 26 poles to a red oak a corner tree of Jno. Pipers from thence S 320 poles to Spanish oak another corner tree of the said Pipers and thence E 200 poles to a red oak standing in the line of the land of Mr. Jno. Watts then S () poles along the said Mr. Jno. Watts his line thence E 200 poles along the said Mr. Watts line thence S 50 poles thence W 426 poles to a red oak standing near Ned the Indians path thence N 550 poles to the place begun...23rd day of October 1669.[21]

John Willis's *patent for 261 acres dated 21 October 1669 adjoining John Washington as cited in Chapter I.*

William Berkeley, etc...to **Phillip Browne** *of the County of Westmoreland in the forest betwixt the rivers of Appomattox and Rappa 200 acres bounded as follows beginning at a red oak a corner tree of a parcel of land surveyed for Jno. Willis extending along a line belonging to Mr. Jno. Foxhall S 130 poles to a red oak standing near to Ned the Indians path from thence W 246 poles from thence N 130 poles to the line of the land of Lt. Col. Jno. Washington finally along the line of the said Lt. Col. Washington and Jno. Willis to the first marked red oak...30th October 1669.[22]*

Although one of the measurements given in Foxhall's patent is unclear, acreages of the other tracts can be computed from the information which is given. For those readers who are unfamiliar with the system used for land surveys in colonial times, one pole was equivalent to 16.5 feet.

The data given in these six patents, supplemented with later deeds and wills, provide several clues to the location of the patents relative to each other at the time the patents were issued.

It may be important that Browne's patent, which was dated nine days after John Willis's patent, stated that John's land had been surveyed but did not specifically say that John was living on it. By law John had three years in which to seat the tract. As it was not repatented and did not escheat, he was probably living on the 261-acre parcel by or before 1672. Browne's and Foxhall's patents did not mention any other landholder on their southern boundaries, so that land may not have been patented yet.

Consequently, in the fall of 1669 John Willis, John Washington, John Piper, John Foxhall, Phillip Browne, Nathaniel Pope, Robert Nurse, and John Watts owned tracts between the Potomac and Rappahannock rivers near Ned the Indian's path (possibly the same as Wariscreek or Warisquock path) and Powetridge (which was found with a variety of spellings in the records, including Portrages, Porotridge, Portridge, Poultridge, Partridge, and perhaps later as Portus or Portis) Creek. I suspect that it may

---

[21]Ibid., 6:276 and Nugent, op. cit., II:70.

[22]Ibid., 6:283 and Nugent, op. cit., II:72.

have been named because it was a convenient route for portaging between the Rappahannock and Potomac rivers. Apparently several branches, including one called Bald Eagle, ran into Portrages Creek which joined Crows Swamp. A 1728 deed mentioned "Indian Ned's but formerly called Powetridge Creek." This may have been an earlier name for Jett's Creek.

One question which remains unanswered is why Westmoreland County was given as the location of the above tracts. Subsequent records place all of Willis's patent, Browne's patent, probably Foxhall's patent, and much of Washington's 1,700-acre patent south of the fall line in what was then Old Rappahannock County and later became Richmond County. I suspect that some of the patentees were residents of Westmoreland County in 1669 and that the ridge line was so indefinite that Westmoreland was used in the patents. According to Eaton, some creeks which flow into the Rappahannock River actually have their headwaters within a mile of the Potomac.[23] Eaton also reported that John Washington, the immigrant, built a hotel and residence called the "Court House" at Mattox Ferry where he held Justices' Court.[24] Although I have not tried to verify that statement, it may account for the fact the earliest records in this area were recorded in Westmoreland County which was more convenient than the Old Rappahannock Court which met several miles downstream. Another possibility which might be explored is that certain areas in this locale were not yet officially open for patenting, and the inference that the tracts were in Westmoreland County and the vagueness of the patents enabled these men to preempt the parcels.

Eaton placed the Washington-Pope patent of 1,200 acres of 4 September 1661 on Sheet #2 (p. 60) between a 1,000 acre patent to Nathaniel Pope (which Eaton said was sold to John Watts in 1665) and a 300 acre patent issued in 1654 to John Hallowes. Although I found some minor discrepancies to this data in the records, the approximate location which Eaton gave to John Piper's and Nathaniel Pope's patents on Sheet #2 compares favorably with what I found for Foxhall's 314 acre patent which seems to have been mostly south of the Piper grant (with the exception of a long, narrow strip which lay between Piper and Washington) and west and south of Pope's grant which Pope sold to Watts.

Nathaniel Pope Sr. died testate in Westmoreland County between 16 May 1659 and 20 April 1660.[25] He left his minor son Thomas his "Clifts" plantation, and his son Nathaniel both the land where Nathaniel Sr. lived and his patent of 1,050 acres at the head of Appomattox Creek. Thomas Pope willed his "Clifts" land to his sons Richard and John in 1685. Nathaniel Pope Jr. repatented the 1,050-acre tract on 13 January 1661/62 and assigned it to John Watts on 1 November 1665 with Watts then selling half of it to Thomas Wilsford.[26]

---

[23] David W. Eaton, *Historical Atlas of Westmoreland County, Virginia (Richmond: Dietz Press, 1942)* p. 28.

[24] Ibid, *p. 44.*

[25] Dorman, *Westmoreland County, Virginia, Records 1658–1661*, p. 53; see Chapter IV.

[26] Dorman, *Westmoreland County, Virginia, Deeds, Patents, etc.,1665–1677*, Part one, p. 13.

Although this tract has not been fully traced, it is known that Wilsford died in 1666 leaving the 525 acres which he bought from John Watts to his son, Andrew Wilsford, stipulating that it would revert to his sons James and Thomas Wilsford if Andrew died without heirs.[27] John Watts was his executor, and Robert Nurse was one of the witnesses to his will. John Watts was deceased by 1679, his will being among the missing Westmoreland County records (see Chapter IV).

It appears that Andrew Wilsford, the son, died without heirs because in 1700 Thomas Wilsford (Andrew's brother?) willed all of his lands and estate to his friend, Richard Watts, who in 1707 sold the entire 1,050 acre Pope patent to Abraham Blagge.[28] Tracing this particular tract is difficult because of the missing deeds and wills, but I suspect the answer lies in a possible relationship between the Wilsford , Watts, and Blagg families.

In 1679 Abraham Blagg paid John Willis 450 pounds of tobacco out of the estate of Mr. Jno. Watts, deceased, by order of the sheriff.[29] The names Watts, Wilsford, and Blagg(e) were not found in later documents with the Willises in Richmond or King George counties, but Nathaniel Pope (alias Bridges, son of Nathaniel Pope Jr.) was called "my friend" by John Willis in a Power of Attorney in 1701 (see Chapter I). No significant references were found for Robert Nurse who died in Westmoreland County, but two of his estate appraisers were William Freake and John Watts which indicates that he probably lived in the Mattox Creek neighborhood.[30]

John Piper Sr. died testate between 25 January 1669/1670 and 17 September 1673 in Westmoreland County leaving his son John "my land which I tooke up this yeare." The records suggest that John Piper Jr. married Margaret Reeds, daughter of Samuel Reeds.[31] Both John Piper Jr. and Samuel Reeds (Sr.) died in 1698, the first intestate and the second testate. Under the law of primogeniture, John Piper Jr.'s land went to his eldest son, another John Piper, who was named as "my grandson" in Samuel Reed's will. John Piper Jr.'s widow, Margaret, then married Thomas Harper who died testate in 1737. Margaret Reeds Piper Harper died testate in 1744, her will naming her sons John Piper, Thomas Harper, George Harper, and Samuel Harper.[32]

In 1716 John Washington and wife Mary of Stafford County sold 171.5 acres, partly in St. Mary's Parish, Richmond County, and partly in Westmoreland County, to Francis Thornton Sr., the tract adjoining land of John Piper, deceased, Thomas

[27] Ibid., p. 26.

[28] Dorman, *Westmoreland County, Virginia, Deeds & Wills No. 3, 1701–1707*, pp. 40 and 58.

[29] Westmoreland County Order Book.

[30] Dorman, *Westmoreland County, Virginia, Deeds, Patents, etc., 1665–1677*, Part two, p. 60.

[31] See Chapter IV for sketch on John Piper.

[32] George H. S. King, *King George County Will Book A-1* (Easley, South Carolina: Southern Historical Press, 1978), p. 127; hereafter referred to as King in footnotes.

Marshall, Thomas Robins, Francis Thornton, and John Willis Sr.[33] Again, the missing Westmoreland records make it difficult to specifically trace this parcel, but the southern boundary of the 171.5 acre tract abutted the northern boundary of John Willis's 261-acre patent. Therefore, the 171.5 acres were probably in the northeastern part of Washington's 1,700-acre patent. As will be seen below, in 1726 Francis Thornton willed this tract to his wife's son, George Riding.

In 1737 John Piper (probably a descendant of the first John) received a grant for 37 acres in both counties on Mattox and Portridges creeks, adjoining John Marshall, George Riding, John Willis, John Jennings, Joshua Farguson, and his own land.[34] This John Willis, probably the son of William and the grandson of John Sr., sold his grandfather's patent to the Church Wardens of Hanover Parish in 1737. John Jennings was the second husband of Mary Coghill Willis Jennings, widow of John Willis Jr. who is discussed in Chapter V.

John Foxhall's 1669 patent is not shown on Eaton's plats of Westmoreland County because most of it was south of the ridge in Old Rappahannock. There has been confusion over Foxhall's land, partly because John Foxhall Sr. died in 1678 in Westmoreland and his will and estate records are among that county's missing records (see sketch in Chapter IV). Reconstruction of his holdings from later documents indicates that in 1670 he bought a 99-year lease on a mill, called Underwood's Mill, from William Underwood, the mill being about eight miles above Southers (or Southerns) Ferry on the Rappahannock. The lease became the property of his son John Foxhall Jr. who was a merchant and died testate in Washington Parish, Westmoreland County, in 1698. Foxhall left his "water mill" to (nephews?) James Vaulx and John Elliott Jr. The mill belonged to several leaseholders through the years, and finally in 1721 John Underwood (heir of William Underwood) and Richard and James Tutt (leaseholders) sold their interests in the mill and 50 acres to John King, Esq., and Company, merchants in Bristol, England.[35] Old maps show that the Bristol Ironworks and Furnace were just below present Bristol Mines Run. Eaton said that by 1729 the Bristol Mines furnace had ceased operations.

Much later (1762) John Jett of Hanover Parish in King George sold a water grist mill which was situated "a little above the place where the Bristol furnace formerly stood" to Jeremiah Murdock.[36] At that time the tract was in Hanover Parish. (In 1732 the upper part of Sittenburne Parish in lower King George County was incorporated into Hanover Parish.[37]) This mill is traced in Chapter IV through the Underwood and Foxhall families. John Willis's tract, which was always in St. Mary's Parish and then in Hanover Parish, and in Old Rappahannock, Richmond, and King George counties

---

[33]See Chapter IV.

[34]Gertrude E. Gray, *Northern Neck Land Grants 1694–1742* (Baltimore: Genealogical Publishing Co., 1988), p. 120. (Northern Neck Grant Book E–11.)

[35]Sparacio, *Deed Abstracts of King George County, Virginia, 1721–1735*, pp. 4–5. (Deed Book 1:14–19.)

[36]King George County Deed Book 4:487 from microfilm.

[37]Cocke, op. cit., pp. 144–145.

as boundaries changed, was west of Foxhall's mill and present Bristol Mines Run.

In 1675 a John Willis was ordered by the Westmoreland County Court to pay John Foxhall 973 pounds of tobacco which was "due by bill,"[38] and in 1687 John Willis was appointed as surveyor of the highways from Foxhall's Mill to Keyes Swamp in Rappahannock County.[39] (The first man may have been the John Willis who died in 1682 in Westmoreland although it is unclear, but the second man was undoubtedly John Willis Sr.) In addition, in 1685 William Underwood gave a performance bond to Nathaniel Pope (alias Bridges) to convey a tract "where Underwood lives near or upon line of John Willis running on outside line of said Underwood's line next to Potomac.[40] William Underwood Sr. acquired several large tracts on the north side of the Rappahannock River prior to the time that John Willis received his 1669 patent. As the only land which John Willis Sr. owned in 1685 was his 261-acre patent, it is assumed that this was the parcel which joined Underwood. Old Rappahannock County wills indicate that William Underwood Sr.'s widow, Elizabeth, married Archidale Coombes (or Archdale Combs) by 1675 and that they were the parents of John Combs, John Willis's adjoining neighbor (see Chapters III and IV).

As will be discussed in Chapter III, John Willis Sr. and John Parsons Sr. jointly received a grant of 158 acres in 1690/91, the tract described as being above (upstream from) Foxhall's mill. This tract appears to have overlapped with Phillip Browne's 1669 patent of 200 acres which escheated for lack of seating and which was later repatented by Randolph Kirk and John Fryer. According to the records, Kirke died before a division was made, and Fryer sold the patent to Thomas Crane. Crane sued for possession, but the Court ruled in favor of Willis and Parsons. The original 1690/91 grant to Willis and Parsons and John Willis's deed to his son John Jr. in 1694 stated that this tract adjoined John's 261-acre patent. The metes and bounds given in Browne's original patent imply that this land was just south of Washington's 1664 patent and Willis's 1669 patent, and west of Foxhall's 1669 patent.

Both Browne's and Foxhall's patents made reference to Ned the Indian's path. Ned (or Edmund) Gunstocker, Indian, received a patent for 150 acres from the Governor on 14 October 1665 in Rappahannock County.[41] Gunstocker's heirs sold it to Nathaniel Pope (alias Bridges, son of Nathaniel Pope Jr.) in 1697.[42] Land records confirm that Gunstocker's tract was later in Richmond (and then in King George) County.

The last and most complex land documents to be discussed here relate to John Washington's 1,700-acre patent. Washington received his patent in 1664 and was named as an adjoining landholder in the 1669 patents to Piper, Foxhall, Willis, and Browne.

---

[38] Dorman, *Westmoreland County Order Book 1675/6-1677/8*, Part one, p. 3.

[39] Sparacio, *(Old) Rappahannock County Orders 1685-1687*, p. 78.

[40] Sparacio, *Deed Abstracts of (Old) Rappahannock County, Virginia, 1682–1686*, p. 88.

[41] Nugent, *Cavaliers and Pioneers, Supplement (1690–1692)*, p. 3; Northern Neck Grant Book 1:566 from microfilm.

[42] See Chapter IV.

In 1674 Washington deeded back 300 acres next to Portridge Creek in the lowermost part of his 1,700 acres to William Freake. In 1675 Washington (whose wife Ann Pope predeceased him) of Washington Parish, Westmoreland County, wrote his will. It was presented in Court in January, 1677/78. He left two tracts to his unmarried daughter Ann including 1,200 acres where Thomas Jordan was living (probably as a tenant) and 1,400 acres where John Frier (Fryer) was living "after Mr. Fricke (Freake) has his quantity out of it."

Consequently, by 1677/78 Washington's original 1,700-acre patent had been disposed of by William Freake's acquisition of 300 acres and Washington's devising the balance (1,400 acres) to his daughter who later became the wife of Major Francis Wright and the mother of John Wright, both of Westmoreland County. Freake's 300 acre parcel will be reviewed first, followed by Wright's 1,400 acres. Documentation and additional information about these men and their heirs will be found in Chapter IV.

William Freake (ffrack) died testate in 1684/85 in Rappahannock County leaving his entire estate to his wife Martha (whose maiden name is unknown) with provisions for "my man" Robert Vincent to have the right to lease his house and ground for seven years rent free.[43] Robert Vincent married the widow Martha, and in 1687 they sold 100 acres to Thomas Tippett. They sold the remaining 200 acres to Joshua Davis who then deeded the same 200 acres back to the Vincents a few days later, the reason for those deeds not being clear.[44]

In 1691 Thomas Tippett sold 100 acres to John Hauxford, and on 7 February 1694/95 the county surveyor was ordered to survey the tract as part of a dispute between Thomas Tippett and Robert Vincent, probably over the boundaries of the tract. At that time the Court ordered Francis Thornton to swear two neighbors to take part in the survey "as also John Willis who is ordered to be present at the time and place aforesaid to a true discovery of what he knows concerning the bounds of the said land."[45] Having lived in the area for twenty-five years, John was probably the oldest living original patentee in terms of years of residency and was knowledgeable about property lines in the neighborhood. (It is noted that in 1694 John Willis Sr. had also deeded part of his 1669 patent and his interest in the Willis–Parsons grant to his son John Willis Jr., so he probably had a vested interest in the survey.)

In March, 1700/01, William Hayberd, son of Ann (Freake) Hayberd (grandson and daughter of William Freake, deceased) sued John Hauxford for title to 300 acres which Freake had purchased from Washington on Portridges Creek (i.e., the southern portion of Washington's 1,700-acre patent). Hayberd claimed that the tract should have fallen to him as heir-at-law to his grandfather. Based upon Freake's will in which Freake specifically left all of his estate, including his land, to his wife Martha, the Court validated Martha's right to deed the tract and validated Hauxford's title.[46]

---

[43] Sparacio, *Will Abstracts of (Old) Rappahannock County, Virginia, 1682–1687*, p. 49.

[44] See Chapter IV.

[45] Sparacio, *Richmond County Orders 1694–1697*, pp. 26–27.

[46] Sparacio, *Richmond County Orders 1699–1701*, pp. 55–56.

Four deeds involving this land were recorded in August and September of 1709. First, John Hauxford and Thomas Tippett traded (deeded to each other) an unspecified number of acres on the dividing line of their tracts. William Willis sold 12 acres of his father's 1669 patent (which John had deeded to him in 1701) to Hauxford. And finally Hauxford and his wife Saints sold 12 acres which were part of Washington's 1,700-acre patent dated 26 March 1664 (the date of Washington's assignment to Freake) to John Willis Jr.[47] When he wrote his will in 1727, John Willis Jr. referred to this as "that tract my brother William exchanged with John Hauxford" and willed it to William Wood (see Chapter V). As seen below, William Willis's son was able to sell the entire 261 acres in 1737, and Frederick Coghill Jr. (nephew of Mary Coghill Willis Jennings, widow of John Willis Jr.) sold the 12 acres to Francis Thornton in 1761. There was undoubtedly some in-house trading which was not properly recorded.

Hauxford received additional land by escheat in 1704. In 1717 he and his second wife Elizabeth sold this tract plus another parcel to Henry Wood who was then married to Sarah (—) Willis, widow of William Willis (see Chapter VI). William Wood (Henry's eldest son and heir-at-law) sold these two tracts to Rush Hudson Sr., the third husband of Sarah (—) Willis Wood Hudson, in 1734 after William Wood had moved to Orange County. In 1746 Rush Hudson Jr. of Orange County sold the two tracts plus two others (including 100 acres which his father had purchased from Richard Butler in 1723 and which was also part of Washington's patent) to Francis Thornton. In the 1746 deed all tracts were described as being on Portrages Creek or Bald Eagle in Hanover Parish, and the 1746 deed mentioned John Washington's patent for 1,700 acres.

In March 1718/19 Elizabeth Hauxford, the last wife of John Hauxford who was then deceased, sold 100 acres to Richard Butler. Hauxford had purchased this parcel from Robert Vincent.[48] In 1726 Butler sold the tract to Rowland Thornton (i.e., the son of Francis Thornton Sr.), the deed stating that it was part of Washington's 1664 patent for 1,700 acres and which was purchased by Butler from John Hauxford (given as Hansford by Sparacio).[49] This tract was part of the 300 acres which Freake had purchased from Washington in 1674 and which Freake's widow, Martha, and her second husband, Robert Vincent, sold to Tippett who sold to Hauxford.

On 5 September 1705 John Wright of Westmoreland County (son of Major Francis Wright and Ann Washington Wright) deeded 1,000 acres to Francis Thornton, the land being "part of a patent granted to Maj. John Washington for 1,700 acres dated 1 June 1664 beginning at the easternmost side of the land that was sold to Wm. Freake out of said patent and next to William Willis's, thence running north a straight course to the line of said patent, thence west and along the several courses of said patent till it comes to the land that did belong to Freake and now in possession of John Hawkford [Hauxford] and Thomas Tippett ... in St. Mary's Parish, Richmond County."[50] The

[47] Sparacio, *Richmond County Deeds 1708–1711*, pp. 36–39.

[48] Sparacio, *Richmond County Deeds 1714–1720*, p. 56.

[49] Sparacio, *Deed Abstracts of King George County, Virginia 1721–1735*, p. 60.

[50] Sparacio, *Richmond County, Virginia, Deeds 1705–1708*, pp. 10–12. (Deed Book 4.)

deed was followed by a release by his father, Francis Wright, of Cople Parish, Westmoreland County. Apparently Ann Washington Wright was deceased at that time.

More detailed information about the Thornton family is found in Chapter IV. For purposes of tracing John Willis's land, it is noted that in 1726 Francis Thornton Sr. willed half of this 1,000 acres to his wife Ann (whose maiden name is unknown to me, but who was the widow of ___ Riding) for life with it to then go to her son, George Riding (in addition to the 171.5 acres discussed earlier) and the other half to his son, Rowland Thornton. His bequest mentioned John Hawxford [Hauxford], Thomas Tippett, and Crows Swamp.[51]

To place these events in context, in 1737 John Willis (son of William and Sarah, and grandson of John Willis Sr.) and his wife Elizabeth (Plunkett) sold his grandfather's 1669 patent to the Church Wardens of Hanover Parish for use as a glebe and moved to Orange County.

In 1741 Rowland Thornton wrote his will, leaving land in both Hanover Parish, King George County, and in Spotsylvania County to his son, Francis Thornton. Rowland's wife Elizabeth (nee Catlett) was to have a life interest in his tract on the upper side of Crows Swamp, and after her death it was also to belong to his son Francis.[52]

In 1766 this Francis Thornton (son of Rowland) willed part of his Crows Swamp land to his son William and the other part to his son Francis.[53] His will mentioned that an unidentified Francis Willis was living on one of the tracts which he left to William, the land lying "in the lowest side of Crows Swamp" and adjoining George Riding's line. Some Willis researchers believe this Francis Willis was the son of John Willis (son of Charles and Matilda Willis) and that Francis later moved to Culpeper County where he died intestate in 1789. Although no direct proofs have been found yet, circumstantial evidence supports this possibility (see Chapter VII).

As shown in Chapter I, in 1767 the Hanover Parish Vestry sold the Willis glebe tract of 261 acres to William Thornton who may have been the son of Francis Thornton who died in 1766.

In 1818 Reuben T. Taylor and wife Mary, Thomas Woodford and wife Sarah (all of Caroline County) and David T. Chevis and wife Elizabeth of King George County deeded 342 acres 3 rods and 12 poles to Nathaniel H. Hoe.[54] The deed described the descent of the tract to three women as heirs of Francis Thornton, deceased, back through Rowland Thornton who died in 1741 and Francis Thornton Sr. who purchased the tract from the Wrights (originally Washington's patent). The deed mentioned Crows Swamp and Portises [sic] Creek.

[51] King, *King George County Will Book A-1, 1721-1752*, pp. 35–37.

[52] Ibid., p. 147.

[53] Sparacio, *King George County Will Book A*, p. 262.

[54] King George County Deed Book 10:470. (Copies of this and later deeds supplied by the King George County Clerk's Office.)

In 1840 Nathaniel H. Hooe sold his interest in the "Bald Eagle" tract which he bought from Francis Thornton's heirs at the head of Porteses [*sic*] Creek to the junction of Crow Swamp Creek to Charles Tayloe.[55]

Porteses (Portises, Portus) Creek is shown on a map (undated) by Warner as Glebe Creek, on the Fry–Jefferson 1775 map as Portus Creek, and on the 1968 USGS Rollins Fork (King George County, Virginia) map as Jett's Creek and was the first major creek above Bristol Mines Run.

In 1897 the Fredericksburg Circuit Court ruled in the matter of the estate of Charles Tayloe. The Bald Eagle tract was judged to be the property of Tayloe's daughter Ella who was then age 65 years, the widow of Thomas R. Waring, who had no living children.[56]

An earlier related deed was found showing that in 1758 Walter Anderson of Washington Parish, Westmoreland County, sold 90 acres in King George County to George Marshall of Hanover Parish, "a burying place of half an acre excepted, joining to the glebe land of Hanover Parish in said county."[57] At that time the glebe belonged to William Thornton and was John Willis's 261-acre patent. It may be that there was a cemetery on the old glebe property, and perhaps it is one of the marked cemeteries on the USGS Rollins Fork map of King George County.[58]

Later land records have not been researched, but there is certainly enough evidence at this point to find the location of John Willis's and John Washington's adjoining patents if someone is interested in pursuing it in depth. In *Historical Atlas of Westmoreland County, Virginia*, Eaton stated that Ann Washington, daughter of John Washington the immigrant and wife of Maj. Francis Wright, inherited a large tract which was patented by her father near Index, now in King George County.[59] This statement is supported by the patents and deeds and suggests that John Willis's 1669 patent, which abutted the southeastern corner of Washington's 1,700 acres, was probably south of present highway 3 and somewhere between present Index and Rollins Fork.

[55] King George County Deed Book 15:302.

[56] King George County Deed Book 28:132.

[57] King George County Deed Book 4:380.

[58] United States Department of the Interior Geological Survey map, Rollins Fork Quadrangle, Virginia, 1968.

[59] Eaton, op. cit., p. 54.

Chapter III

Other Grants and Deeds for John Willis Sr.

In addition to his 1669 patent John acquired three other tracts between January 1687/88 and March 1696/97 on the north side of the Rappahannock River. This chapter will discuss those documents, the possible location of the tracts, and later disposition of the land.

Although John's first patent was on the south side of the ridge line in Old Rappahannock County, his name was not found in that county's records until 1684, leaving a fifteen-year period when virtually nothing is known about him. Clues suggest that during that time John may have been more closely associated with the families on Mattox Creek. If that was the case, the loss of the Westmoreland County records between 1671 and 1691 may present problems in tracing his parents, his previous wife or wives, and the mother or mothers of his children.

Besides the 1684 performance bond of William Underwood to Nathaniel Pope for a tract adjoining John Willis as given in Chapter II, the following records were found in Old Rappahannock County for John Willis Sr.[1]

> *6 November 1684, reference granted between Jno. Willis, Plaintiff, and Walter Anderson til next court north side of the river.*

> *4 May 1687, ordered that John Willis officiate as surveyor of the highways from Foxhall's Mill to Keys Swamps this ensuing year.*

> *4 May 1687, ordered that John Willis, John Parsons, and Moses Hubbart be paid by the executrix of Josias (Josiah) Mason, deceased, for one day's attendance for proof of Mason's will.*

Other connections between John Willis and Parsons, Anderson, Foxhall and Underwood are discussed below. Underwood was executor of Josias Mason's will. Saints Gay (or Jay), a legatee of Josias Mason, married John Hauxford who bought part of Washington's 1,700 acre patent from Thomas Tippett.

All of John Willis's later grants and deeds were for tracts in that part of Old Rappahannock which became Richmond and then King George County. For ease in referencing the different parcels, they will be numbered chronologically and identified by those numbers in the text.

> Tract #1: On 21 October 1669 John Willis received his first patent for 261 acres as reported in Chapter I.

---

[1] Sparacio, (Old) Rappahannock County Order Books.

Tract #2: On 27 January 1687/88 Mallachy Peal(e) of Stafford County, merchant, deeded 403 acres to John Willis, Thomas Kendall, and Thomas Goff jointly and acknowledged his deed at the March session of County Court.[2]

Tract #3: On 27 February 1690/91 John Willis and John Parsons, both of Rappahannock County, were granted 158 acres in that county adjacent to a tract which was surveyed for Henry Fleete above Foxhall's Mill.[3] A previous article in the Willis–Gordon–Garnett and Allied Families Association *Journal* erroneously states that it was 185 acres (probably due to transposition).[4]

Tract #4: On 19 March 1696/97 John Willis of Richmond County was granted 210 acres on the Rappahannock River adjoining Mary Gunstocker (Indian), Thomas Goff(e), and John Combs.[5]

No locators were given for tract #2, but later deeds suggested that both #2 and #4 were on or near the Rappahannock River and south of tract #3 and John's first patent, #1. Tracts #2 and #4 also adjoined a large parcel which was owned by Ralph Wormley whose tract was on the north side of the river and across from Port Tobacco.[6]

The grantor of tract #2, Mallachy Peal(e), was a prominent land broker in the Northern Neck whose named appears frequently in the records. He would buy random tracts and sometimes either break them up or combine them when he sold, so it is difficult to determine when and how he obtained this tract or combination of tracts.

In 1676 Mallachy Peale (who was about 28 years old, making him approximately the same age as John Willis) witnessed the will of a William Browne in Old Rappahannock County.[7] Browne left his land to his three sons (William, John, and Maxfield Browne) and named his wife Elizabeth and "the rest of my children." Elizabeth Browne and Evan Morgan were the executors of his will. Morgan married the widow Elizabeth and died testate in Old Rappahannock County. Morgan's will was witnessed by Josiah Mason, Thomas Jones, and Thomas Booth. His executors were "my loving wife Elizabeth and my loving friend Mallachy Peal." In June 1684 his estate appraisers were Thomas Arnold, Adam Woffendall, Francis Thornton, and William Strother.

---

[2]Sparacio, *Deed Abstracts of (Old) Rappahannock County, Virginia 1686–1688*, p. 79.

[3]Nugent, *Cavaliers and Pioneers*, Supplement, p. 3, and Northern Neck Grants, Book 1:43, from microfilm.

[4]See Chapter I.

[5]Northern Neck Grants, Book 2:264–265, from microfilm of the original document (see below).

[6]Sparacio, *(Old) Rappahannock County Deed Book 1672–1676*, Part II, p. 88. (Deed Book 5:331–333.)

[7]Sweeney, William Montgomery, *Wills of Rappahannock County, Virginia 1656–1692*, p. 47. Sparacio, *(Old) Rappahannock County Will Book 1682–1687*, pp. 30–31 and 38–39.

Evan Morgan's will identified his residence as lying in the freshes of the Rappahannock River. He bequeathed 120 acres (which was part of a 220 acre tract) to "my Godson, Maxfield Browne, my wife's youngest son," livestock to his wife's other children—Elizabeth Browne, John Browne, and William Browne—and the balance of his estate to his wife and his friend Mallachy Peale.

Tract #2 which Willis, Kendall, and Goffe jointly purchased from Peale in 1687/88 was also in the freshes.[8] Maxfield Browne and William Browne (heirs of both their father and stepfather) later owned land which lay to the north of Washington's 1,700 acre patent. As those tracts which joined Washington's tract were not in the freshes, it may be that Elizabeth (—) Browne Morgan and Mallachy Peale sold the tract where Morgan lived.

In 1686 Henry Fleet (Jr.) and his wife Elizabeth of Northumberland County deeded a parcel in St. Mary's Parish, Rappahannock County, to Mallachy Peale of Stafford County, Gentleman. The land was on the north side of the Rappahannock River in the freshes bounded by Tankard's line to Indian Ned's corner, running with Indian Ned's line (but excluding Ned's 150 acres) up the river to the mouth of a small creek near Warasquick Indian Town, then up the creek and main branch to Mr. Underwood's line and corner to Underwood and Tankard, except 200 acres granted by said Henry Fleet to Joshua (Josiah) Mason and the land called Indian Ned's (Gunstocker).[9] The Fleets had deeded to Josiah Mason in 1684/85, the deed stating that the land had been granted to Henry Fleet, father of Henry (Jr.).[10]

The acreage in the above deed was not given, but in 1694 Henry Fleet of Christ Church Parish, Lancaster County, Gentleman, deeded 2,000 acres to Edwin Conway, also of Christ Church Parish, the land being in Richmond County (which was created in 1692) on the Rappahannock River near Warasquit Indian Town.[11] The tract was first granted in 1655 to Nicholas Meriwether who assigned it to Col. Henry Fleet (Sr.), father of the above Henry, "excepting 200 acres of said tract granted to Joshua Mason, 100 acres to Peter Butler, and 300 acres to Malachi [sic] Peale by the said Henry Fleet, party to these parts." Edwin Conway, who died in 1698, was the first husband of Elizabeth Thornton, eldest daughter of Francis Thornton Sr.[12] Conway's first wife was Sarah Walker, daughter of Col. John Walker and Mrs. Sarah Fleet, widow of Henry Fleet Sr. This 1694 deed from Fleet to Conway would later affect John Willis's title in tract #3.

When comparing these wills and deeds with other records for John Willis, Thomas Kendall, Thomas Goff(e), and John Combs, I believe that Peale may have combined

[8] According to Webster's *New Twentieth Center Dictionary* (unabridged, 2nd ed.), the term *freshes* referred to "the mingling of fresh water with turbid or salt water, especially the mingling of the waters of a river or brook with the salt water of a bay or estuary."

[9] Sparacio, *(Old) Rappahannock County Deed Book 1686–1688*, pp. 26–27.

[10] Sparacio, *(Old) Rappahannock County Deed Book 1682–1686*, p. 102.

[11] Sparacio, *(Old) Rappahannock County Deed Book 1692–1694*, p. 80.

[12] For additional information see George H. S. King, *Marriages of Richmond County 1668–1853* (Easley, SC: Southern Historical Press, 1964, repr. 1986).

the 300 acres from Fleet with 103 acres from Morgan's estate and deeded the 403 acres to Willis, Kendall, and Goff in 1687/88. Grants to these three men and John Combs in 1696/97 described their tracts as located in the freshes of the river and joining Gunstocker's patent and each other.

Edmund Gunstocker will be discussed in Chapter IV. He was known as Ned the Indian and was a member of the Nanzatacons of Rappahannock. Ned was friendly to the settlers and was given a patent of 150 acres by the Governor in 1665.[13] Gunstocker wrote his will on 22 October 1676, and it was proved in May or June of 1686. Ned willed his 150 acre patent to his wife Mary, and in 1697 his heirs sold the patent to Nathaniel Pope alias Bridges.[14]

In his history of Westmoreland County, Norris placed the Indian villages of Warisquock (Warasquick), Nansatico, Nanzimond, and Portobaco in this area across from Portobago Bay.[15] Wariscreek path, which was mentioned in William Freake's 1662 patent and John Washington's 1664 patent, was probably the same as Indian Ned's path which was mentioned in the 1669 patents to Foxhall and Browne. Warner also placed Jett's Creek (earlier name unknown) as flowing into Portobago (Port Tobacco) Bay "east of old Nanzatico Town."[16] I do not know if Jett's Creek was first known as Indian Ned's or Portridges Creek as the records are unclear, but the evidence strongly suggests that tracts #2 and #4 were in the area between present Jett's Creek and Bristol Mines Run, both names not appearing in the records until much later.

In January, 1692/93, John Willis deeded a tract in Richmond County adjoining Indian Mason and Joseph Mason to Thomas Kendall.[17] The land was described as being on the river up to the first swamp, then up a run to an Indian path and then to Thomas Kendall's land. This was probably part of tract #2 because later disposition of previously acquired tracts can be accounted for. On the same day John Coombes (Combs) and wife Anne deeded a tract to Thomas Kendall on the north side of the river and lying between the swamp, John Willis, and John Coombes [*sic*]. The acreage was not given in either of these deeds.

Research on tract #3 produced some interesting results and emphasized the importance of land records in genealogical research. Detailed information regarding the descent of title to tract #3 is found in Richmond County Deed Book 4 (pp. 102a–103) when in 1706/07 John Willis Jr. and Walter Anderson divided the tract.[18] Consequently, it is possible to re-construct the sequence of events from the time the grant was issued on 27 February 1690/91.

---

[13] Nugent, op. cit., I:566.

[14] See Chapter IV.

[15] Norris, op. cit., p. 27.

[16] Thomas Hoskins Warner, *History of Old Rappahannock County, Virginia 1656–1692*, p. 169.

[17] Sparacio, *Richmond County Deeds 1692–1693*, pp. 51–52.

[18] Sparacio, *Richmond County Deeds 1705–1708*, pp. 80–81.

The original grant to John Willis (Sr.) and John Parsons (Sr.) recorded in the Northern Neck Land Grants (vol. 1, p. 43) is almost unreadable due to ink blots and poor condition. Gray's transcription states that it was 154 acres which appears to be incorrect. The original document on microfilm was reviewed, and the acreage was 158. It was adjacent to a tract which had been surveyed for Henry Fleet above Foxhall's Mill. Readable portions of the grant mention the main branch of Poltridges [sic] Creek and indicated that it adjoined a line of 190 perches along John Willis's line. This probably referred to the southern boundary of Willis's 261-acre tract (#1) which was 190 perches (or poles), and it agrees with the bounds given in Phillip Browne's 1669 patent.

John Willis Sr. deeded his interest in tract #3 (plus 100 acres of tract #1) to his son John Jr. in 1694. John Parsons Sr. willed his share to his son John Parsons Jr. and Walter Anderson. According to Sweeney, John Parsons Sr. wrote his will on 12 April 1688, and it was proved on 6 November 1689. He devised two tracts of land to his *son* Walter, the tract where he (John Parsons Sr.) lived to his son John, and certain legacies to his grandchildren. It may be that Walter Anderson was his stepson or son-in-law as no records were found for a man named Walter Parsons and the Andersons were known neighbors for many years (see sketch in Chapter IV).

In the 1706/07 division of the tract, the document stated that Walter Anderson had purchased John Parsons Jr.'s share so that Walter Anderson and John Willis Jr. owned the tract[19]. When they divided it, Anderson got the eastern part, and John Willis Jr. got the western part. The division made reference to Fleet's line and an unnamed branch which ran through the land as being the dividing line between Willis and Anderson. Nathaniel Pope was one of the witnesses both in 1698 when John Parsons Jr. deeded his share to Walter Anderson and again in 1706/07 when the division was made. The deed gave the acreage as 158 which agreed with the acreage given in the original grant from microfilm.

A John Parsons was mentioned in early Westmoreland County records with two unidentified Willis men there—a John Willis who died in 1682 and a William Willis who died in 1720—so our Willis family may have been related to the Willises of Westmoreland County (see Chapter X).

Apparently this tract was a target of litigation from the time that Willis and Parsons first claimed it. The first action was brought by Thomas Crane against John Willis Jr. and Walter Anderson on 4 June 1696 when Crane asked for 10,000 pounds of tobacco in damages.[20] Crane stated that Willis and Anderson were occupying a tract in St. Mary's Parish on the north side of the Rappahannock River, that the land was patented by Phillip Brown who defaulted, and that the land was granted to Randolph Clark/Kirke and John Fryer of Westmoreland County by Order dated 24 September 1680. According to Crane's testimony, Clark/Kirke died before he and Fryer divided the land, and the tract then became Fryer's by right of survivorship. Fryer sold the

---

[19] Sparacio, *Richmond County Deeds 1695–1701*, p. 66.

[20] Sparacio, *Richmond County Orders*.

tract to Crane who received title from the Proprietors Office on 2 October 1694. Willis and Anderson produced their grant from the Proprietors Office dated 27 February 1690/91, and the Court ruled for Willis and Anderson. It may be important that John Washington's 1675 will mentioned that a man named John Fryer was living on one of the tracts which Washington left to his daughter Ann (later Wright).

Several documents were found which related to this suit. Randolph Kirk(e) was deceased by 22 February 1681/82.[21] His will, which is in the missing wills of Westmoreland County, was proved by Thomas Tanner and John Watts. In 1689 John Fryer and wife Rosamond deeded 125 acres to Thomas Crain (Crane).[22] The Rappahannock County Orders of 8 May 1690 contained the entry, "Reff. Inter Tho. Crane Plt. and Jno. Willis & Walter Anderson till next Court." On 2 September 1691 the County Orders stated, "The suit depending between Tho. Crane Plt. and John Willis & Walter Anderson Defts. for an uncertainty in the declaracon [declaration] is dismist [dismissed] and ordered that the Plt. pay all cost of suit." These references to Randolph Clark/Kirk/Kirke and John Fryer also suggest a possible relationship between the John Willis who died in 1682 in Westmoreland County and John Willis Sr. who died in 1715 in Richmond/King George County.

John Willis Jr. held title to half of tract #3 for approximately twelve years after the division was made. On 27 March 1719 Edwin Conway of Lancaster County (probably the son of Edwin, deceased, and his second wife, Elizabeth Thornton, who was then the wife of Jonathan Gibson Sr.) sold to John Anderson a parcel containing by estimation 117 acres in Hanover Parish "and being most part their part of a patent of land formerly granted unto John Willis Sr. and John Persons [Parsons] which bears (date) the 27th day of February 1690 as by the said patent may fully appear, and being by a late survey made by said Conway taken into a patent of the said Conway's for 2,000 acres of land." This was probably part of the above 1694 deed from Fleet to Conway. The lease and release stated that the tract began near the head of Poultridges Creek, running thence along a line of trees formerly called Fleet's line to a red oak corner to the said Willis and Parsons, then north to the back line of the said Conway and to the beginning near the head of Poultridges Creek.[23]

John Anderson (brother of Walter Anderson) died testate in King George County in 1721.[24] Part of his will was eaten away by insects, but readable parts indicate that he left his home place which contained about 120 acres to his underage son who was also named Walter. If his son Walter died without issue, the farm was to go to his brother Walter who was undoubtedly the Walter Anderson who divided tract #3 with John Willis Jr. Anderson's will also mentioned a horse which formerly belonged to John Combes who owned neighboring land (see note below and Chapter IV).

As a result of Conway's survey, John Willis Jr. and Walter Anderson lost their title to

[21] Dorman, *Westmoreland County, Virginia, Order Book 1675/6–1688/9*, Part two, p. 76.

[22] Sparacio, *(Old) Rappahannock County Deeds 1688–1692*, p. 55.

[23] Sparacio, *Richmond County Deeds 1714–1720*, p. 86. (Deed Book 7:401–403.)

[24] King, *King George County Will Book A-1*, pp. 5–7.

most of tract #3. John Willis Jr. still had the 100 acres from his father's 1669 patent, and he had leased another 100 acres from George Green in 1709, the last parcel being adjacent to William and Maxfield Brown (see Chapter V).

At the same time that John Willis Sr. received his last grant for 210 acres (tract #4), three adjoining grants were recorded. John Combs received his grant six days prior to the other three men, so his did not mention Willis, Kendall, or Goff. A comparison of the four grants shows that they adjoined each other and Mary Gunstocker, widow of Edmund Gunstocker (Ned the Indian). Later records prove that these men were neighbors for many years.

Abstracts of these grants can be found in Gray's *Virginia Northern Neck Grants*. Because the entire grants were needed for information and landmarks, I went to the original books on microfilm. The first number given is the number of the grant book, and the second number is the page. Spelling, capitalization, and punctuation have been retained. Highlighting and underlining have been added.

> 2:263, *Margaret, Lady Culpeper, Thomas Lord Fairfax, etc. ... Whereas know ye that we for and in consideration ... do give and grant unto* **John Combs** *of the County of Richmond ... bounded as followeth/viz/beginning at a hickory by the river side on the line of a pattent of one William Yarrett now in the occupation of Mr. Tankard, and running along said line north, north west twelve perches to a stake and white oak thence along another line of Yarretts, north, north east three quarter of a degree East three hundred and twenty perches to a red oak corner tree to Underwood and Yarrett, thence along a line of Underwoods north nine degrees, west fifteen perches to a stake by a small hickory, thence west fifteen degrees north one hundred and two perches to a white oak and a branch, thence south south west three quarter of a degree west three hundred and eight perches to a chestnut oak, upon the bank of the river on the north side of a branch near Indian Neds old field, thence down the river its several courses to the first mentioned station containing and being now laid out for* **two hundred acres** *... to have and to hold yielding and paying four shillings yearly ... dated the thirteenth day of March one thousand six hundred and ninety 6/7 [sic].*

> 2:264-5, *Margarett Lady Culpeper, etc., ... Know ye ... that we for and in consideration of the composition ... do give and grant unto* **John Willis** *of the County of Richmond ... bounded as followeth/viz/beginning at a marked hickory corner tree to this land, and (to) the land of Mary Gunstocker Indian standing upon Rappahannock river side in the clivis extending thence north six degrees east one hundred and sixty poles to a marked white oak corner tree to this land and the land of the said Gunstocker, thence west by north eighty poles to a marked red oak corner tree on the lines of the land of the said Gunstocker, and dividing this land from the land of* <u>Thomas Goffe</u> *thence north four and half degrees East, one hundred and fifty eight poles to a marked locust corner tree, thence south seventy six degrees East two hundred and eleven poles to a marked white oak corner tree to this land, and the land*

*of <u>John Combs</u>, thence South twenty nine and half degrees, West three hundred and twenty two poles to a marked corner chestnut oak standing by the said River, thence along the said river side to the dwelling house, the aforementioned beginning place, containing and being now laid out for **two hundred and ten acres**, Together ... Royal mines excepted, To have and to hold ... yielding and paying five shillings yearly ... dated the nineteenth of March one thousand six hundred and ninety 6/7.*

2:265, Margarett Lady Culpeper, Thomas Lord Fairfax ... Know ye that wee for and in consideration of the composition ... do give and grant unto **Thomas Kendall** *of the County of Richmond ... bounded as followeth/viz/beginning at a marked hickory corner tree standing upon the north side of a pocoson (swamp) which falleth into Rappahannock river being a corner to this land, and the land of Mary Gunstocker Indian in the clivis, extending thence north by East one hundred and fifty four poles to a locust (post) being a corner to this land & the land of the said Gunstocker, thence East by south sixty poles to a marked White Oak, standing in the back line of the land of the said Gunstocker, thence north four and a half degrees East one hundred and thirty three poles to a marked corner Spanish oak standing upon the said pocoson swamp, dividing this land from the land of <u>Thomas Goffe</u>, thence down the meanders of the said pocoson swamp to the aforementioned beginning place containing and being now laid out for* **a hundred and five acres** *... To have and to hold ... yielding and paying three shillings yearly provided ... dated the nineteenth day of March one thousand six hundred and ninety 6/7.*

2:266, Margarett Lady Culpeper, Thomas Lord Fairfax ... Know ye that we for and in consideration of the composition ... do give and grant unto **Thomas Goffe** *... of the County of Richmond ... bounded as followeth/viz/beginning at a marked corner white oak to the land of <u>Thomas Kendall</u> standing in the back line of Mary Gunstocker in the clivis extending thence East by North one hundred and seven poles to a marked red oak corner tree to this land and the land of <u>Mr. John Willis</u> standing in the said Gunstocker line thence north seventy six degrees west ninety poles to à marked white oak upon the east side of the pocoson swamp near the head of Warasque Creek, thence down the meanders of the said swamp to a marked Spanish oak, dividing this land from the land of the said <u>Kendall</u> being on the said swamp, thence south four and a half degrees West one hundred and thirteen poles to the aforementioned beginning, containing and being now laid out for* **one hundred and five acres**, *Together ... Royall mines excepted ... To have and to hold ... Yielding and paying three shillings yearly ... dated the nineteenth day of March one thousand six hundred and ninety 6/7.*

The exact location of these tracts has not been determined, but they almost certainly were somewhere between present Jett's Creek and Greenlaw Wharf on the USGS Rollins Fork, King George County, Virginia, map. A careful review of all the land records for John Combs, Thomas Kendall, and Thomas Goffe might clarify the issue.

In summary, documents show that between 1669 and 1696/97 John Willis obtained title to approximately 684 acres, all of which lay in what is now King George County. His tracts included (1) a 1669 patent for 261 acres, (2) a 1687/88 deed from Mallachy Peale for 403 acres which John held jointly with Kendall and Goff(e), (3) a 1690/91 grant for 158 acres held jointly with John Parsons Sr. and (4) a 1696/97 grant for 210 acres.

In 1694, by which time John owned all or part of the first three tracts, he deeded 100 acres of his 1669 patent (#1) plus his interest in the Willis–Parsons grant (#3) to his son John Jr. In 1701 he deeded the remaining 161 acres of his 1669 patent to his son William. John Willis Jr. died testate without issue, and William Willis died intestate but with two sons, the eldest being John who later moved to Orange County. At the death of John Willis Jr. his portion (100 acres) of the 1669 patent reverted to William's son John who sold the entire tract to the Church Wardens of Hanover Parish in 1737. William's son John would also have inherited his uncle John Jr.'s interest in the Willis–Parsons grant (#3), but most of it was lost to Edwin Conway in 1719 by resurvey.

Regarding tracts #2 and #4, John Willis Sr. sold part of his interest in the 403 acres (#2) to Thomas Kendall in January 1692/93. It is assumed that this was part of the 403 acres as the other land which John owned at the time can be identified. In 1716/17 Thomas Kendall deeded 20 acres to his son William (who married Elizabeth Combs).[25] In 1721 William Kendall sold 20 acres to his brother, Samuel Kendall, for "love and affection," the tract being in Hanover Parish on the lower side of Poultridges Creek, and part of a patent to Thomas Kendall for 100 acres joining lands of Edwin Conway and John Green.[26] John Green sold 50 acres on Poultridges Creek adjacent to Conway (formerly known by the name of Mary Grimstecker's line, *i.e.*, Gunstocker) to William Pitman in 1706.[27] In 1727 Samuel Kendall sold 20 acres to William Pittman, the land being described as adjoining Ralph Wormley, Thos. Dickson, and John Willis Jr. and as being part of a patent granted to John Willis Sr. late of King George County.[28] I believe that this land was close to the area shown as Pitman's Landing on the 1737 map which is found in George H. S. King's *King George County Will Book A-1* or near Greenlaw's Wharf on the current USGS Rollins Fork, King George County, map.

Therefore, by the time that John Willis Sr. wrote his will in 1715, he had deeded his 1669 patent (#1), his interest in tract #3, and an unknown portion of tract #2, leaving him with his remaining interest in tract #2 and his last grant #4.

John Willis Sr. devised two plantations, including the tract where he was then living, to his son Charles for life with the land then to go to Charles' son John. A portion of one of these plantations was willed to his daughter Mary James, and another part was left to Mary Cullins whose share reverted to John's heirs when she died without issue. In his will John described his land as joining Mr. John Wormley, Isaac Arnold (son-in-law of Thomas Goff), and John Combs (who died in 1716/17).

---

[25] Sparacio, *King George County Deeds 1714–1720*, pp. 68–69.

[26] Sparacio, *King George County Deed Book 1*, pp. 11–12.

[27] Ibid., p. 50.

[28] Ibid., p. 65.

John Willis (probably the son of Charles) and wife Elizabeth sold 60 acres to Isaac Pitman in 1736/37.[29] William James (John's grandson and the son of Mary and Thomas James) sold 20 acres to Jeremiah Murdock in 1742.[30] Both deeds mentioned Wormley's line. John Willis (son of Charles) mortgaged 170 acres to the executors of Harry Turner, deceased, in 1752.[31] The names of adjacent landowners and other data in these deeds correspond with John Sr.'s will. Other records for Charles Willis's family and Charles' son John will be reviewed in Chapter VII.

The evidence is very strong that John's 261-acre tract was near or south of present Highway 3 between the present towns of Index and Rollins Fork, that tract #3 lay just south of the first patent, and that tracts #2 and #4 touched the river and perhaps joined each other. It is possible that at some point in time John's adjoining tracts stretched from present Highway 3 to the Rappahannock River.

In 1758 Walter Anderson of Washington Parish, Westmoreland County (undoubtedly a descendant of John Anderson who became the owner of most of the Willis–Parsons grant) deeded 90 acres in King George County to George Marshall. The deed excluded "a burying place joining to the glebe land of Hanover Parish."[32] In 1758 the glebe land was still John Willis's 1669 patent which his grandson, John Willis, had sold to the Hanover Parish Vestry in 1737 and which the Vestry sold to William Thornton in 1767 (see Chapter I).

Records which were found for neighboring families will be discussed in Chapter IV, not only to shed more light on the specific area of the Willis holdings, but also to explore possible family relationships.

---

[29] King George County Deed Book 2:142–147.

[30] Ibid., pp. 398–402.

[31] King George County Deed Book 3:499–502.

[32] King George County Deed Book 4:380.

Chapter IV

The Willis Community
in Old Rappahannock, Richmond, and King George Counties

While John Willis Sr.'s land records were interesting, they did not provide the answers to the basic questions of my search. When did John immigrate to Virginia? Who were his parents? Did he have siblings? Who was (or were) the mother(s) of his children? What was the maiden name of Sarah who married John's son William and whose descendants moved to Orange County?

Many of the early immigrants who settled in rural areas of the Northern Neck were related to each other in various ways, and their children frequently married the neighbor's son or daughter. At this point in my research both the evidence and the laws of probability suggested that there must have been a connection between John Willis Sr. and one of these early groups. The records show that no other Willis family lived in that specific locale when John received his 1669 patent. If he had relatives living nearby, they may have been through his mother's line, his wife's family (assuming that he was married at that time) or a married sister.

In order to better understand John's community and to find the answers to my questions, I began to compile data for adjoining patentholders and landowners so that I could cross-reference the names and identify related families. By listing those names chronologically and charting them, I was able to reduce the list to a few families who owned adjoining tracts through changes in county and parish lines from 1669 when John received his patent until 1737 when his grandson sold the tract to the Church Wardens.

This chapter summarizes John Willis Sr.'s community on the Northern Neck. Due to the volume of my notes at this point, they have been condensed into a few brief comments and limited to what I consider to be the most important findings. Some of these records have been cited in previous chapters. Other sources are given below in the footnotes.

The records identify two rather discrete clusters of people who owned land adjoining John Willis Sr. with a few families overlapping into both groups. The earliest group migrated up the Potomac and settled in Westmoreland County on the north side of the ridge. It included John Washington, Nathaniel Pope, John Watts, John Piper, John Foxhall, Phillip Browne, and William Freake. Patents issued to those men have been discussed and will not be included here except to note that in every case the location of the patents was given as Westmoreland County when, in fact, some were south of the ridge in the Rappahannock watershed.[1] The families represented in this group will be discussed first, followed by a review of the second group which developed a few

---
[1] Chapter II.

45

years later and owned land south of the ridge.

The first link I found between John Washington and John Willis Sr. was Willis's 1669 patent as given in Chapters I and II. The location, configuration, and timing for Washington's and Willis's adjoining patents raise some questions. The area where Washington and Willis received their patents was sparsely settled before 1669, and they appear to have been the first patentholders on these tracts. Why was John Willis's tract a rectangular plot which perfectly joined the lower corner of Washington's 1,700 acres even though Washington received his patent five years earlier? Why didn't someone else patent John Willis's tract between 1664 when Washington received his patent and 1669? Was there a prior connection between John Willis and the Washingtons, Popes, or William Freake? Is it significant that William Freake, John Hallowes, and James Willis were on the Northern Neck in 1648–1652 or that William Freake and a Richard Willis were listed as headrights in John Hallowes' 1650/51 patent?[2]

The second link I found between the two men was a 1675 entry in the Westmoreland County records when Col. [John] Washington, John Willis, Mr. Wm. Butler, Mr. Bridges, and the orphans of Abram Field were paid out of the estate of Corderoy Ironmonger in Westmoreland County.[3] The original document shows that Washington and Willis were paid 490 pounds of tobacco and 600 pounds of tobacco respectively for "corne" (corn). When I initially saw this entry, I assumed that it referred to the John Willis who died in Westmoreland County in 1682. Later research suggested that he may have been John Willis Sr., but the records are still unclear (see Chapter X). In his will Col. Francis Willis also mentioned relatives by the names of Ironmonger and Butler (see Chapter XII).

John Washington the immigrant was born *circa* 1630 and died testate in 1677 leaving three children by his wife Ann Pope (the daughter of Nathaniel Pope Sr.) who predeceased him.[4] Ann Pope Washington was the sister of Nathaniel Pope Jr. who married Mary Lisson and died *circa* 1670 leaving an underage son, Nathaniel, later called Nathaniel Pope *alias Bridges* in the records. Mary Lisson Pope, married secondly (William?) Bridges, third Lewis Nicholas, and fourth David Whitlife (Wickliffe).[5]

---

[2] See Chapter II.

[3] Dorman, *Westmoreland County, Virginia, Deeds, Patents, etc., 1665–1677*, Part three, p. 41, and microfilm.

[4] Dorman, *Westmoreland County, Virginia, Deeds, Patents, etc., 1665–1677*, Part four, pp. 32–34. Also see Dorman, *Westmoreland County, Virginia, Records 1658–1661*, pp. 30 and 52 (Deeds & Wills 1:88 and 1:115–116). Washington's other wives are not discussed here. Additional sources reviewed for data on the Washington family included Henry Fitz-Gilbert Waters, ed., *Genealogical Gleanings in England*, vol. I; Douglas Southall Freeman, *George Washington: A Biography*, vols 1 and 2; David W. Eaton, *Historical Atlas of Westmoreland County, Virginia*; Nell Marion Nugent, *Cavaliers and Pioneers*, vols. 1 and 2; and Westmoreland County records as abstracted by John Frederick Dorman, and original records on microfilm through a local LDS Family History Center (see Bibliography).

[5] Dorman, *Westmoreland County, Virginia, Deeds, Patents, etc., 1665–1677*, Part three, p. 41; *Westmoreland County Order Book 1675/6–1688/9*, Part two, p. 14; *Westmoreland County, Virginia, Deeds, Patents, etc. 1665–1677*, Part four, p. 6; *Westmoreland County, Virginia, Deeds & Wills No. 2*,

Nathaniel Pope alias Bridges witnessed John Willis's deeds to his sons in 1694 and 1701 and Willis gave Pope his Power of Attorney to acknowledge the deeds in Court. Records suggest that Nathaniel may have been related to another William Willis of Westmoreland County, and that Nathaniel's uncle, Thomas Pope (who was a merchant living in England before his death in 1685) seemed to connect to the John Willis who died in 1682 in Westmoreland County (see Chapter X).

One of the earliest references I found for a John Willis in the Westmoreland County records was in February 1668/69 when the inventory of Phillip Silvester, deceased, was presented in court "to be delivered in kind to Mr. Daniel Liston [Lisson] for use of Margaret Silvester, daughter of Phillip, etc." including "a calf about John Willis's."[6] Again, it is difficult to determine whether this was the John Willis who died in 1682 or John Willis Sr.

Nathaniel Pope alias Bridges married Jane Brown(e), daughter of Original Brown and Jane Brooks [Higden] who was the daughter of Henry Brooks and his wife Jane. Jane Brooks married first Richard Higden, second Original Brown, and third James Campbell. Records for these families are found primarily in Westmoreland County; although they were reviewed, they will not be discussed in this manuscript. However, it is significant that the names of Nathll [Nathaniel] Pope and James "Compll" [Campbell] appear on John Willis's deed to his son William in 1701 and his Power of Attorney (see Chapter I). At that time Campbell was married to Pope's mother-in-law. This particular group exemplifies but one of the many incredibly complex families found on the Northern Neck.

In 1662 James Coghill (probably the father of Mary Coghill Willis Jennings) witnessed two deeds in Westmoreland County from Henry Brooks and his wife Jane to their daughters Jane Higden, and Liddia Abbington (wife of Laurence).[7] Coghill later received a patent on the south side of the Rappahannock River, but the fact that his name appears in the Westmoreland records suggests that he may have known the Mattox group earlier.

In 1684 William Underwood signed a performance bond to Nathaniel Pope to convey a tract on the back (or Potomac side) of his land in or near the line of John Willis.[8] In 1694 Nathaniel Pope and a William Willis witnessed a deed from John Willis Sr. to his son John Jr. in Richmond County (see Chapter I). In 1696/97 John Willis was granted 210 acres adjoining Mary Gunstocker, Indian; and in 1696/97 Willis and Pope became neighboring landowners when Nathaniel Pope bought Indian Ned

---

pp. 74–75; *Westmoreland County, Virginia, Deeds & Wills No. 2*, pp. 22–23; and Fothergill, *op. cit.*, p. 168. Mary Lisson Pope's maiden name was been transcribed as "Sisson," probably because the written "L" was misinterpreted as an "S."

[6] Dorman, *Westmoreland County, Virginia, Deeds, Patents, etc. 1665–1677*, Part one, pp. 45–46; also see Chapter XI.

[7] Dorman, Westmoreland County, Virginia, Records 1661–1664, pp. 8–9.

[8] Old Rappahannock County Deed Book 7:179.

Gunstocker's 150 acre patent from Gunstocker's heirs.[9]

Original Browne's will, which was written in 1697/98, names his wife Jane, son William, daughters Jane Pope (*i.e.*, wife of Nathaniel), Judith Roe, and Mary (who was under sixteen), plus some other legatees.[10] George Tunbridge's will (written in 1698) also names Mary Browne, daughter of Original and Jane Browne, who was underage and unmarried.[11]

In 1712 a Mary Willis (identified as the widow of William Offile) and her husband, William Willis, of Westmoreland obtained letters of administration of Offile's estate with Nathaniel Pope, Gent., and Charles Smith as their securities.[12] Men who posted bond for estate administrations were often related to one of the parties involved. Westmoreland County Orders suggest that this William Willis died intestate in 1720 (see Chapter X). It is possible that Mary Browne, sister-in-law to Nathaniel Pope, was the same Mary who married first William Offile and second (by 1712) William Willis which would explain many of the entries although not his exact relationship, if any, to John Willis Sr.?

Nathaniel Pope died by March 1719/20 in when an inventory of his estate was presented in Court by John Elliott, Augustine Washington, and Robert Valux.[13] Two of these men (Elliott and Valux) were descendants of the Foxhalls through their maternal lines, and Augustine Washington married as his first wife Jane Butler, daughter of Caleb Butler and Mary Foxhall.[14]

In summary, we find Nathaniel Pope alias Bridges in the records with John Willis Sr. and his sons John Jr. and William, as well as with another William Willis of Westmoreland County who died in 1720. Because of possible links, those records in early Westmoreland County will be explored further in Chapter X.

A limited amount of research was done on John Watts and his descendants because some of their important documents are among Westmoreland's missing records. Interest in the Watts family stems from the proximity of John Watts' 1669 patent to John Willis Sr.'s neighboring landowners, the fact that a Robert Franke's name is found in related records, and later connections between the Watts and Willis families in Madison County, Virginia. Robert Franke was probably the father of Frances Franke who married John Plunkett and became the parents of Elizabeth Plunkett who married John Willis, son of William and Sarah Willis, in 1734/5.[15]

---

[9]Sparacio, *Richmond County Deeds 1695–1701* (Deed Book 3), p. 48.

[10]Dorman, *Westmoreland County, Virginia, Deeds & Wills No. 2, pp. 63–64*; Fothergill, op. cit., p. 22.

[11]Ibid., pp. 64 and 76; Fothergill, op. cit., pp. 22 and 26.

[12]Dorman, *Westmoreland County, Virginia, Deeds & Wills No. 5*, p. 11. See Chapter X.

[13]Dorman, Westmoreland County, Virginia, Deeds & Wills No. 6, p. 94

[14]In 1697/98 John Foxhall Jr. named his "loving brother" [*brother-in-law*] Caleb Butler as executor of his will; see Dorman, *Westmoreland County, Virginia, Deeds & Wills No. 2, pp. 59–60*.

[15]See Chapters VI and IX.

Watts' tract at the head of Mattox Creek was originally patented by Nathaniel Pope Sr. who willed it to his son Nathaniel (father of Nathaniel Pope alias Bridges) who sold it to Watts in 1665. Watts then sold half of it to Thomas Wilford who died in 1666. Metes and bounds given in the patents indicate that the western boundary of Watts' tract joined John Piper and that the southern boundary of Watts' tract joined John Foxhall. Watts and Willis lived within two or three miles of each other, but Watts' land lay on the dividing ridge and was mostly in Westmoreland County where records for this tract are found.

When John Watts received a patent for 750 acres in Westmoreland County in 1664, one of the headrights was Robert Francke [*sic*]. At that time Watts was married to Elizabeth Vaughan, daughter of John Vaughan who died in 1664 with Thomas Wilsford being one of Vaughan's executors.[16] After Vaughan's death, John Watts and wife Elizabeth sold a patent of 600 acres on Attopin Creek which Elizabeth had inherited from her father to John Bocock with John Washington and William Freake witnessing the deed.[17] In 1673 Robert Franke witnessed the will of John Bocock, and John Watts was one of Bocock's executors.[18] In 1679 John Willis sued Abram Blagg who paid Willis 450 pounds of tobacco from the estate of John Watts, the reason for the payment not stated in the Orders.

The loss of the Westmoreland records makes it difficult to trace the Watts' tract, but extant documents imply that there were family connections between the Watts, Wilsford, and Blagg families. It seems that Andrew Wilsford probably died without heirs and his share became the property of his brother Thomas Wilsford Jr. who willed it to "my friend" Richard Watts in 1700. Richard sold it to Abram (or Abraham) Blagg(e) in 1707, the land then becoming known as the "Blagg land."[19] No connections between John Watts and John Willis have been found beyond those cited above, but Willis descendants married into a Watts family later and three of the grandchildren of Robert Franke migrated to Orange County with the extended Willis family.

As given in Chapter II, in 1669 both John Piper and John Willis Sr. received patents adjoining John Washington. John Piper Sr. died between 25 January 1669/70 and 19 September 1673 in Westmoreland County at which time his son John was under twenty-one.[20] Apparently John Piper Jr. married Margaret Reeds, daughter of Samuel Reeds whose 1698 will names his daughter Margaret and "two grandsons David and John Piper," both under ten years of age.[21] Samuel's son, William Reeds, was

---

[16]Dorman, *Westmoreland County, Virginia, Deeds, Patents, etc., 1665–1677*, Part one, p. 1.

[17]Dorman, ibid., p. 3. See Chapter VII for information that Charles Willis, son of John Willis Sr., sold tracts on Attopin (an earlier name for Rosier's) Creek in 1714/15 and 1719. The basis of Charles' title to these tracts has not been found.

[18]Dorman, *Westmoreland County, Virginia, Deeds, Patents, etc., 1665–1677* Part three, p.11.

[19]Dorman, *Westmoreland Deeds & Wills No. 3*, p. 58, and No. 4, and *Westmoreland County, Virginia, Deeds, Patents, etc., 1665–1677*, Part four, p. 39; also Eaton, op. cit, p. 44.

[20]Dorman, Westmoreland County, Virginia, Deeds, Patents, etc., 1665–1677, Part two, p. 73.

[21]Dorman, op. cit., p. 84.

probably the man who appraised William Willis's estate (see Chapter VI). John Piper Jr.'s inventory was taken on 24 February 1699/1700 by Joseph Henings [Hemings, Hemmings] and Anthony Rallins [Rawlings] and returned on 25 June 1707. Piper's widow married Thomas Harper.[22]

A 1716 deed from John and Mary Washington to Francis Thornton, which was recorded in Richmond County, indicates that Piper's land adjoined John Willis at the northeast corner of Willis's 261-acre patent.[23] In 1737 John Piper (probably grandson of the first John and son of John Jr. and Margaret) was granted an additional 37 acres in Westmoreland and King George counties on branches of Mattox and Portridges creeks and joining John Marshall, George Riding, John Willis, John Jennings, Joshua Farguson, and Piper's former land (see below).[24]

In 1740 John Piper of Westmoreland County sold 15 acres on a branch of Poultereges [Portridges] Creek adjoining the glebe land "whereon the Reverend Mr. William Mackay now liveth" to Joshua Farguson. The tract was part of two patents—one granted to Piper's grandfather in 1662, and the other granted to said John Piper in 1737. Witnesses were William Plunkett (probably the elder brother of Elizabeth Plunkett who married John Willis), John Farguson Jr., and James Scurlock.[25] Mackay was probably the same man who witnessed John Willis's deeds in 1737.

The records were searched extensively for John Foxhall's family, but my findings will be limited here to a few comments.[26] It may be important that the Foxhalls can be connected to both John Willis who died in 1682 in Westmoreland County and to John Willis Sr. of Old Rappahannock and Richmond counties.

John Foxhall Sr. was a merchant on Pope's Creek. His 1669 patent of 314 acres joined Washington, Piper, Watts, and Browne; and Browne's patent joined Foxhall, Washington and Willis (see Chapter II). As already shown, John Willis Sr. was appointed surveyor of roads from Foxhall's Mill to Key's Swamp in Old Rappahannock County in 1687, and in 1690/91 John Willis Sr. and John Parsons Sr.

[22]Fothergill, p. 42, and Westmoreland County records.

[23]Sparacio, *Richmond County Deeds 1714–1720*, p. 51 (Deed Book 7). Various records reviewed for these families can be found in both Westmoreland and King George counties; of particular interest see Dorman, *Westmoreland County Deeds & Wills No. 6*, p. 1; and King, *King George County Will Book A-1*, pp. 92 and 96–97.

[24]Northern Neck Grants E–11.

[25]Sparacio, *King George County Deeds 1735–1752*, p. 32 (Deed Book 2).

[26]For data on Foxhall family, see Eaton, op. cit., pp. 45, 47, and 51; Sparacio, *Old Rappahannock County Deed Book 1682–1686*, pp. 96–97., and *Richmond County Deeds 1695–1701*, p. 45 (Deed Book 2); Dorman, *Westmoreland County, Virginia, Deeds, Patents, etc., 1665–1677*, Part two, p. 59, and *Westmoreland County Deeds & Wills No. 2*, pp. 59–60; Lothrop Withington, *Virginia Gleanings in England* (Baltimore: Genealogical Publishing Co., 1980), pp. 170 and 601–602. Mary Foxhall Vaulx Gorge Duddleston Butler Blagg's will (1712/13) is found in Westmoreland County Deeds and Wills 5:221 with her estate inventory in Book 5:310. .

were granted 158 acres above Foxhall's Mill.[27]

One of the records connected John Foxhall to the John Willis who died in Westmoreland County in 1682. As discussed in Chapter X, this John Willis purchased 200 acres on a branch of Herring Creek from Andrew Read in 1668 and assigned 100 acres of it to Phillip White in 1668/69. In 1674 White sold the tract to John Foxhall with John Crabb and Corderoy Ironmonger as witnesses. In November 1697 John Foxhall Jr. sold the 100 acres to Charles Smith of Nomony in Cople Parish (perhaps the same Charles Smith who posted bond with Nathaniel Pope alias Bridges for the unknown William Willis cited above). This was the last land record which I found for the Foxhalls as John Jr. died without male heirs the following year. The Foxhall name ceased to exist on the Northern Neck due to lack of male heirs, but there were many connections between them and the Washington, Pope, Elliott, and Butler families.

Phillip Brown(e)'s 1669 patent is the only one which specifically names John Willis (see Chapter II). It abutted Foxhall on Browne's eastern boundary and Washington and Willis on Browne's northern boundary.

Browne's will was proved in Westmoreland County on 25 February 1670/71.[28] He left his entire estate, including 200 acres lying and "being upon Rappahannock in the forest" to his wife Joane. Browne died without seating his 1669 patent and it escheated, later becoming the property of Randolph Kirk (given erroneously as Clark in one entry) and John Fryer. Kirk died before a division was made between them, and Fryer became the sole owner by right of survivorship. Fryer sold it to John Crane who brought suit against John Willis Jr. and Walter Anderson for trespass, and the court ruled for Willis and Anderson. However, Willis and Anderson lost most of the tract to Edwin Conway in 1719 when Conway sold it to John Anderson, brother of Walter Anderson, when the land was described as being near the head of Poultridges Creek. This tract was in Rappahannock (later Richmond, then King George) County.[29]

No connection was found between John Willis Sr. and Phillip Brown, Randolph Kirk, or John Fryer, although a William Browne was named in the Westmoreland County records with Robert Nurse and a George Browne with Andrew Reade. Nothing was found which linked this Phillip Brown(e) to William Browne who died in Rappahannock County leaving all of his land to his three sons— Maxfield, John, and William Browne .[30] As shown in Chapter V, John Willis Jr. leased a tract joining Maxfield Browne in 1709. Also I have not established a connection between Phillip

---

[27]For information on Foxhall's (Underwood's) mill, see Sparacio, *(Old) Rappahannock County Deed Book 1682-1686*, pp. 52–53 (Deed Book 7); *Deed & Will Abstracts of (Old) Rappahannock County 1677-1682*, Part II, p. 97; *(Old) Rappahannock County Deeds 1682-1686*, pp. 96–97 (Deed Book 7); *Deed Abstracts of (Old) Rappahannock County, Virginia, 1686-1688*, p. 52; *Deed Abstracts of Richmond County, Virginia, 1695-1701*, p. 45 (Deed Book 2); and Chapter III.

[28]Dorman, *Westmoreland County, Virginia, Deeds, Patents, etc.,1665-1677*, Part one, p. 62.

[29]See Chapter III.

[30]Sparacio, *Deed & Will Abstracts of (Old) Rappahannock County, Virginia, 1677-1682*, Part 1, pp. 11 and 107; *Will Abstracts of (Old) Rappahannock County, Virginia, 1682-1687*, pp. 30–31; *Deed Abstracts of (Old) Rappahannock County, Virginia, 1686-1688*, p. 28.

Brown(e) and Original Brown(e) who married Jane Brooks Higden (and whose daughter Jane married Nathaniel Pope alias Bridges). However, the evidence should not be considered as conclusive at this point.

The second group identified as neighbors of John Willis Sr. settled in the Rappahannock watershed south of the ridge. Several Indian villages were in that region for some time which may account for the fact that this particular area was settled later than the land north of the ridge in the Potomac watershed. Norris stated that in 1655 the Indian towns of Ausaticon (Nanasatico) and Warisquock were mentioned in patents as being on the north side of the Rappahannock River across from Portobago Bay. Also while land was being patented in Old Rappahannock County, actual settlement by the colonists west of Bristol Mines Run was either prohibited or limited until after 1669.[31]

Early patentees in the Rappahannock group in that area which eventually became King George County included Edmund Gunstocker (Indian Ned), William Underwood, and several nonresident landholders (including Henry Fleet) who sold or willed their land to various people. By the 1680s the records show that William Underwood, William Freake, Josiah (Josias, Joshua) Mason, John Combs, Thomas Kendall, Thomas Goffe, John Parsons, John Willis, and Ralph Wormley owned land which either adjoined or was situated close to each others in Old Rappahannock County.

Records for William Freake were found in Northumberland County by 1750/51 and then in Westmoreland County after its creation in 1653. His will was proved on 5 March 1684/85 in Old Rappahannock (see Chapters II and III). Freake appears to have been about the same age as the John Willis who died in 1682 in Westmoreland County, and, like the Washingtons, Popes, Lissons, Watts, and others, was originally a part of the old Mattox Creek community. Little is known about Freake's family except that he was married at least twice and had a daughter, Ann, who married Capt. John Haeberd (or Hayberd) of Stafford County.[32] Like John Foxhall Jr. William Freake seems to have died without male heirs.[33] Freak's widow, Martha, married Robert Vincent.

Although no direct relationship was found between William Freake and John Willis, Sr., they were known to have been neighboring landowners and the possibility of a connection should not be ignored—especially since Freake's age was suitable for having a daughter who could have been a wife of John Willis Sr. The fact that John Willis named his second son William and also had a daughter named Susannah (for which *Ann* is a diminutive) should also be considered.

[31] Norris, op. cit., pp. 26–27.

[32] See Chapter III.

[33] For William Freake, see Dorman, *Westmoreland County, Virginia, Records 1661–1664*, p. 7; *Westmoreland County, Virginia, Deeds, Patents, etc., 1665-1677*, Part two, pp.66 and 81; *Westmoreland County, Virginia, Deeds, Patents, etc., 1665–1677*, Part three, p. 38; *Westmoreland County, Virginia, Deeds, Patents, etc.*, Part four, pp. 32–34. Also Sparacio, *Richmond County Order Book*, 6 March 1700 (1701); *Will Abstracts of (Old) Rappahannock County, Virginia 1682–1687*, p. 49; *Richmond County Deed Book* 5:128–129 and 5:131–135.

Thomas Tippett became John Willis's neighbor in 1687 when Tippett purchased land from Robert and Martha Vincent.[34] Locators given in the records show that this tract was the westernmost part of Freake's 300 acres on the branches of Portridges Creek and lay in the southern portion of John Washington's original 1,700-acre patent before Freake's purchase from Washington (see Chapter II). Tippett died in 1710 and was survived by his wife Catherine (whose maiden name is unknown to me) and at least three children—William, Abigail (who married John Green), and Ann (who married Edmund Donahoe or Donohoe).[35] Although no relationship was found between this family and the extended Willis family, they were neighbors for many years, and John Green was one of the appraisers of William Willis's estate.

One of the most unique members of this community was Edmund Gunstocker, also called Ned the Indian or Indian Ned. He appears to have been a remnant of the Nansatico tribe (called Nanzatacons in his grant) who accepted the settlers and their Christian faith. By special order of the Governor on 14 October 1664 Edmund Gunstocker was granted 150 acres in the freshes of the Rappahannock River, the patent being dated 14 October 1665.[36] His tract is described as being in Rappahannock County on the north side of the river in the freshes beginning near a branch called Comisstanck on the easternmost side, running north by east ... to a marked ash near a branch called Weequionendike, etc. Several related patents and deeds mentioned Ned the Indian's path or land, Indian Ned's old field, or Gunstocker's patent.

On 22 October 1676 when he was "about to depart on an expedition with the English against my countrymen, the Indians," Gunstocker wrote his will leaving his land and all his personal property to his wife, Mary. It was proved in Rappahannock Court in July 1686, so Gunstocker must have survived the expedition.[37]

As discussed in Chapter III, the 1696/97 grants to John Combs, John Willis, Thomas Kendall, and Thomas Goffe joined Mary Gunstocker, Edmund's widow. In 1697 Gunstocker's heirs (Numpskinner/Numkinner and Betty Nonomiske, the niece of Ned Gunstocker and wife of Numpskinner, and Pattiawaske) sold Edmund's patent to Nathaniel Pope alias Bridges.[38] Witnesses were Tho. Smyth, Jno. Linto [sic], and Jane Brown(e) who was probably the mother-in-law of Nathaniel Pope alias Bridges. Jane was also identified as one of the heirs' interpreters.

Gunstocker's tract provides new information regarding the location of John Willis's

[34] Sparacio, *Deed Abstracts of (Old) Rappahannock County, Virginia, 1686–1688*, p. 56.

[35] For Tippett, Green, and Donahoe records, see Headley, op. cit., p. 19; King George County Deed Book 2:237–238 with plat from microfilm; Sparacio, *Deed Abstracts of King George County, Virginia, 1735–1752*, pp. 66 and 101–102; King, *King George County Will Book A-1*, pp. 161–162 , and *Marriages of Richmond County, Virginia*; also King George County Deed Book 4, pp. 447 ff., and Chapters V and VI.

[36] Nugent, op. cit., I:566. Note that John Washington's patent for 1,700 acres was issued on 1 June 1664.

[37] Dorman, *Will Abstracts of (Old) Rappahannock County, Virginia, 1682–1687*, p. 75.

[38] Sparacio, *Deed Abstracts of Richmond County, Virginia 1695–1701*, pp. 1–2.

land. It appears that the Nansatico and Warisquock Indians were still living in villages across from Portobago Bay on the north side of the Rappahannock River in 1669, but that most of them had left the area by 1696/97 when Willis, Combs, Kendall, and Goff received their grants next to Mary Gunstocker. Those grants and Gunstocker's patent were on the Rappahannock, and the metes and bounds indicate that Gunstocker's tract was actually surrounded by Willis, Kendall, and Goff (see Chapter III).

After an extensive review of the land records for men who owned land in the area of Portridges Creek, I have concluded that the name was initially used to describe a rather large watershed which included Bald Eagle swamp (or run) and several smaller creeks. It lay east of Chingoteague and west of present Bristol Mines Run. I also believe that the main branch of Portridges Creek was probably an earlier name for what became known as Jett's Creek (a name which is not seen in the records until much later) and that Indian Ned's property and the above patents to Willis, Kendall, Goff, and Combs were between present Jett's Creek and Greenlaw's Wharf as shown on the 1968 USGS Rollins Fork, King George County, map. This would place John Willis's 1669 patent near the present town of Index and his other tracts somewhere between that patent and the Rappahannock River.

One of the first neighbors found in the Old Rappahannock records was Josiah (or Josias) Mason. His will, written on 28 March 1687 and proved that May, was witnessed by John Parsons, John Willis, and Moses Hubbert who were paid for one day's attendance to prove it in Court.[39] Mason's name appears infrequently in the Old Rappahannock records, but related deeds prove that he was a neighbor to Edmund Gunstocker, and his will shows that his legatees were his underage daughter Ann and Saynty Gay/Jay [sic] who then married John Hauxford. Mason's executor and guardian of Ann Mason was William Underwood.[40] Nothing more is known about his daughter, Ann, although there is the possibility that she became the wife of John Combs whose youngest son was named Mason (*q.v.*).

Of all the families reviewed, the Underwoods seemed to be the longest neighbors of the Willises with their association spanning almost seventy years. At the time John Willis received his first patent in 1669, William Underwood, then a minor, also held patents for land on the north side of the Rappahannock River as his father's son and heir. No references were found showing the proximity of the two families until 1685 when William Underwood gave a performance bond to Nathaniel Pope to convey part of a tract where Underwood lived "near or upon the line of John Willis."[41] Two years later Underwood and Willis were involved in the estate of Josiah Mason.

---

[39] William Montgomery Sweeney, *Wills of Rappahannock County, Virginia*, pp. 135–136. I do not find this will reported by Sparacio. For payment to Willis, Hubbard, and Parsons, and the appointment of Francis Sterne and Tho. Swinburne as appraisers of Mason's estate, see Sparacio, *(Old) Rappahannock County Orders 1685–1687*, pp. 78–79.

[40] Other data for Mason can be found in Sparacio, *(Old) Rappahannock County Deeds 1682–1686*, p. 102; *(Old) Rappahannock County Deeds 1686–1688*, p. 27; and (Old) Rappahannock County Orders 4 March 1684/85, 6 May 1685, 1 July 1687, and 4 March 1689/90..

[41] Sparacio, *(Old) Rappahannock County Deed Book 1682–1686*, p. 88.

Although the records do not suggest that there were marriages between the Underwoods and Willises, in 1715 Francis Slaughter, Richard Tutt, and John Combs—who were all connected to the Underwood family—appraised the estate of John Willis Sr. (see Chapter I). One immediate question is why these men were appointed as appraisers rather than some of the other neighbors whose names are found so frequently in documents with the Willis family.

In an attempt to find out if there was a relationship between the two families, I went to a variety of sources. I found that Eaton's *Historical Atlas of Westmoreland County* contains several errors regarding the Underwoods. A comprehensive, documented account of the family by Augusta B. Fothergill was discovered in *Virginia Historical Magazine* (volumes 38–40). Fothergill's data, together with George H. S. King's *Marriages of Richmond County* and *King George County Will Book A-1* (the latter which was not available to Eaton and Fothergill or to King when he compiled his first volume) and information in county records made it possible to clarify many of the discrepancies and to identify the three appraisers of John Willis's estate. This sketch will not attempt to discuss all of the references found for the Underwood family, but some of them have been noted below.[42]

The most significant links I found between the extended Underwood family and John Willis Sr. are summarized as follows. First, Willis's neighbor, John Combs, was the son of Archdale Combs and Elizabeth who was the widow of William Underwood who died in 1662. (Contrary to Fothergill's report, she was not Elizabeth Moseley. William's first wife, Mary, was probably a Moseley, and Elizabeth's maiden name has not been found.[43]) Second, John Willis Sr. is known to have owned land on Underwood's "back line" in 1685 (although this was not mentioned in John's patent and Underwood probably acquired it after 1669). Third, the names of Catherine and William Pullen, who were leasing land from John Willis Sr. in 1715, are found as witnesses on various Underwood documents. And finally, in 1767 when the Hanover Parish Vestry sold John Willis Sr.'s 1669 glebe tract to William Thornton, they replaced it with a 339 acres which they bought from Richard Tutt (Jr.), son and heir of Richard Tutt Sr. who died testate in 1766 in Spotsylvania County (see Chapter I). Tutt

---

[42]Augusta B. Fothergill, "Underwood Family of Virginia," *Virginia Historical Magazine*, vols. 38–45 (which is highly recommended to anyone who is researching the Underwood family); Dorman, *Westmoreland County, Virginia, Deeds, Patents, etc., 1665–1677*, Part one, p. 62; Headley, pp. 4 and 37; King, *Marriages of Richmond County* and *King George County Will Book A-1*, pp. 52–53; Sparacio, *Deed Abstracts of (Old) Rappahannock County, Virginia, 1672–1676*, Part II, pp. 60, 85–86; *Deed & Will Abstracts of (Old) Rappahannock County, Virginia, 1677–1682*, Part II, p. 97; *Deed Abstracts of (Old) Rappahannock County, Virginia, 1682–1686*, pp. 52–53 and 102. *(Old) Rappahannock County Will Book 1683–1687*, pp. 39–40; *Deed Abstracts of (Old) Rappahannock County, Virginia, 1688–1692*, p. 59; *Deed Abstracts of Richmond County, Virginia, 1695–1701*, p. 45; *Richmond County Orders 1697–1699*, p. 45; Richmond County Deed Book 6:5; King George County Deed Book 1:14–19, 1:81–85 and 1:106.

[43]In 1663 William Underwood's (son of William who d. 1662) guardian was his uncle, William Moseley, which has caused confusion. In a later deed William Underwood later called Elizabeth Combs his *mother-in-law* [*i.e.*, stepmother]. It appears that Elizabeth and William Underwood Sr. had no issue and that there was no blood relationship between his son William (by his first wife) and Elizabeth's children by Archdale Combs. See discussion on John Combs below.

was a descendant of William Underwood and first wife, Mary Moseley.[44] The 339 acres which Tutt deeded to the Vestry was a portion of a 454 acre tract which Richard Tutt had purchased from Nicholas Smith and Nathaniel and Lucy Pope. This Nathaniel Pope was the grandson of Nathaniel Pope alias Bridges of the above 1685 performance bond. The deeds trace the 454 acres back to a deed from Tankard (formerly Yarrett's land) to Nicholas Smith and Nathaniel Pope in 1708.[45]

While no specific relationship was found between the Willis and Underwood families, this line of research is being continued because of the myriad of clues including the appraisers of John Willis Sr.'s estate, the Combs connection, the proximity of the two families for three generations, the names of William and Catherine Pullen on both Willis and Underwood documents, and the fact that some of these descendants also migrated to Orange and Culpeper counties.[46]

The next five families—Thomas Kendall, Thomas Goff, John Combs, John Parsons, and John Hauxford—comprised the "heart" of the Willis community for fifty years and deserve special attention for obvious reasons. As noted in Chapter III, in 1687/88 John Willis Sr., Thomas Kendall, and Thomas Goff jointly purchased 403 acres from Mallachy Peal(e). Thomas Kendall and Thomas Goff were brothers-in-law. The records show that these men were of the same generation. Combs, who was born after 1662, was probably the youngest.

In 1690/91 John Willis Sr. and John Parsons Sr. jointly received a grant above Foxhall's mill. In 1691 John Hauxford purchased a tract adjacent to John Willis from Thomas Tippett (which was part of Washington's patent that he sold to William Freake). In 1692/93 John Willis and John Combs each deeded tracts to Thomas Kendall. In 1696/97 Willis, Kendall, Goff, and Combs received grants adjoining each other and Mary Gunstocker. When John Willis wrote his will in 1715, he mentioned his land which joined Isaac Arnold (who was given a tract by his father-in-law, Thomas Goff) and John Combs. In the ensuing years these families deeded land to each other, witnessed each other's documents, appraised each other's estates, and married into each other's families. John Combs' daughter Elizabeth married Thomas Kendall's son William, and Thomas Goff's daughter Margaret married Isaac Arnold. Hauxford became the guardian of John Plunkett, father of Elizabeth Plunkett who married John Willis, son of William and Sarah.

Many questions regarding this closely knit group remain unanswered. When and how did John Willis Sr. become acquainted with the others? Was he related to any of them? Was there any significance in his joint purchase of land with Kendall and Goff, or in his joint grant with John Parsons Sr.?

---

[44] Crozier, op. cit., pp. 23–24; King George County Deed Book 4, p. 30, and Deed Book 5, pp. 685–686, from microfilm.

[45] One of the locators in the 1696/97 grants to John Willis, Thomas Kendall, Thomas Goff, and John Combs was "Yarrett's, now Tankard's land;" see Chapter III.

[46] Other members of the early Underwood family of interest include Col. William Peirce/Pierce who married Sarah Underwood (sister of William Underwood who died in 1662) and who lived on Cos Cos Creek in Westmoreland County near John Willis who died there in 1682.

John Willis and the Combs family were living in the area by 1669, and their names are frequently found together on documents until John Combs' death in 1716/17.[47] Combs was the eldest son of Archdale Combs (shown with a variety of spellings) and Elizabeth (—), the widow of William Underwood who died in 1662. The records show that John Combs had a younger brother named William.[48]

Archdale Combs descended from John Comb [sic] and wife Margaret Archdale, daughter of Thomas Archdale and his first wife Mary Clifton of London where Thomas was described as a draper (a dealer in cloth and drygoods). Margaret Archdale married John Comb(s) on 11 December 1587. Thomas Archdale died in 1611; his will names his daughter Margaret Combe [sic] and his grandson Archedale Combe [sic] who was underage.[49] I believe that this family may also have been related to the Abram or Abraham Combs whose name is found in early Rappahannock records, and it is noted that between 1665 and 1674 Archdale Combs' name was found as a witness to documents of James Coghill's in Old Rappahannock County . Archdale and Elizabeth were probably deceased by September 1684 when William Combs was bound to William Underwood until he reached the age of twenty-one by order of the Sittenburne Parish Vestry.

William Willis, son of John Sr., was deceased on 5 December 1716 when the Richmond County Court ordered John Combs, John Green, William Pitman, and William Reeds, or any three of them to inventory and appraise his estate (see Chapter VI). When it was returned, the inventory was signed by the last three men as Combs had died in the interim.

John Combs wrote his will on 11 December 1716 and it was proved in Richmond County on 7 February 1716/17.[50] Both his and William Willis's estate inventories were presented in Court on 3 April 1717. Combs' will names his wife Hannah, his youngest son Mason (suggesting a possible relationship to Josias Mason), his daughter Elizabeth Kendall, his son Archedale [sic], and his daughters Judith, Mary, Sarah, and Aime (with no last names given). Mason and Aime were under eighteen. Executors were his wife and John Anderson; witnesses were Isaac Arnold, Charles Willis, and Mary (Willis) James. Mason received 200 acres in Essex County (probably John's interest in a tract which his mother received in exchange for The Mount, part of Underwood's estate), and Archedale was given the home plantation which joined Willis's land in Hanover Parish.

Archedale Combs, son of John, died testate in 1735 in King George County leaving his estate to his wife Mary, eldest daughters Ann Combs and Mary Combs, and youngest

[47] Headley, op. cit., pp. 34–35.

[48] Fothergill, op. cit, "Underwood Family of Virginia," , vol. 39, pp. 74–75; Sparacio, op. cit., *Deed Abstracts of Old Rappahannock County 1672–1676*, Part 2, p. 60; *Old Rappahannock Deed Abstracts 1682–1686*, pp. 60 and 85–86; *Deed Abstracts of Richmond County, Virginia, 1692–1695*, p.2.

[49] Lothrop Withington, *Virginia Gleanings in England* (Baltimore: Genealogical Publishing Co., 1980), pp. 316–319. It is noted that this is another connection to the merchandising class (see discussion in Chapter XII).

[50] Headley, op. cit., pp. 34–35.

daughter Ezabell Combs. His will also names his sister Amey who was a widow.[51] In 1737/38 John Willis (probably the son of Charles) and his wife Elizabeth sold 60 acres to Isaac Pitman, the tract joining the line of Archdell Combs, deceased.[52] As Archdell received his father's home place, it is assumed that these tracts referred to the adjoining 1696/97 grants discussed in Chapter III.

Besides the Underwoods, another obvious connection between the Combs and Willis families was found through William and Catherine Pullen. John Willis's 1715 will mentioned both Combs and Pullen, the latter holding a ten-year lease on a tract belonging to Willis. The Pullens witnessed William Underwood's will in 1717 with John Willis Jr. signing the estate inventory. In 1722 Pullen was one of the witnesses to the will of John Underwood (son of William) whose wife was Margaret Slaughter (daughter of Francis). In 1725 John Plunkett and John Gilbert (who married Sarah Underwood) were two of the appraisers of Mary Cullins' estate; Mary's mother was Catherine Pullen, and Mary's will named both Catherine and William.[53] In 1728 William and Catherine Pullen witnessed John Willis Jr.'s will, and Richard Tutt was one the appraisers. In addition, William Pullen witnessed the will of John Jennings (second husband of Mary Coghill Willis) in 1728/29, Jennings' will being written in King George and his estate being probated in both King George and Orange counties in 1735 (see Chapter V). While the records do not prove any direct relationship, they confirm the proximity of the Willis, Underwood, and Combs families.

Further research on the Combs family is difficult because Archdell (son of John) left his land to his wife and daughters in 1735, and the married names of his daughters are unknown. However, several questions arise with the clues given in documents. Was Combs' wife Hannah the same as Ann Mason, the unmarried daughter of Josias Mason who died in 1687, which would explain why he named a son Mason? And was Combs' daughter Sarah the wife of William Willis? Combs' will offers no clarification, but it implies that Aime (Amie) was his only unmarried daughter in 1716.

The next family to be discussed is that of John Parsons Sr. On 27 February 1690/91 John Willis Sr. and John Parsons Sr., both of Rappahannock County, were jointly granted 158 acres adjacent to a tract which had been surveyed for Henry Fleet above Foxhall's Mill (see Chapter III).[54] The connection between the two men is unknown. However, the Willis, Parsons, and Anderson families are found together in several documents, and their relationship may have extended into early Westmoreland County. According to a deposition which John Parsons gave in Westmoreland County in 1674/75 apparently involving a land dispute between Clement Spillman (or Spilman) and John Foxhall, Parsons was born *circa* 1646 which means that he was about the same age as John Willis Sr.[55] In the fall of 1674 Clement Spillman and John Crabb

---

[51] King, *King George County Will Book A-1*, pp. 80–81.

[52] Sparacio, *Deed Abstracts of King George County, Virginia, 1735–1752*, p.15, and microfilm.

[53] See King, *King George County Will Book A-1*.

[54] The term "above" implies that it was upstream, or west of present Bristol Mines Run.

[55] Dorman, *Westmoreland County, Virginia, Deeds, Patents, etc., 1665–1677* Part three, p.27.

witnessed a deed from Jno. Viccars to Rob[ert] Sanford in Westmoreland County.[56] This and other records suggest that Parsons was at least acquainted with the John Willis who died in Westmoreland in 1682.[57]

The first appearance of John Willis's name in the Old Rappahannock records was in 1684 with an item in the Court Orders involving John Willis vs. Walter Anderson.[58] The reason for this suit was not given. In 1687 John Parsons and John Willis witnessed the will of Josias Mason. The following year the Court ordered a non-suit to John Parsons, Attorney of Walter Anderson, against John Foxhall.

John Parsons Sr. wrote his will on 12 April 1688 and it was proved on 6 November 1689.[59] He left land to both of his *sons* (see below), Walter and John Jr. Walter received a point of land where he (Walter) lived plus another point of land next to it, John Jr. inherited the home place, and other bequests were made to his grandchildren. Witnesses to Parsons' will were Joseph Hemings and Thomas T. Spilman. No other records were found for a Walter Parsons, and I believe that the will referred to Walter *Anderson* who was Parsons' son-in-law or stepson.

In 1689 John Parsons (Jr.) was ordered by the Rappahannock County Court to "remain and abide with his *brother-in-law* Walter Anderson until he can show sufficient cause for his departure." No reason for the order was given, but John was probably underage. In May 1690 the Court referred a suit between Thomas Crane, plaintiff, and John Willis and Walter Anderson, defendants, until the next session. On 2 September 1691 the Court Orders state that the suit was dismissed "for an uncertainty in the declaration" and that Crane was to pay all costs. Crane again sued John Willis Jr. and John Parsons (Jr.) on 4 June 1696. The records show that Willis and Parsons produced their earlier patent and retained title with Crane appealing (see Chapters I–III).

In July 1698 John Willis Jr., Walter Anderson, Thomas Kendall, and Nathaniel Pope or any three of them were ordered to appraise the estate of William Wheeler, deceased, whose will was proved by the oaths of Pope and Anderson.[60]

On 26 October 1698 John Parsons Jr., who was living in Essex County at the time, deeded his interest in the Willis–Parsons patent to Walter Anderson.[61] Nathaniel Pope was one of the witnesses. John Willis Jr. and Walter Anderson divided the tract in March 1706/07, the deed of division giving the full descent of the land to that date. John Willis Jr. took the western part, and Anderson got the eastern part (see Chapters III and V).

---

[56] Ibid., p. 14.

[57] See Chapter X.

[58] Sparacio, *(Old) Rappahannock County Orders 1683–1685*, p. 47.

[59] Sweeney, op. cit., p. 8.

[60] Sparacio, *Richmond County Orders 1697–1699*, p. 45; Sweeeney, op. cit., pp. 3–4.

[61] Sparacio, Deed Abstracts of Richmond County, Virginia, 1695–1701, p. 66. Anne Wheeler married Robert Goff, Thomas Kendall's brother-in-law, according to Newman A. Hall (personal correspondence) and Westmoreland County Will Book 5:623.

It appears that John Parsons Jr. moved to Westmoreland County where he, another William Willis, and John Niccols [*sic*] with others served on a jury before Justice Joseph Bayly on 2 May 1713. Other records suggest that this William Willis had married Mary Offile, the widow of William Offile and perhaps the sister-in-law of Nathaniel Pope alias Bridges (see above and Chapter X). A 1715 deed suggests that Parsons was probably a tenant on a tract which belonged to Brookes Abbington on Pope's Creek . An inventory of the estate of John Parsons (Jr.?), deceased, was reported to Joseph Bayly by Nathaniel Washington, Anthony Baxter, John Higdon (or Higden), and James Creed in 1715.[62]

As given in Chapter III, before 27 March 1719 Edwin Conway of Lancaster County had gained title to most of the Willis–Parsons grant by resurvey and deeded 117 acres of it to John Anderson, brother of Walter Anderson. The tract was described as near the head of Poultridges (Portridges) Creek. Conway's title was based upon his 1694 deed from Henry Fleet (Jr.) for 2,000 acres and an earlier patent. This Edwin Conway (Jr.) was the stepson of Elizabeth Thornton (daughter of Francis Thornton Sr.) and the son of her first husband, Edwin Conway Sr., by his first wife who was Sarah Walker.[63] Sarah Walker (wife of Edwin Conway) was the daughter of Col. John Walker and his second wife, Mrs. Sarah Fleet, the widow of Henry Fleet Sr. The history of that patent will not be included here except to say that this was one of the many instances where early patents held by non-residents preempted later grants or deeds.

John Anderson died testate between 2 November and 1 December 1721 leaving the tract which he purchased from Edwin Conway to his son Walter Anderson who was underage. According to his will, if his son Walter died without issue, "every part and parcel thereof (was) to revert descend and return to my loving brother, Walter Anderson."[64] John Anderson's will was proved on the oaths of Isaac Arnold, William Pullen, and William Harvey. William Brown was executor and Arnold was his co-bondsman. John Willis (Jr.), Joshua Farguson, William Pitman, and Robert Rankins were ordered to appraise Anderson's estate according to the County Orders.

In 1758 a Walter Anderson of Washington Parish in Westmoreland County sold 90 acres in King George County to George Marshall of Hanover Parish, excepting "a burying place of half an acre" and adjoining the glebe land of Hanover Parish.[65] At that time the Hanover Parish glebe was the old 1669 Willis patent of 261 acres, and the boundary between Westmoreland and King George counties was still the dividing ridge. King states that this Walter lived in Cople Parish, Westmoreland County, and married Ann Thornton, daughter of Thomas Thornton and Susannah Smith, who predeceased her husband and her son John Anderson, but those records were not reviewed.[66]

---

[62] Dorman, *Westmoreland County, Virginia, Deeds & Wills No. 5*, pp. 51, 90, and 117.

[63] See King, *Marriages of Richmond County, Virginia, 1668–1853*, for additional information on these families.

[64] King, *King George County Will Book A-1*, pp. 1–3.

[65] King George County Deed Book 4:380, from microfilm.

[66] See King, *Marriages of Richmond County 1668–1853*.

In conclusion, John Parsons Sr. and John Willis Sr. knew each other as early as 1684, and patented land together in 1690/91. John Parsons Jr. sold the land he inherited from his father to Walter Anderson who divided the tract with John Willis Jr. in 1706/07. Most of the patent was lost to Edwin Conway who then sold 117 acres to John Anderson, brother of Walter. The two families were neighbors to each other and to John Combs for many years. Documents found in Westmoreland County for the Parsons and Willis families will be discussed in ChapterX. Researchers may want to review these families more thoroughly as they could have been related to John Willis Sr. by marriage. In particular, John Parson's 1688 will should be examined for the names of his grandchildren as it is possible that John Willis married Parsons' daughter.

Another neighbor who deserves attention is John Hauxford (also seen as Hawkford, Hawksford, Hoxford, and Oxford) who, according to the Rappahannock County Orders, was living in the area by 1685. Sometime between then and July 1687 Hauxford married Saint (or Saints) Jay, legatee of Josias Mason, and the Court ordered Mr. William Underwood, who was Mason's executor, to deliver Saints' legacies to them. John Willis and John Parsons witnessed Mason's will.

In January 1699/1700 the Court bound (apprenticed) John Plunkett, an orphan without estate, per indenture dated 3 January 1697/98 to serve John Hauxford and his wife Saints until he (Plunkett) arrived at the age of twenty-one and to learn the trade of a carpenter.[67] This John Plunkett is assumed to be the father of Elizabeth Plunkett who married John Willis, son of William and Sarah (see Chapter VI).

In 1691 Robert Vincent, who had married Martha Freake (widow of William Freake), sold 100 acres to Hauxford. Although the deed is missing in both the Rappahannock and Richmond County records, two later Richmond County deeds refer to it. As Vincent's land (formerly Freake's which he bought from John Washington) joined John Willis Sr., this was the first indication that Hauxford lived next to the Willises. Hauxford continued acquiring adjoining tracts by grant in 1695, 1704, and 1705, the parcels either part of or adjoining Washington's original 1,700-acre patent.[68] In 1705 when Francis and John Wright, husband and son of Ann Washington Wright, deceased, deeded 1,000 acres of Washington's patent to Francis Thornton, their deed mentioned William Freake's portion of Washington's patent and said that the tract was next to William Willis, John Hauxford, and Thomas Tippett.[69] As an aside, these deeds are examples of the rich source of information sometimes found in land records when explored in depth. The Willis family is mentioned only once in these documents and probably would not have been named in the index.

In 1707 Thomas Tippett was granted 37 acres on Indian Ned's Creek in Richmond County adjoining Maj. (Francis) Wright and John Hauxford.[70] This grant is one of the

[67] Richmond County Order Book.

ee Gray, op. cit., 2 173, 3–67, and 3–100 (read from microfilm) and Richmond County Order Book 6 March 1700/01.

[69] Sparacio, *Richmond County Deeds 1705–1708*, pp. 10–11.

[70] Gray, op. cit., 3–167, and microfilm.

first records I found that mentioned Bald Eagle swamp which lay in the watershed of Portridges Creek. Indian Ned's Creek was undoubtedly named after Edmund Gunstocker, and the 1696/97 patents to Willis, Kendall, and Goff adjoined Gunstocker. John Washington's 1664 patent was also described as being on Porotridge [*sic*] Creek (see Chapters II and III).

In August and September of 1709 four "swaps" of small parcels were made between Hauxford, Thomas Tippett, William Willis, and John Willis Jr. with William and Sarah Willis giving John Combs their Power of Attorney to acknowledge their deed in Court. The last two deeds in effect exchanged 12 acres of Washington's original patent of 1,700 acres for 12 acres of John Willis's patent of 216 acres (see Chapter VI).

By 1717 John Willis Sr., his son William, John Combs, and Saints Hauxford had all died. Sarah, the widow of William Willis, married as her second husband Henry Wood who was a widower. In December of that year John Hauxford and wife Elizabeth (maiden name unknown) deeded 100 acres on the eastern and lower side of Portridges Creek to Henry Wood.[71] At Henry Wood's death this parcel and another tract descended to his eldest son, William Wood, who sold the two tracts to Rush Hudson Sr., Sarah (—) Willis Wood's third husband. At Rush Hudson's death his son Rush Jr. inherited the tracts and sold them to Francis Thornton after the Hudson, Willis, and Turberville families moved to Orange County (see Chapters VI and IX).

John Hauxford (Hoxford) wrote his will in August 1718 leaving his estate to his wife Elizabeth. Henry Wood was one of the witnesses.[72] In March 1718/19 Elizabeth Hauxford sold the 100 acres where she was living on Portridges Creek adjoining Henry Wood, Rowland Thornton, and William Tippett to Richard Butler, the tract being part of Washington's 1,700 acre patent which was purchased by John Hauxford from Robert Vincent in 1691.[73]

Nothing further is known about Elizabeth Hauxford, and no record was found to prove that Hauxford had any children by either Saints or Elizabeth. However, the records do support the possibility that Sarah, wife of William Willis, could have been the daughter of John and Saints Hauxford.

John Hauxford may have been a little younger than John Willis Sr., but he was older than Willis's children. His land was west of the Willises, and they were neighbors for thirty-three years during the time when John Willis Sr.'s children were growing up. John and Saints were appointed guardians to John Plunkett. William and Sarah Willis sold a tract to Hauxford; and after William Willis's death and Sarah's remarriage to Henry Wood, Hauxford sold a tract to Wood. Hauxford's records make it possible not only to trace the southern portion of Washington's 1664 patent and John Willis's adjoining 1669 patent, but to also identify the area where Sarah (—)Willis Wood Hudson Turberville lived from the time she married William Willis until she, her

---

[71] Sparacio, Richmond County Deeds 1714–1720, pp. 2–3.

[72] Headley, op. cit., p. 42.

[73] Sparacio, *Richmond County Deeds 1714–1720*, p. 56.

children, and her last husband, Edward Turberville, migrated to Orange County (see Chapter VI).

Several documents were found which connected John Willis, Thomas Kendall, and Thomas Goff and their descendants beginning in 1687/8 when Mallachy Peale deeded 403 acres to the three men jointly (see Chapter III). The three men seem to have been about the same age. From data found to this point, it is assumed that John Willis Sr. was born by 1648, and he died in 1715. According to Hall, Thomas Goff was born *circa* 1660 and may be the man who died intestate in Richmond County in 1716.[74] Thomas Kendall was born by 1650. However, in spite of the fact that the three men lived adjacent to each other for approximately fifty years, no record was found to suggest that they were related.

Hudson family researcher Newman A. Hall states that Thomas Kendall married Martha Goff (sister to Thomas Goff) and that their son William Kendall married Elizabeth Combs (daughter of John Combs).[75] Kendall' s date of death is not known, but he was living on 4 March 1716/17 when he deeded land to his son William.[76]

Although I have not thoroughly researched the Kendall and Goff families, I extracted a few entries for them as I was working in the records. In 1692/93 John Willis and Thomas Goff each sold tracts to Thomas Kendall. Since Willis's other land can be accounted for, it is assumed that the land he sold to Kendall was part of his joint purchase from Mallachy Peale. The grants which Kendall, Goff, Willis, and Combs received in 1696/97 were on the Rappahannock River and probably just east of present Jett's Creek (see Chapter III). In 1716/17 Thomas Kendall deeded two tracts—one to John Green (son of George Green and husband of Abigail Tippett) on Poultridges [*sic*] Creek adjoining Thomas Goff (witnessed by Charles Willis and William Kendall); and the other to his son William Kendall who married Elizabeth Combs, daughter of John Combs. In 1721 William Kendall sold this tract to his brother Samuel. Locators in these and later Kendall deeds mentioned Portridges Creek, Bald Eagle Run (a branch of Portridges Creek), lands of Mr. Edwin Conway and Isaac Pitman, and others.[77]

In 1727 Samuel Kendall deeded 20 acres to William Pitman; it lay on the river in Ralph Wormley's line (*cf.* John Willis Sr.'s will) and went up the branch which divided Kendall's land from John Willis, Jr. The deed stated that the tract was part of a patent to John Willis Sr., so it was probably part of Willis's 1696/97 patent.[78] It may have been close to Pitman's Landing as shown on a 1737 King George County map in King's *King George County Will Book A-1*. In 1730 Samuel Kendall sold 12 acres of

---

[74] Headley, op. cit., p. 34.

[75] Newman A. Hall, personal correspondence.

[76] Sparacio, *Richmond County Deeds 1714–1720*, pp. 68–79.

[77] Sparacio, *Deed Abstracts of Richmond County, Virginia, 1692–1695*, pp. 51–52; *Richmond County Orders 1697–1699*, p. 45; *Deed Abstracts of Richmond County 1711–1714*, pp. 73–75; *Richmond County Deeds 1714–1720*, pp. 29 and 68–69; Headley, op. cit., p. 34.

[78] Sparacio, *Deed Abstracts of King George County, Virginia 1721–1735*, p. 65.

Kendall's patent to Murdock, and the deed mentioned Indian Ned's land.[79] In 1741 Samuel Kendall and wife Sarah sold 50 acres on Portrages [*sic*] Creek and adjoining the land of Isaac Pitman to Murdock, it being part of 105 acres which Thomas Kendall patented on 19 March 1696/97 and then sold by Thomas to his son William in 1716/17.[80] The Kendalls were selling land in King George as late as 1761.[81]

The surname "Goff" is given in the records as Goffe, Gough (because it rhymes with "cough," I suppose), Goss, and Gost (probably due to clerical or transcribing errors because of confusion over the script form of the double "s" at the time). It is most frequently seen as Goff which will be used here.

The Goffs and Kendalls lived on the south side of the Rappahannock River prior to moving to the north side of the river. Newman A. Hall has identified Thomas Goff as the brother of Martha Goff (who married the above Thomas Kendall) and of Robert Goff (who married Anne Wheeler, daughter of Thomas Wheeler), both children of William Goff and Martha (—) who married secondly John Prosser.[82] Hall estimates that Thomas Goff was born around 1660 and married Margaret (—) around 1685. Thomas and Margaret had at least four children: Margaret Goff who married Isaac Arnold; Thomas Goff who married Sarah (—); John Goff who married Anne (—); and William Goff.

In 1687/88 Thomas Goff, Thomas Kendall, and John Willis jointly purchased a tract of 403 acres from Mallachy Peale on the north side of the river in Old Rappahannock County. No partition of that tract was found in the deed books. In 1696/97 the three men received three separate contiguous grants which appear to have been in the same area. Based upon the land records and the fact that Goff and Kendall were brothers-in-law, it is possible that at least one of them was related to John Willis Sr. The Goffs also owned land over the dividing ridge in Westmoreland County, but those records will not be discussed here.[83]

Thomas Goff Sr. may have died intestate in Richmond County in 1716, and William Goff may have died by 1717.[84] Thomas Goff Jr. probably died intestate in 1734 in King George County with another Thomas Goff administering his estate.[85] As with many families, repetition of the same Christian names over several generations confuses the records.

---

[79] Ibid., p. 94.

[80] Sparacio, *Deed Abstracts of King George County 1735–1752*, p. 39.

[81] King George County Deed Book 4, p. 51.

[82] Newman A. Hall, personal correspondence; also see Sparacio, *Deed Abstracts of (Old) Rappahannock County Virginia 1672–1676*, Part one, pp. 74–75 and Westmoreland County Deeds & Wills 5:623; Margaret, the second wife and widow of John Prosser, married Symon Miller who died testate in Old Rappahannock County in 1683.

[83] Dorman, *Westmoreland County, Virginia, Deeds, Patents, etc., 1665–1677*, Part four (with Deeds & Wills No. 4), p. 35; Sparacio, *Deed Abstracts of (Old) Rappahannock County, Virginia 1688–1692*, pp. 84–85,; Westmoreland County Deed Book 8:192; Gray, E–9.

[84] Headley, op. cit., pp. 34–35.

[85] King, *King George County, Virginia, Will Book A-1, 1721–1752*, p. 238.

In February 1707/08 Thomas Goff (Sr.) and wife Margaret deeded 40 acres to Isaac Arnold and his wife Margaret who was the daughter of said Thomas Goff, in St. Mary's Parish, Richmond County, for "love and affection." This tract was on the boundary between John Willis Jr. and Thomas Goff, running to Gunstocker's line (which at that time was owned by Nathaniel Pope alias Bridges), and was part of Goff's 1696/97 patent.[86] The Goffs gave the Arnolds lifetime interest in the land with it then to go to their son Isaac Arnold Jr. Witnesses were John Hauxford, William Duff, and Edward Turberville. This was the earliest entry I found which linked Turberville to the Willis community. He would become the fourth and last husband of Sarah, the widow of William Willis, Henry Wood, and Rush Hudson Sr. and would move to Orange County with the extended Willis family.

Thomas Goff (perhaps the son of Thomas Sr.) was named as guardian of John Willis (son of Charles Willis?) in 1728/29 after John's first guardian, John Willis Jr., died.[87] This Thomas Goff seems to have died intestate in 1734 when administration of his estate was granted to his son Thomas with Thomas Ammon and Isaac Pitman as his securities.

Newman A. Hall reported that in 1737 John Goff (son of Thomas Sr.) obtained two parcels of land in Orange County and that John and his wife Anne later obtained an additional 70 acres. According to Hall, John Goff sold 215 acres in Orange County to Peter Rucker in 1750 in exchange for land in Albemarle County.[88] In her book, *The Rucker Family Genealogy*, Sudie Rucker Wood also cites records for the Goff family which shows connections between them and the Ruckers, Goffs, and David Rosser..[89]

There were other family connections in Orange and Amherst counties. Isaac Rucker (brother of Peter Rucker) married Mildred Hawkins Plunkett (daughter of Benjamin Hawkins and Sarah Willis, assumed daughter of William and Sarah Willis). Mildred Hawkins Plunkett was the widow of John Plunkett Jr. who was the brother of Elizabeth Plunkett Willis (wife of John who was the son of William and Sarah).[90] John Plunkett Jr. and Elizabeth Plunkett are believed to have been the children of John Plunkett Sr. who was apprenticed to John Hauxford and his wife Saints in 1699/1700. John Plunkett Sr. married Francis Frank, daughter of Robert Frank. The Plunkett family is currently being researched and will not be included here.

One man whose name frequently appears on documents for the extended Willis family is Isaac Arnold who married Margaret Goff, daughter of Thomas Goff. Members of the Arnold family also migrated to Orange County where their name is again found with the Willis family.

---

[86] Richmond County Deed Book 4:126–127a.

[87] See Chapter V.

[88] Personal correspondence.

[89] See Orange County records including Deed Book 11:217, Albemarle County Deed Book 1:382, and Amherst County Orders.

[90] See Chapter IX.

The date of the Arnold family's immigration to the colonies has not been established. Newman A. Hall states that a Thomas Arnold was included in the headrights for a patent to James Keyes on the north side of the Rappahannock River in 1678 and that a Thomas Arnold began acquiring land from Adam Woffendall on Gingoteague [Chinoteague]Creek in 1679.[91] In 1684 Thomas Arnold, Francis Thornton, William Strothers, and Adam Woffendall were ordered to appraise the estate of Evan Morgan who had married the widow of William Browne, and Josias Mason was one of Morgan's witnesses to Morgan's will.[92]

Thomas Arnold wrote his will on 27 December 1725 at age 77, giving him a birthdate of 1748 and making him approximately the same age as John Willis Sr. His will names only his wife Grace and sons James and John who was the youngest. Grace was given a lifetime interest in part of Thomas's home place with it to descend to his son James after her death. The balance of Thomas's tract was given to his son John. The will was witnessed by Isaac Arnold and James White and was proved the following May.[93] Isaac Arnold's relationship to James and John Arnold was confirmed by a 1732 deed which included a Power of Attorney from Margaret Arnold, wife of John (son of Thomas), to "my loving friend and brother," Isaac Arnold.[94] Hall does not rule out the possibility that Thomas Arnold Sr. had other children besides James, John, and Isaac, and believes that Isaac was an older son who had already received land from his father-in-law Thomas Goff (see above). Similarly, John Willis Sr. did not leave land to his sons John Jr. and William in his will because he had deeded to them previously.

Grace Arnold died intestate in King George County in 1732/33. Isaac Arnold was appointed administrator of her estate with Rush Hudson (Sr.) as security.[95] At that time Rush Hudson was married to Sarah (—) Willis Wood Hudson.

James Arnold seems to have died intestate in King George County by 1 March 1727/28 when his wife Sarah (nee Weedon), William Harrison, and Neal McCormick posted bond for the administration of his estate. Appraisers were Will Harrison, Fran. Woffendall, and Fran. Settle. Later deeds prove that their eldest son was Weedon Arnold who was living in Washington Parish, Westmoreland County, in 1743 when he deeded two tracts including land by his grandfather Thomas Arnold from Adam Woffendall in 1694/95 and which was bequeathed to Weedon's father, James Arnold.[96] Sarah Weedon Arnold was still living in 1771.

John Arnold was married to Margaret (maiden name unknown) in 1732 and living in Prince William County when they sold 50 acres to William Duff, the land having been willed to him by his father, Thomas Arnold, late of King George County, deceased.[97]

---

[91] Personal correspondence.

[92] Sparacio, *Will Abstracts of (Old) Rappahannock County 1682–1687*, pp.30–31.

[93] King, *King George County Will Book A-1*, pp. 29–30.

[94] King George County Deed Book 1A:222.

[95] King George County Order Book 1:632.

[96] King George County Deed Book 2:463.

[97] Sparacio, *Deed Abstracts of King George County, Virginia (1721–1735)*, pp. 117–118.

The tract lay on a western branch of Gingoteague joining a tract which was given by Thomas (Sr.) to his son James. John was still living in 1744 and had a known son also named James.

Newman A. Hall estimates that Isaac Arnold, the son-in-law of Thomas Goff, was born 1680–1685 in that part of Rappahannock County which later became Richmond, then King George, County. Isaac wrote his will on 15 September 1757 and it was presented in Court on 4 May 1758.[98] His present wife, Mary, was named executor and was given a life interest in their home place and another piece of land after the death of his daughter Diana Wharton, wife of Samuel Wharton. Also named in his will are his eldest son Isaac (who received the land "where I formerly lived in Hanover Parish adjoining land of Capt. Joseph Murdock and Moses Pittman, given to said Isaac Arnold my son by Thomas Goff, grandfather to the said Isaac"), sons William, Benjamin, and Mark (who turned 18 the previous July), and daughters Sarah Moran, Isabell Rogers, Mary Arnold, Jemima Arnold, and Susanna Arnold. Witnesses were Robert Walker, Robert Walker Jr., and William Kendall. To this list of Isaac Arnold's children Hall adds a son named Thomas based upon a 1727 deed from Isaac to his son Thomas which gave Thomas and his wife Mary a lifetime interest in a tract with it then to descend to Thomas's son Humphrey.[99]

It is often difficult to distinguish between Isaac Arnold Jr. (who was born before 1707/08, son of Isaac Sr.) and his nephew Isaac (son of Thomas) in the records. Hall believes that the latter Isaac (son of Thomas and grandson of Isaac Sr.) is the one who is found in the Orange County records beginning in November 1750. The other children of Isaac Arnold Sr. will not be discussed here.

Because Isaac was a neighbor to the Willises and his name appears in most of the significant Willis records, I first speculated that Sarah (—) Willis Wood Hudson Turberville might have been his sister. However, no proofs were found to either substantiate or disprove my theory. Sarah's estimated birthdate was probably between 1680 and 1690, and Hall estimates Isaac Arnold's birthdate as between 1680 and 1685. Based upon circumstantial evidence, Hall believes that Sarah was the daughter of David Rosser and wife Sarah Sherwood (see Chapter VI).

Isaac was married to Margaret Goff, daughter of Thomas Goff, and living in St. Mary's Parish in Richmond County before February 1707/08 at which time they had a son (Isaac Jr.) when her parents (Thomas and Margaret Goff) deeded 40 acres to them and gave their Power of Attorney to John Hauxford to acknowledge the deed in Court.[100] This 40 acres was part of Goff's 1696/97 patent adjacent to John Willis and Gunstocker's line (see Chapter III). It would be logical to assume from the wording in the deed that Isaac Jr. was the eldest son of Isaac and Margaret, but Hall places their son Thomas as the eldest and Isaac as their second son.

---

[98]King George County Will Book A:89.

[99]King George County Deed Book 1:452–453.

[100]Richmond County Deed Book 4:126–127a.

From the records it is obvious that Isaac Arnold Sr. was a gregarious and respected neighbor. His name is found frequently as a witness, executor or administrator, appraiser, bondsman, or in a Power of Attorney on documents in Richmond and later King George County, only a few of which will be mentioned here.

As shown above, Arnold and John Willis witnessed a deed from William Willis and wife Sarah to John Hauxford, and Arnold and John Pitman witnessed a deed from John Hauxford to John Willis Jr. in 1709. The same year Isaac, Charles Cullins, and William Goff witnessed a lease from George Green to John Willis Jr. In 1715 John Willis Sr. wrote his will and named his son John Jr. and Isaac Arnold as executors. He also appointed Isaac Arnold and his son William Willis as guardians of Mary Cullins. While a few earlier family historians speculated that Arnold was the son-in-law of John Willis Sr., I found no evidence that this was the case.

Arnold's name appears in several deeds involving the Butler, Wood, Hauxford, Kendall, and Pitman families and with Charles Willis and Mary (Willis) James as witnesses to John Comb's will in 1716. In 1721 Isaac Arnold, William Pullen, and William Harvey witnessed the will of John Anderson *(q.v.)*, and Arnold was security for John Plunkett in his administration of the estate of Joseph Littlefield. Arnold, Thomas Dickason, and Moses Knighton witnessed the will of Archdell Combs (son of John) in 1734/35 (see above). In 1736 Isaac witnessed Neal McCormick's will and a deed from John Willis (son of Charles?) and wife Elizabeth to Isaac Pitman.[101]

Although he was neither an appraiser nor bondsman in William Willis's estate (as John Willis Jr. and Charles Willis co-signed Sarah's bond), Arnold provided security for Rush Hudson and his wife Sarah in the administration of the estate of her second husband, Henry Wood, in 1722. In 1735 Arnold, Neal McCormick, Thomas Thatcher, and Benjamin Berryman provided bond for Edmund Turberville and wife Sarah's administration of her third husband Rush Hudson's estate. Other entries are found in the King George County records through 1751/52 when Isaac Arnold Sr. and Isaac Arnold Jr. were on the list of voters in Hanover Parish.[102]

Sometime before 15 September 1757 when he wrote his will, Isaac Arnold Sr. moved from his home place. In his will Isaac Sr. gave his eldest son Isaac Jr. "land where I formerly lived in Hanover Parish adjoining land of Joseph Murdock and Moses Pittman and which was given to my son Isaac Arnold by Thomas Goff, grandfather to the said Isaac Arnold."[103] Isaac Jr. married Sarah (—) and died before 1772 at which time Sarah was still living in King George County. James Arnold, son of Isaac Jr., was living in Fauquier County by 1761 and was still living there in 1772.

Continued research on the Arnold family is indicated for several reasons. Isaac Arnold

---

[101] King, *King George County Will Book A-1*, pp. 120–121.

[102] Ibid., p. 288.

[103] A related deed is found in King George County Deed Book 4:425, when in 1759 Moses Pitman sold 60 acres in King George County to Joseph Murdock (from microfilm). The tract being conveyed was sold to Pitman in 1746 by Thomas Gough [Goff] and lay on Crows Swamp. Moses Pitman married Margaret Riding, stepdaughter of Francis Thornton Sr.

Sr. and his wife Margaret Goff(e) lived adjacent to the Willises in Richmond/King George County, and his name is found repeatedly on Willis documents. When John and William Willis (sons of William), their mother Sarah (—) Willis Wood Hudson Turberville, and their extended family migrated to the Rapidan River in Orange County, the Arnolds were again neighbors. William Willis (son of William and Sarah) placed an attachment on the estate of Isaac Arnold in Orange County Court in November 1758, and in April 1759 the Court ordered James Arnold to pay William Willis the debt from the estate of Isaac Arnold (see Chapter VI). The reason for this debt is unknown, but the records show that this unidentified Isaac's estate was not probated in Orange County.

The last neighbor of John Willis Sr. to be discussed is Francis Thornton Sr. who died in 1726. Several factors suggested that the Thornton family records should be reviewed. They lived adjacent to the Willises in Richmond/King George County. Descendants of both Francis Thornton Sr. and John Willis Sr. moved to Orange County. Land formerly belonging to the Wood and Hudson families was sold to the Thorntons in 1746/47. And John Willis's 1669 patent became the property of William Thornton, grandson of Francis Thornton Sr., in 1767.

Francis Thornton Sr.'s acquisition of 1,000 acres out of John Washington's 1,700-acre patent has been given above. It is noted that Thornton bought this tract thirty-six years after John Willis Sr. received his adjoining patent. Since Washington's family did not live on the tract and it never escheated, it is assumed that it was occupied by tenants between 1664 when Washington received his patent and 1705 when his heirs sold it to Thornton. From that time onward, the Thorntons were neighbors, and by 1750 the Thornton family owned much of the land which had belonged to the extended Willis–Wood–Hudson family.

The first entry I found in the records linking Francis Thornton and John Willis Sr. was dated February 1694/95 when the Richmond County Court ordered Capt. William Moseley, surveyor, "in the presence of two honest men of the neighborhood" to view 100 acres which Robert Vincent and his wife Martha (formerly the widow of William Freake) sold to Thomas Tippett in 1687 in order to determine the boundaries of the tract. The Court also ordered that "Mr. Francis Thornton is requested to swear the two neighbors chosed [*sic*] to their due survey as also John Willis who is ordered to be present at the time and place aforesaid to a true discovery of what he knows concerning (the bounds of said land)."[104]

According to George H. S. King, Francis Thornton Sr. (1651–1726) of Richmond, Stafford, and King George counties, was the son of William Thornton and the cousin of Rowland Thornton who died in 1701 in Richmond County.[105] Francis was married three times. His first wife was Alice Savage, the daughter of Anthony Savage, and she

---

[104] Sparacio, *Richmond County Orders 1694–1697*, pp. 26–27, and *(Old) Rappahannock County Deeds 1686–1688*, p. 56.

[105] Primary sources for data on the Thornton family were George H. S. King's two volumes (*Marriages of Richmond County, Virginia*, and *King George County Will Book A-1*) and various county records.

was the mother of all of Francis's children. About 1701 Francis married secondly Jane Harvey, widow of John Harvey who died in 1700/01 in Stafford County. In 1706 Francis Thornton and his wife Jane deeded 684 acres which she inherited from her former husband to four of Francis's sons—Anthony, Francis, Rowland, and William—with Francis and Jane to hold lifetime occupancy rights.[106] Three of the tracts lay in Stafford County and one was in Westmoreland County. His last and surviving wife, Ann (—) Riding, had two known children by a previous marriage—George Riding and Margaret Riding (who married Isaac Pitman).

Francis Thornton's will was dated 10 May 1726 and presented into Court for probate on 7 October 1726. Witnesses were Thomas Turner, Thomas Moore, and John Kendall (whose relationship, if any, to Thomas Kendall is unknown to me).[107] He left a tract of "800 & odd acres" at the foot of the Lower Falls of Rappahannock River which he had bought from Mr. John Hawkins to his sons Francis Thornton and Rowland Thornton. He also gave his son Rowland half of the tract which he bought from John and Francis Wright in Richmond County adjoining the lines of John Hawxford [Hauxford] and Thomas Tippett on both sides of Crows Swamp. He gave the other half of this tract to his wife Anne during her lifetime and then to her son George Riding. In addition, he gave George Riding about 170 acres which he had purchased from Capt. John Washington in King George County (i.e., 171.5 acres in 1716 as reported in Chapter II). Other heirs named were his eldest son William Thornton, eldest daughter Elizabeth Gibson, daughter Sarah Taliaferro, daughter Margaret Strother, son Anthony Thornton, grandson Francis Conway (i.e., son of his daughter Elizabeth Thornton Conway Gibson by her first husband Edwin Conway), and his wife's daughter, Margaret Riding.

Therefore, after 1726 Rowland Thornton and George Riding owned that portion of Washington's 1664 patent which adjoined that part of John Willis's 261-acre patent which then belonged to John Willis, the eldest son of William Willis who died in 1716.

According to King, Francis Thornton's daughter Elizabeth (not to be confused with Elizabeth Catlett Thornton, her sister-in-law and wife of Rowland Thornton who died in 1741–1742) was born in 1674. She married first Edwin Conway (d. 1698) of Lancaster and Richmond counties after the death of Conway's first wife, Sarah Walker. From the records it is assumed that the above Edwin Conway was the same man to whom Henry Fleet (Jr.) deeded 2,000 acres in 1694 and impacted upon the Willis–Parsons grant of 1690/91.[108]

Edwin Conway (Sr.) and his first wife, Sarah Walker, had two children—Col. Edwin Conway (1681–1763) and Mary Conway (1686–1730).[109] Edwin Conway (Sr.) and his second wife, Elizabeth Thornton, had one son, Francis Conway (1696–1732), who married Rebecca Catlett and became the parents of Nelly Conway who married James

---

[106]Sparacio, *Stafford County Deeds & Wills 1699–1709*, p. 18.

[107]King, *King George County Will Book A-1*, pp. 35–37.

[108]Richmond County Deed Book 2:59. Also see Chapter III.

[109]King, *Marriages of Richmond County, Virginia, 1668–1853*, pp. 248 and 251.

Madison. Elizabeth Madison, sister of James Madison, married John Willis the elder, said to have been the son of Col. Henry Willis of Fredericksburg and his first wife, Ann Alexander Smith (see Chapter XII).

After Conway's death in 1698, Elizabeth (Thornton) Conway married Jonathan Gibson Sr. and by him had Jonathan Gibson Jr. (who married Margaret Catlett and died in 1745 in Orange County), Alice Gibson (who married John Catlett who died in 1744 in Orange County), Rachel Gibson (who married Col. George Taylor), and Sarah Gibson. Jonathan Gibson Sr.'s will of 1727 and Elizabeth Thornton Conway Gibson's will of 1732 are found in *King George County Will Book A-1.*

A Francis Conway received a grant for 576 acres on the southeastern side of Chestnut (now Clark's) Mountain in Spotsylvania (now Orange) County on 30 June 1726 adjoining Alexander Spotswood's large Spotsylvania grant where John Willis's descendants moved and adjacent to patents held by Lawrence Taliaferro, John Taliaferro, Thomas Taylor, and Benjamin Porter.[110] I believe that this Francis Conway may have been the son of Elizabeth Thornton and Edwin Conway Sr., and the grandson of Francis Thornton Sr.

Rowland Thornton, son of Francis Sr., married Elizabeth Catlett and lived on the Crows Swamp tract in King George where he died in 1741/42.[111] Because of his proximity to the Willis family and the fact that Rowland was probably about the same age as William Willis and John Willis Jr. (sons of John Sr.), his will and the descent of his land are important. Rowland bequeathed to his son Francis his land "near the Great Falls" in Spotsylvania County and 300 acres where Francis was living in King George County. Besides personal property, Rowland gave his wife Elizabeth the use of his "dwelling plantation with all the land belonging to it on the upper side of Crows Swamp" during her lifetime with it then to go to his son Francis. To daughter Elizabeth Thornton he left two tracts—his share of 500 acres in Caroline County which he purchased with his father-in-law, Col. John Catlett, and 250 acres "if recovered from the heirs of Charles Smith who mortgaged the same to Micajah Perry, Merchant in London, of whom the said Catlett and I made the purchase." His daughter Alcey was to have the use of his quarter with the land adjoining it below Crows Swamp until she married, after which the land was to go to his son Francis. Executors were his son Francis and his brother Anthony Thornton. Witnesses were John Moore and Wm. Mackay—probably the same Mackay who witnessed John Willis's deed to the Church Wardens in 1737.

Rowland's widow Elizabeth (Catlett) Thornton died testate in 1751.[112] Her will names her son Francis Thornton, son-in-law John Fitzhugh, daughter Alce Fitzhugh, grandsons William Thornton and Francis Thornton, and daughter Elizabeth Thornton. Witnesses were John Brown and George Riding.

---

[110] Patricia J. Hurst, *The History and People of Clark Mountain, Orange County, Virginia* (Rapidan: author, 1989), p. 5; and personal correspondence.

[111] King, *King George County Will Book A-1*, pp. 108–110.

[112] Ibid, pp. 204–205.

In 1761 Frederick Coghill (Jr.) of Essex County (*i.e.*, the nephew of Mary Coghill Willis Jennings) sold 12 acres which his uncle, John Willis Jr., had purchased from John Hauxford in 1709 to Francis Thornton of King George County.[113]

Francis Thornton, son of Rowland and Elizabeth (Catlett) Thornton, died in King George in 1767.[114] He left part of his land below Crow Swamp adjoining Joseph Murdock, being part of the land he bought from John McCormack on the lowest side of Crows and "back of my log house where Francis Willis now lives," plus other land to his son William Thornton who had married Elizabeth Fitzhugh. To his son Francis Thornton he left the residue of his land in King George plus other tracts. He also made bequests to Judith and Nanny Settle, daughters of Emma Settle, with William Settle as trustee. Executors were his son Francis and Col. Presley Thornton (probably his cousin and son of Anthony Thornton and wife Winifred Presley). Witnesses were Thomas Lendrum, John Jett, and John Triplett.

The identity of this Francis Willis is unknown. He may or may not have been the son of John Willis, son of Charles. According to Torrence, John Willis died intestate in King George County in 1753.[115] Elizabeth Willis, assumed to be John's widow, died testate in 1767. Elizabeth's will (found immediately preceding Francis Thornton's in King George County Will Book A) names grandchildren William, Elizabeth, Willis, and Younger Johnson with the bulk of her estate to go to her son Francis Willis during his life and then to her granddaughter Jane Willis, daughter of Francis. Witnesses were William Chapman and William Thornton.

By comparing the above data on the Thornton family with various deeds and wills, it is clear that they were not only neighbors for many years, but that they eventually purchased four tracts from Rush Hudson Jr. after he and Willis family moved to Orange County. Landmarks in the deeds such as Crows Swamp, Portridges (Poultridges) Creek, and Bald Eagle Run indicate that the tracts were in the watershed of present Jett's Creek. Based upon a review of these and other records for that period, it can be assumed that by 1760 most of John Willis Sr.'s land and that of his early neighbors belonged to the Thornton, Riding, Turner, and Murdock families and the Church Wardens of Hanover Parish.

In 1767 the Church Wardens sold the Willis patent, which had been the church glebe since 1737, to William Thornton.[116] Consequently, one hundred years after John Washington and John Willis received their adjoining patents, the Thornton family owned most of these tracts.

In 1818 the heirs of a Francis Thornton (nephew to Francis who was son of Francis, son of Rowland, son of Francis Thornton Sr.) deeded 342 acres 3 rods and 12 poles

[113]See Chapters V and VI; King George County Deed Book 4:460.

[114]King George County Will Book A:262–265.

[115]Clayton Torrence, *Virginia Willis and Administrations 1632–1800* (Baltimore: Genealogical Publishing Co., 1990).

[116]King George County Deed Book 5:684–685 from microfilm; see Chapter I.

in King George County at the head of Portises (Portridges?) Creek, down the creek to the junction of Bald Eagle swamp, etc., to Nathaniel H. Hooe.[117] According to a document from the Circuit Court in Fredericksburg, part of this land may have belonged to the heirs of Chas. Tayloe, deceased, in 1897. I have not reviewed all of the later Thornton family deeds and wills, but a study of those records could very well pinpoint the exact location of John Willis's first patent.

While scrutiny of John Willis Sr.'s neighbors did not provide the names of his parents, the mother(s) of his children, or the maiden name of William Willis's wife, Sarah, it gave me a much better picture of his community as it evolved over three generations. I learned that John was initially connected to the people of Appomattox Creek in Westmoreland County, and that his alliances with the Old Rappahannock County group south of the ridge were not evident until the 1680s. Consequently, after reviewing the records of his known descendants in Richmond, King George, Orange, and Culpeper counties (which will be discussed in Chapters V through IX), I turned to early Westmoreland and then to its parent, Northumberland County (which are reviewed in Chapters X and XI).

John's first wife was probably from Westmoreland County, and I strongly suspect that his father was John Willis who died in Westmoreland in 1682 although this assumption must be based on circumstantial evidence because his will is missing. Sarah, the wife of William Willis, was probably the daughter of one of his neighbors; but that, too, is still unclear. As the records do not tell us, other factors must be considered such as proximity, probability, naming patterns, and the families who migrated to Orange County with the extended family.

---

[117]King George County Deed Book 10:470, 10:499, 15:302, 15:331, 20:567, 25:547, and 28:132, from microfilm.

Chapter V

John Willis Jr.

A s John Willis Jr. was the eldest son of John Willis Sr., his records will be reviewed first, followed by the records for his next eldest brother, William, and then for the rest of his siblings (or half-siblings). Assuming that John Jr. was at least twenty-one years old when his father deeded to him in 1694, he was born by or before 1673. This suggests that his father was approximately 25 years old when John Jr. was born. John Jr. was probably in his early forties when his father and brother William died and in his middle fifties when he himself died. During those thirteen years between 1715 and 1728 John Jr. was the "head" of the family in King George County although either or both of his known sisters could have been older than he was. He married Mary Coghill, daughter of James Coghill and his second wife, Mary, sometime before 1698. As will be shown, Mary Coghill was born before 1685, married secondly John Jennings, and died in 1748.

Our knowledge about John Willis Jr. was enhanced when King George County Will Book A-1, which had disappeared during the Civil War, was found, restored, and transcribed by George H. S. King in 1978. Family historian George B. Loeffler either did not know about this discovery or did not report it when he conducted his research for his article in the Willis–Gordon–Garnett and Allied Families Association *Journal* in 1982, so the wills of John Jr., his wife Mary (Coghill), and Mary Cullins provide new insights into the family.

John Jr. died testate in King George County between 6 February 1727/28 and 3 May 1728. He and Mary may have had children who predeceased them, but both his and Mary's wills indicate that they did not leave surviving issue. His will, as transcribed by George H. S. King, is given below.[1]

> *In the name of God Amen I John Willis of the Parish of Hanover in the County of King George, being sick in body but of perfect sense and memory thanks be to God for the same, do make my last Will & Testament in manner and form following, that is to say ... I give unto William Wood that parcel of land my brother William Willis exchanged with John Hawxford to him and his heirs forever. I give and bequeath unto my loving wife Mary Willis all that parcel of land whereon my now dwelling plantation is to her and her heirs forever. I also give unto my wife Mary all and singular my other land & tenements for and during the term of her natural life, and as touching my personal estate my two slaves and all other movables I give unto my wife Mary Willis for and during her natural life. It is my will that after my wife Mary's death my two slaves and other movables then left be equally divided amongst both my Relations and her Relations as she shall think fit at that*

---

[1] King, *King George County Will Book A-1*, p. 49.

time between them. I hereby make constitute and appoint my loving wife Mary Willis full and sole Executrix of this my last Will & Testament, revoking all other Wills by me formerly made. I desire that my estate may not be brought to an appraisement. In witness whereof I have hereunto set my hand and seal this twenty sixty day of February 1727 (1728).

Signed: John Willis

Witnesses: William Pullen
            Catherine (her mark) Pullen
            Elizabeth (her mark) Harly

At a Court held for King George County the 3ʳᵈ day of May Anno Dom. 1728 the Last Will & Testament of John Willis, deceased, was presented into Court by Mary his Widow & Executrix who made oath thereto and the same was proved by the oaths of William Pullein [Pullen] and Catherine Pullein [Pullen] witnesses thereto subscribed and admitted to record. Attest: Turner, Cl. Cir.

An inventory of John's estate was presented in Court on 7 June 1728 by his widow, Mary Willis.[2]

By 20 February 1728/29 Mary Coghill Willis had married John Jennings, a widower with children. As she was born before 1685, Mary Coghill Willis was beyond her childbearing years when she married Jennings, and they left no issue. Jennings died testate in Orange County, Virginia, in 1735 and his will was probated in both counties.[3] It may be that Jennings accompanied William Wood to Orange County to look for land *circa* 1734 and died while he was there (see Chapter IX). His will is given here as abstracted by Ruth and Sam Sparacio.[4]

John Jennings of Hanover Parish, King George County; wr. 20 February 1728/9, rec. 15 June 1735; executor wife Mary; witnesses William Pullen, Elisha Harly, Elizabeth Harly; to children John, Ann, Margaret, Mary, and Elizabeth (Orange County Will Book 1:6).

The names of the witnesses indicate that Jennings made his will in King George County. Inventories of his estate were recorded in both Orange and King George. In Orange County John Hawkins and Isaac Smith provided bond, and an appraisal was made of his estate there on 16 July 1735.[5] John Hawkins was probably the son of John and Elizabeth (Butler) Hawkins of Richmond County and the brother of Benjamin Hawkins who married Sarah Willis, assumed daughter of William and Sarah Willis.

Mary Coghill Willis Jennings (also given as Ginnings) wrote her will on 16 July 1745,

---

[2] Sparacio, King George County Inventories.

[3] King, *King George County Will Book A-1*, p. 245.

[4] Sparacio, *Digest of Orange County, Virginia, Will Books 1734–1838*, p. 58.

[5] Ibid.; Orange County Will Book 1:6 and 1:8–9.

and it was produced in King George County Court on 7 October 1748.[6]

In the Name of God Amen the 16th day of July Anno Dom: 1745, I Mary Ginnings of the Parish of Hanover in the County of King George being in health of body and of perfect mind and memory thanks be given unto God therefore, calling to mind the mortality of my body and knowing that it is appointed for all people once to die do make and ordain this my last Will & Testament—

Item: I leave the plantation whereon I live to John Willis, the son of Charles Willis, during his natural life and after his decease I give my land and plantation to my cousin [sic] Frederick Coghill Junr. and his heirs forever.
Item: I give to John Willis, the son of Charles Willis, one Negro man named Adam and two Negroes he has in possession to him and his heirs forever.
Item: I give to Elisha Harley one bed and furniture and one pot.
Item: I give to John Ginnings a young mare to him and his heirs forever.
Item: I give to John Dickerson one cow and calf, the son of Sarah Dickerson.
Item: I give all my wearing cloths [sic] to Elizabeth Peynon.
Item: I give to my cousins Susannah Miller and Mary Hawes and Sarah Samues [sic] each a ring ten shillings price.
Item: I leave to my brother Frederick Coghill four Negroes and their increase during his natural life and then I give them to my two cousins Thomas Coghill and Frederick Coghill Junr. to be equally divided to them and their heirs forever.
Item: I give all of my personal estate to my brother Frederick Coghill to him and his heirs forever.
I have divided my estate as I thought proper and it is my desire that my estate may not be praised to fullfill my former husband's will. I make and appoint my brother Frederick and my cousin [sic] Frederick Coghill, Junr. my full and sole Executors, ratifying and confirming this and none other to be my last Will and Testament. In Witness whereof I have hereunto set my hand (and) seal the day and year first above written. Signed Sealed & Delivered by the said Mary Ginnings to be her last Will & Testament.

Signed: Mary (mark) Ginnings

John McCormic
Wm. (mark) Turner
Sarah (mark) Dickerson

On 7 October 1748 Mary's will was presented by Frederick Coghill the Elder and proved by the oaths of John McCormic and Sarah McDonald (late Dickerson) and admitted to record.[7] On the same date the Court ordered Mary's estate to be appraised and bond was posted by Frederick Coghill for his administration with Benjamin Strother Sr. as his security in the amount of 400 pounds. The inventory was taken by Francis Thornton, George Riding, and Henry Ware who listed six slaves (Hannah,

---

[6] King, *King George County Will Book A-1*, pp. 158–160.

[7] King George County Court Orders.

Bob, Dick, Tom, Frank, and a girl), household items, four hives of bees, a large bible, and some old books with a total value of 195 pounds 6 shillings 3 pence.[8] It is noted that the Frederick Coghill, Jr. and Thomas Coghill who are named in Mary's will were not cousins, but nephews.

Returning to John Willis Jr., the first time he is named in the records was in 1694 when his father deeded his interest in the Willis–Parsons grant plus 100 acres of his 261-acre patent to him. The wording of the deed implies that John Jr. was unmarried at the time.

In 1715 John Willis Jr. and Isaac Arnold were executors of his father's estate in 1715. That year John and his brother-in-law Frederick Coghill were also executors of Mary (__) Coghill Ducksberry's will in Essex County, so in one year John and Mary each lost a parent. In December 1716 John and his brother Charles co-signed Sarah Willis's bond for her administration of their brother William's estate.

County Orders show that in 1718 John Willis and Christopher Edrington were appointed surveyors of roads from Gravelly Run to Crows Swamp.[9] In 1719 John was appointed surveyor of roads from Gingoteague (Chingoteague) to the lower end of the parish, and in 1720 he was reappointed to the same position.

John's brother Charles was deceased by 6 August 1725 and left at least one son who was also named John and who was close in age to William's son John. After Charles' death, his son John chose his uncle John Willis (Jr.) as his guardian; and after his uncle's death in 1728, Charles' son John chose Thomas Goff(e) as his guardian. Those records will be discussed in more detail in Chapter VII.

Because John Jr. did not leave any children, his line ended with his death. John Jr. is very important, however, in proving the lineage of his nephew John (son of William and Sarah) who sold John Willis Sr.'s patent to the Church Wardens in 1737 and moved to Orange County. In addition, the Coghill connection may account for later marriages between collateral lines and the Rucker and Hawkins families—connections which continued into Orange and Culpeper counties and then into Kentucky for several generations.

John's wife, Mary Coghill, was the daughter of Old Rappahannock (later Essex) County immigrant James Coghill whose will, dated 5 October 1684 and proved in September 1685, is briefly summarized below from Ruth and Sam Sparacio's transcription.[10]

> *To my wife Mary Coghill, life interest in my plantation where I now live with all livestock and a horse; to my eldest son (William?) 225 acres and a mare with all coopers and carpenters tools to be divided between William and James; to son James, 225 acres, a gun, and a sword; to son David, 200 acres*

[8] King George County Inventories from microfilm.

[9] Richmond County Order Book 8:36 (see note below).

[10] Sparacio, *Will Abstracts of (Old) Rappahannock County, Virginia 1682–1687*, p. 63.

*and a gun; to son Frederick, 200 acres and a mare; to unborn child if a boy,
200 acres (otherwise to return to above four sons); land to be equally divided
according to age; to daughters Margrett and Mary, 600 acres lying in
another dividend, 200 acres of this land to unborn child if a girl (otherwise
to remain with Margarett and Mary, each of them (to have) one mare of one
year old; I appoint David and Frederick to be at age at 18 and to enjoy their
estate if their mother marryeth; my loving wife to be full and sole executor;
witnesses Christopher Man, Thomas Fenley.*

James Coghill's name is found in both Westmoreland and Old Rappahannock records,
and he was married more than once. In 1665 his wife was Alice, and by 1673 he was
married to Mary. It appears that Frederick and Mary were the children of James and
his second wife, Mary, and that the other children named in James' will were children
from a previous marriage.

After Coghill's death his widow, Mary, married Henry Duckberry and died testate in
1715. Mary Duckberry's will names her sons Frederick Coghill and George
Duckberry, her daughter Mary Willis and son-in-law John Willis, and Susannah
Coghill, Thomas Coghill, and Mary Coghill, the last three probably the children of her
son Frederick. Frederick Coghill and John Willis were her executors.[11] George
Duckberry died shortly after his mother. His will names his "brother" [stepbrother or
half-brother] Frederick Coghill, Frederick's daughter Susannah, John Kendall, Hugh
Crutcher, Richard Booker, John Willis, and John Pellow. Duckberry's executors were
Frederick Coghill and Richard Booker.[12] I do not know if this John Kendall was
related to the Kendalls who were neighbors to the Willises on the north side of the
Rappahannock River.

Old Rappahannock County deeds suggest that James Coghill's sons William and James
were living in Charles City, Maryland, in 1689 when they sold 250 acres on Portobaco
Creek in Rappahannock County adjoining Coghill's plantation and all cattle, hogs, and
household items to a Johanna Hudson.[13] In 1691 Johanna sold to Richard Booker of
Gloucester County with Mary Ducksberry as one of the witnesses.[14] This is probably
the same Richard Booker who was named in George Duckberry's will.

It is not known when John and Mary Willis married or how they met as James Coghill
lived on the south side of the Rappahannock River. However, Coghill may have been
the same man who witnessed deeds from Henry Brooks and wife Jane to their daughter
Jane Higdon (who later was the mother-in-law of Nathaniel Pope alias Bridges) and
Lawrence Abbington in 1662 in Westmoreland County, so prior connections to the
Mattox group in Washington County are possible.[15] Clues were also found connecting
the Coghills and Archdale Combs who witnessed Coghill deeds in 1665, 1666, and

[11]Essex County Deeds & Wills 14:428.

[12]Ibid., p. 430.

[13]Sparacio, *(Old) Rappahannock County Deed Book 8 1688–1692*, pp. 12–13.

[14]Ibid., p. 122.

[15]Dorman, *Westmoreland County, Virginia, Records 1661–1664*, pp. 8–9.

1673.[16] As discussed in the sketch on the Combs family in Chapter IV, the name of an Abraham Combs of Maryland was found in Old Rappahannock records in 1665 and 1683. Considering that two of James Coghill's sons were living in Maryland in 1689, they may have been related in some way.

Two interesting entries were found in the Essex County records in 1698. First, John and Mary Willis (who are given as residents of Essex County although this was probably not the case) sold 289 acres which she inherited from her father to Thomas Ramsey.[17] John Willis (Jr.) gave his lands in Richmond County as collateral on the bond to Ramsey. Secondly, John Parsons (Jr.) of Essex County sold his share of the Willis–Parsons patent to Walter Anderson (who was John Parsons Jr.'s brother-in-law, half-brother, or stepbrother).[18] Other records clearly show that both John Willis Jr. and John Parsons Jr. were residents of Richmond County. John Parsons Jr. was the son of John Parsons Sr. (see Chapter III). Also named in related Essex County deeds in 1698 were Cornelius Noell and Bartholomew Vawter who owned land adjacent to Coghill's patent. The Noell and Vawter families married into the Rucker family, and Frederick Coghill and wife Susannah deeded land on Cockleshell Creek to the Ruckers in 1707.

In 1712 an unidentified William Willis of Westmoreland County and his wife Mary (daughter and heir of Thomas Kirk, deceased, of Essex County) sold a tract to Charles Brown adjoining Coghill's 1664 patent.[19] This tract appears to have been on Cockleshell Creek where Kirk was living in 1682. Although these records are still fragmented and inconclusive, they may be significant in our search for other members of John Willis Sr.'s siblings or family.

There are several records which name John Willis Jr. in Richmond and King George counties. In 1694 John Willis Sr. deeded 100 acres of his 261 acre patent plus his interest in the Willis–Parsons grant to his eldest son John. The two parcels adjoined and were located in what was then St. Mary's Parish, Richmond County, and which later became Hanover Parish, King George County. As noted in Chapter III, title to the Willis–Parsons tract was disputed by Crane, but the Court ruled for John Willis Jr. and Walter Anderson who divided it in 1706/07.

In 1709 George Green sold John Willis Jr. a lease for 100 acres in St. Mary's Parish for the lifetimes of John and his wife Mary.[20]

2 September 1709, George Green, Planter, of St. Mary's Parish to John Willis Jr., Planter, of St. Mary's Parish, a lifetime interest in 100 acres more or less in St. Mary's Parish on the north side of the Rappahannock River corner to Maxfill (Maxfield) Brown, south to line of Mr. Francis Thornton to

---

[16]Sparacio, *Deeds & Wills of (Old) Rappahannock County 1665–1677*, p. 18, and others.

[17]Sparacio, *Essex County Deeds & Wills 1699–1701*, pp. 5–6.

[18]Sparacio, *Richmond County Deeds 1695–1701*, p. 66.

[19]Beverley Fleet,*Virginia Colonial Abstracts*, vol. VIII, Essex County Wills & Deeds 1711–1714 (Baltimore: Genealogical Publishing Co., 1971), p. 10.

[20]Sparacio, *Richmond County Deeds 1708–1711*, p. 53 (Deed Book 5:173–174).

*line of William Thornton, to line of Thomas Newton, to Maxfill Brown, during
the natural lives of John Willis Jr. and his wife Mary Willis and no
longer—after death of John and Mary to return to me [George Green] and
my heirs; witnesses Isaac Arnold, Charles Cullins, William Goffe.*

George Green was issued a grant for 885 acres in Richmond County on 15 December
1708.[21] The original document states that it joined Major (Francis) Wright, Bald Eagle
Neck, the estate of Esq. Wormely who was then deceased, Francis Slaughter, William
Brown, Maxfield Brown, and land surveyed for William Thornton. The metes and
bounds of Green's grant show that it lay directly west of Washington's 1,700-acre
patent (which the Wrights sold to Francis Thornton) and confirms the approximate
location of Bald Eagle Run as a branch of present Jett's Creek. The tract which Green
leased to John was in the northeast corner of his grant. This lease is one of several
documents which proves that Maxfield Brown (who was named in Evan Morgan's
1683 will in Old Rappahannock County) owned land adjacent to the Willises. After
Mary (Coghill) Willis Jennings' death, this tract reverted to George Green's heirs, and
John Green sold 70 acres out of it to William Dodgin in 1750.[22]

In 1709 William Willis sold 12 acres to John Hauxford, and the following day
Hauxford sold 12 acres to John Willis Jr.[23] Those deeds intermingled John
Washington's and John Willis Sr.'s early patents, and the "exchange" of these parcels
is mentioned in John Willis Jr.'s will.

Consequently, in the fall of 1709 John Willis Jr. held by deed or lease a total of 291
acres in Richmond County. However, he and Walter Anderson lost most of their claim
to the Willis–Parsons tract in 1719 to Edwin Conway (Jr.), and in 1719 Conway sold
117 acres of the tract, including most of the Willis–Parsons grant, to John Anderson,
the brother of Walter Anderson. So after 1719 John Willis Jr. was left with whatever
acreage was spared in Conway's resurvey plus 100 acres of his father's 261-acre patent
(which eventually descended to William's son John), the 100 acres which he leased
from George Green (which reverted to the Green heirs upon Mary's death), and the 12
acres which he bought from John Hauxford.

By the time that John Jr. wrote his will in 1727/28, many changes had taken place in
the family. John's parents and his wife Mary's parents were deceased. His brother
William had died, after which William's widow Sarah had married Henry Wood,
become widowed a second time, and then married Rush Hudson. His brother Charles
Willis was deceased, and John had been appointed guardian to Charles' son John.
Mary Cullins was also deceased with her legacy from John Willis Sr. reverting to John
Sr.'s heirs. It is not known if his sister Susannah was still living in 1727/28, but his
sister Mary James seems to have been living in King George in 1736 (see Chapter VI).

John Jr. specifically named only two legatees in his will—his wife and William Wood

---

[21] Northern Neck Grant Book 3:208 from microfilm.

[22] Sparacio, *King George County Deeds 1735–1752*, p. 114 (Deed Book 3:366–369).

[23] Chapter II and Richmond County Deed Book 5:133–135.

who was the eldest son and heir-at-law of Henry Wood Sr. (the second husband of Sarah—Willis) by a previous marriage. Why John chose to leave land to William Wood is unknown. In Chapter IX, which reviews the transition from King George to Orange County, it will be seen that William Wood and John Jennings preceded the others to the Rapidan River area, and that William Wood sold his land in King George County to Rush Hudson Sr., his stepmother's third husband.

William and Catherine Pullen witnessed John's will, and William Pullen witnessed John Jennings' will. They also witnessed William Underwood's will in July 1717, and John Willis Jr. signed Underwood's estate inventory.[24] William Pullen and Samuel Wood proved the will of William Underwood's son John in 1723. William and John Underwood both lived in Sittenburne Parish, but various deeds and wills suggest that they owned land on both sides of present Bristol Mines Run.

Catherine (Cullins) Pullen was the mother of Mary Cullins as proved by Mary Cullin's will which was written on 12 February 1725/26 and proved on 1 April 1726.[25] Elizabeth Harly was a witness in John Willis's and Mary Coghill Willis Jennings' wills, and Elisha Harley was mentioned in both Mary's and John Jennings' wills.

In 1732 the General Court awarded John Willis 53 pounds 14 shillings in a judgment against John Jennings who, with William Grant as his security, posted bond to John Willis in the amount of 100 pounds and appealed. The reason for the judgment was not given, and it is unclear which John Willis was involved.[26] It may have been John (son of Charles) with the suit relating to John Willis Jr.'s guardianship account, or it may have been John (son of William) who was suing for another reason.

Mary Coghill Willis Jennings must have continued to live on John's home tract under the conditions of the 1694 deed from John Willis Sr. because her lifetime interest in 108 acres was noted in the 1737 deed from John (son of William and Sarah) to the Church Wardens.

In March 1736/37 the King George County Orders note a suit which was brought by John Willis (probably the son of Charles) against Mary Jennings at the same time that Edward and Sarah Turberville were administering the estate of her third husband Rush Hudson Sr. In April the following record appears in the Orders:

> In the action of account rendered between John Willis, plaintiff, and Mary Jennings, executrix of the last will and testament of John Willis, deceased, Capt. Joseph Strother, Samuel Skinner (Skinker?), and Thomas Turner, Gentlemen, or any two of the are appointed to audit and settle the accounts and differences and make their report to the next Court, and it is also ordered that the auditors settle the amount [or account] of the administration of the

---

[24] See sketch on Underwood family in Chapter IV.

[25] King, *King George County Will Book A-1*, pp. 28–29; Richmond County Orders 2 February 1703.

[26] Sparacio, *King George County Deeds 1721–1735*, p. 116 (Deed Book 1-A).

estate of John Jennings, deceased.

The Orders do not give the reason for the suit, but it was continued for lack of the auditors' report until October 1737 when the Court ruled that John Willis was to receive 3,288 pounds of tobacco from Mary Jennings, executrix of John Willis.[27] Again in February 1737/38 the Court ruled that John was to receive 3,288 pounds of tobacco, etc., from Mary Jennings, executrix of the last will of John Willis, with auditors Joseph Strother, Benjamin Strother, and Thomas Turner signing. John may have been attempting to recover some property which his uncle held for him when he was John's guardian, or it could have been over some undivided portion of the personal estate of John Willis Sr.[28]

In her will Mary Coghill Willis Jennings gave a life interest in her home farm to John Willis, son of Charles and grandson of John Sr., with the tract to become the property of her "cousin" [nephew] Frederick Coghill Jr. at John's death. As Mary left no children, her other legatees included her brother Frederick, nephews and nieces, Jennings heirs, and perhaps cousins and friends. Ann Ginnings [Jennings] was named in both Mary's will and John Jennings' will. She was probably John Jennings' daughter by his previous marriage and Mary's stepdaughter.

After Mary's death, her life interest in her first husband's share of John Willis Sr.'s 261-acre patent, her remaining life interest in the Willis–Parsons patent (which was divided with Anderson and then preempted by Conway), and the lease on 100 acres from George Green all expired. Thus it appears that the only Willis land which was included in Mary's estate was the 12-acre parcel which her nephew John Willis (son of Charles) held until his death in 1753, the tract then devolving to Mary's nephew, Frederick Coghill Jr. In 1761 Frederick Coghill sold the 12 acres to Francis Thornton.[29] The deed fully describes the descent of the land from John Hauxford to John Willis Jr. to his wife Mary to Frederick Coghill. According to the 1709 deed from Hauxford to John Willis Jr., this 12 acres was part of Washington's 1664 patent and seems to have been that part which Washington sold to William Freake and which Freake's widow Martha (who had married Robert Vincent) sold to Hauxford in 1691.

No attempt was made to trace this specific tract beyond 1761. However, I believe that the area of Washington's and Willis's adjoining patents could easily be identified by reviewing later deeds, especially those for William Thornton who purchased the glebe tract in 1767 (see Chapter I).

We are deeply indebted to the John Lee and Lillian Thomas Pratt Foundation of Fredericksburg, Virginia, who purchased the King George County Will Book A-1

[27]King George County Orders 2:132, 7 October 1737.

[28]Many records for these families in the Richmond and King George County Order Books (specifically Richmond Co. Books 6, 7, and 8, and King George Co. Books 1 and 2) plus selected inventories were abstracted from microfilm by Mrs. Norris Groves of Rochelle, Illinois in 1977 and 1978, but, to my knowledge, have not been published.

[29]King George County Deed Book 4:460 from microfilm.

when it was found and to George H. S. King, now deceased, for his transcription.[30] King also provided us with much information in his 1964 compilation, *Marriages of Richmond County, Virginia, 1668–1853.*[31]

---

[30]Southern Historical Press, 1978.

[31]Southern Historical Press, reprinted in 1986.

Chapter VI

William Willis

W illiam Willis was the second son of John Willis Sr. The name of his mother is
not known. Also unknown is whether William, John Jr., Charles, Susannah,
and Mary Willis were full or half siblings. It is possible that William had other
brothers or sisters who were named in his father's will as "all my sons and daughters,"
although none have been found. William died intestate in 1716 in Richmond County
leaving a widow, two sons, and a daughter.

Much of the following data on William and his wife Sarah was not reported by George
Loeffler in his article on the Willis family in the 1982 issue of the
Willis–Gordon–Garnett and Allied Families Association *Journal*, but Loeffler's article
provided me with invaluable background information as a basis for my research.

Although William was still a relatively young man when he died, his name appears in
several Richmond and King George County documents. Proofs of his identity were
given in Chapter I and will not be repeated here.

If William was at least twenty-one years old when his father deeded to him in 1701,
he was born by 1680. He died intestate before 5 December 1716 when his widow,
Sarah, and his brothers John and Charles, all of Richmond County, posted bond in the
amount of 100 pounds sterling for the administration of his estate.[1] The bond was
recorded in a deed book which is somewhat unusual. According to the Order Book,
John Coombs [Combs], John Green, William Pitman, and William Reed or any three
of them were directed to appraise William's estate after taking oath before William
Thornton, Gent., or any other justice of the peace "as also Sarah Willis the
administrator for her true discovery thereof."

On 3 April 1717 the following is recorded in Richmond County Will Book 3, page
306, as transcribed from a microfilmed copy of the original:

> *In obedience to an Order of Richmond County Court bearing date the fifth
> day of December, 1716, we the subscribers being first sworn by Col. William
> Robinson, one of his Majesty's Justices of the Peace for the County aforesaid,
> did on the (28th?) Day of March 1717 meet at the house of William Willis,
> deceased, and did () and there apprize all and () the estate of the aforesaid
> William Willis in (manner) which was presented to our view as the following
> articles sheweeth.*

Several items in the inventory are not readable, but it included 7 barrows and sows, 2
shoats, 10 pigs, an old mare, a gelding, 4 cows and 3 yearlings, 2 large heifers, 2 young

---

[1] Richmond County Deed Book 7:173–174 and County Order Book 7:76 from microfilm.

bulls, a great coat, several items of fabric, furniture and bedding, 2 hireling servants "which are to serve until 25th of December next," a parcel of pewter and a "razer," looking glass, 2 guns, saddle, cooper's tools, lumber, spinning wheel, and other items. It was signed by Sarah Willis as administrator, Wm. Reeds, William Pittman, and John Green.

An initial appraisement of William Willis's estate was returned and recorded in County Court on 3 April 1717, the same day that John Combs' estate inventory was presented.[2] A second inventory for tobacco and a hog was reported to the Court by appraisers William Pittman and John Green on 6 July 1722 by Sarah Hutson [Hudson] in the amount of 33.10.6 and ordered recorded.[3] Inventories by appraisers William Reede [Reeds], Willm. Pittman, and John Green amounting to 74.11.10 ½ were ordered recorded in Court on 3 August 1722 at which time Sarah Hutson [Hudson], administratrix of Henry Wood, deceased (Sarah's second husband), also presented an inventory and appraisement of Wood's estate for 173.15.11 ½ which included one servant, one Negro woman, and some old books and was signed by Thos. Strother, Wm. Strother, Rowl[and] Thornton, and William Howard.[4]

No guardianship records were found for Sarah's children by William Willis or for her son Henry Wood Jr. although Henry Wood's eldest son, William, was bound out to Richard Butler (see below).

Sarah was married four times and widowed each time. Fellow researcher Newman A. Hall, who descends from Sarah and her third husband, Rush Hudson Sr., estimates the birthdate of Sarah's last child, David Hudson, as *circa* 1727.[5] Consequently, she was probably born between 1685 and 1690 and was between seventy and seventy-five years old when she died in 1761. As her will names seven surviving children and three grandchildren, it will be given before continuing with the records for William Willis.

The following is a transcription of Sarah's will dated 18 June 1760 and presented in Court on 28 May 1761 from a microfilmed copy of the original in Orange County Will Book 2, pages 310–311.

In the Name of God Amen I Sarah Turbervile [sic] of Orange County in the Colony of Virginia being sick of Body but of perfect mind & memory Thanks be to God for all, do make & ordain this my last Will & Testament in Manner and form following viz:

Item: I give to my son John Willis one shilling sterling.
Item: I give to my son William Willis ten shillings.
Item: I give to my son Henry Wood two pounds.

---

[2] Richmond County Order Book 7:98 as abstracted by Mrs. Norris Groves; see King's notes in *King George County Will Book A-1.*

[3] King George County Inventories and County Orders.

[4] King George County Inventories 1:15 and 1:17.

[5] Personal correspondence.

Item: I give to my son David Hudson one shilling sterling.
Item: I give to my son Joshua Hudson one shilling sterling.
Item: I give to my daughter Sarah Hawkins all my wearing clothes with a book called William Beverage Sermons.
Item: I give to Rush Hudson's daughter Mary one chest and his daughter Elizabeth one trunk. I give to my son Rush Hudson one Negro Woman named Winny during his life & afterwards I give the said Winny & her increase to Rush Hudson Jr. I give to my son Rush all the rest of my goods to dispose with as he shall think property and (finally) I make & ordain my son Rush Hudson full & whole Executor of this my last Will and Testament revoking all other will or wills by me made In Witness whereof I have hereunto set my hand & seal this 18th day of June in the year of our Lord God 1760.

Signed: Sarah

(her mark) Turbervile
Signed sealed & delivered by the
said Sarah Turbervile for her last
Will & Testament in the presence of
Benjamin Hawkins Jr.
Moses (his mark) Harwood
Kezia (her mark) Rosser
N.B.[6] it is my desire that my Estate shall not be appraised.

Signed: Sarah (her mark) Turbervile

N.B. interlined before signed (I give Winny's first born to Elizabeth Hudson and the next to Mary Hudson).

At a Court held for Orange County on Thursday the 28th day of May 1761 This Last Will & Testament of Sarah Turbervile dec'd was presented into Court by Rush Hudson the Executor herein named & proved by the oaths of Benjamin Hawkins Jr., Moses Harwood & Keziah Rosser witnesses thereto & ordered to be recorded & on the motion of the said Executor who made oath according to a law certificate was granted him for obtaining Letters of probate thereof in due form giving security on which he with Joshua Hudson & John Morton his Securities entered into & acknowledged their Bond for the same in the sum of Twenty pound's current money. Teste: Geo. Taylor C.O.C. (Clerk of Orange County Court)

An inventory of the estate of Sarah Turberville, deceased, was returned by her son Rush Hudson and recorded in Orange County on 26 November 1761.[7] It included one Negro named Winney, furniture, three head of cattle, one trunk and chest, and some old books.

Returning to Richmond County, the first record which I found for a William Willis was as a witness on a deed in 1694 from John Willis Sr. to John Willis Jr. as given in

---

[6] N.B. means *nota bene* and was used to emphasize or to give special attention to something.

[7] From microfilm; also see Sparacio, *Digest of Orange County, Virginia, Will Books 1734–1838*, p. 114.

Chapter I. William and John Jr. also witnessed John and Matilda Willis's Power of Attorney to Nathaniel Pope on that date. While this may have been a different man named William Willis, it could have been John Sr.'s son. A person did not have to be of legal age to act as a witness. It could also have been the William Willis who was found in the Westmoreland County records during this time (see Chapter X).

On 26 April 1701 John Willis Sr. deeded the remaining 161 acres of his 1669 patent of 261 acres to his unmarried son William, John (Sr.) having deeded the other 100 acres to his eldest son John Jr. in 1694.[8] John Sr. entailed the tracts to his sons in both deeds with the words "unto my said son and his heirs legally begotten or to be begotten of his body forever" and giving their wives, if they should marry, lifetime occupancy rights. If either died without issue, the tracts were to revert to the legal heirs of John Willis Sr. When William died intestate about a year after his father's death, William's eldest son John (who was underage) became heir of his father's, portion of his grandfather, John Sr.'s, patent, although he held the 161 acres *en tail* and his mother Sarah had lifetime occupancy rights. When William's brother John Jr. died without issue in 1728, William's son John also became heir-at-law to the 100 acres (part of John Sr.'s 1669 patent) which John Sr. had given to his eldest son, John Jr., in 1694. Deeds for the sale of this tract in 1737 are given in full in Chapter I.

Three documents containing William Willis's name are found in the Richmond County records between 1703 and 1705. The first of these is an item in the County Court Orders on 2 February 1703 when Catherine Cullins, servant to William Willis, was ordered to serve her master eight months past her stated indenture for having a child out of wedlock.[9] William appeared on behalf of his father John Willis and "confest judgment to the Church Wardens of St. Maryes Parish for the use of said parish for five hundred pounds of tobacco in caske, the same being the find of Catherine Cullins." This child was undoubtedly the Mary Cullins of John Sr.'s will, and Catherine Cullins was undoubtedly the same person as Catherine Pullen.

On 5 April 1704 William Willis "brought his information in court against John Willis for concealing Joseph Ducker, a tythable, contrary to the 7th Act of Assembly ... and the defendant (*i.e.*, John) appeared and offering nothing material against the matter contained in said information, judgment (is) granted to said William Willis against said John Willis for the said Joseph Ducker according to the tenor of the said Act of Assembly."[10] It is unclear if this was John Sr. or John Jr., but the latter was more likely. As indentured servants were counted as taxable tithables, it was not uncommon for people to conveniently forget to report them, and many such infractions are seen in the county records. No other references to Joseph Ducker were found.

On 5 September 1705 Francis Thornton purchased 1,000 acres from John and Francis Wright. As shown above, the land was part of a 1,700-acre patent granted to Major John Washington on 1 June 1664 and adjoined John Willis Sr.'s 261 patent in 1669.

---

[8] Richmond County Deed Book 3:135, given in its entirety in Chapter I.

[9] Sparacio, *Richmond County Orders 1702–1704*, p. 84.

[10] Ibid., p. 104.

Washington sold 300 acres of his patent to William Freake and willed the remaining 1,400 acres to his daughter Ann who later became the wife of Maj. Francis Wright and the mother of John Wright. The parcel was located in St. Mary's Parish and in 1705 joined lands of William Willis, John Hawkford [Hauxford], Thomas Tippett, and Harrison's plantation.[11]

In 1709 William and Sarah Willis sold 12 acres, which was described as being part of John Willis's 1669 patent, to John Hauxford. Witnesses were Isaac Arnold and John Willis (although he is not identified as Sr. or Jr.). Sarah Willis gave her Power of Attorney to John Combs to release her dower and acknowledge the deed in Court. This was followed by a deed from John and Saint Hauxford to John Willis Jr. for 12 acres which was part of John Washington's patent of 1,700 acres. Witnesses to that deed were Isaac Arnold and John Pittman.[12] Hauxford's tract was undoubtedly part of the 300 acres which Washington sold to Freake whose widow married Vincent with the Vincents selling to Thomas Tippett and Tippett selling to Hauxford. The deeds indicate that the land being deeded by Hauxford in 1709 was in the southern portion of Washington's patent which abutted the western boundary of John Willis Sr.'s 261-acre patent.

In his will which was written in 1727 and proved in 1728, John Willis Jr. left the land which his brother had "exchanged with John Hauxford" to William Wood, the acreage not being given. This implies that John Jr. presumed to hold title to the 12 acres which William sold to Hauxford in 1709 because in 1727 both his brother William and John Hauxford were deceased. William Wood's records do not clarify the issue. In 1734/35 he sold two tracts to Rush Hudson Sr. who was then married to Sarah (the widow of William Willis and Henry Wood). One of the tracts was 100 acres which his father Henry Wood Sr. had purchased from John Hauxford and had descended to William Wood as his father's heir-at-law.[13] In 1746/47 Rush Hudson Jr., as heir-at-law of his father, sold four tracts to Francis Thornton, two being the above parcels his father bought from William Wood and one being "30 acres more or less" which was part of a patent to John Washington for 1,700 acres, etc.[14]

In 1761 Mary Coghill Willis Jennings' nephew Frederick Coghill sold 12 acres which John Jr. had purchased from John Hauxford to Francis Thornton (see Chapter V), so inconsistencies appear. As William Willis's tract was entailed by his father, I do not know how he was able to sell it and I have not found any other deeds which clarify this discrepancy except for the possibility that the John Willis who witnessed William's deed to Hauxford in 1709 was his father who approved the sale or "exchange." In 1737 William's son John sold the entire 261-acre patent to the Church Wardens, and no mention was made that any part of it was previously part of Washington's patent in spite of the fact that the deeds are very explicit.

---

[11]Sparacio, *Richmond County Deeds 1705–1708*, pp. 10–12 (Deed Book 4:11a–13a) and Chapter II.

[12]Sparacio, *Richmond County Deeds 1708–1711*, pp. 38–40 (DeedBook 5:133–135).

[13]King George County Deed Book 1A:324.

[14]King George County Deed Book 3:173.

Returning to earlier records for William Willis, in 1715 his father named William in his will and left his crop of Indian corn and tobacco to be divided between his sons William and Charles out of which they were to pay their sister Susannah and an unidentified Mary Gardner each five hundred pounds of tobacco. John Willis Sr. also stipulated that his son William and Isaac Arnold were to be the guardians of Mary Cullins, who was under the age of sixteen, and were to watch over her share of the estate which included the rent William Pullen was to pay for ten years on the ground he leased from John Willis Sr.

Because William died the following year when his children were still minors, it was necessary to shift the research to William's widow, Sarah, who has proved to be a remarkable woman. Although her maiden name has not been conclusively proved, she was undoubtedly the daughter of a neighboring family. I first thought that she might be the sister of Isaac Arnold. However, Hudson family researcher Newman A. Hall believes that Sarah was the daughter of David Rosser Sr. and his first wife Sarah Sherwood.[15] Several clues in deeds and wills seem to support Hall's thesis although the evidence is circumstantial rather than direct. It is ironic that more is known about Mary Coghill Willis Jennings' family, even though she left no surviving issue, than is known about Sarah's family when Sarah left many descendants.

Sarah's first three husbands died in Richmond/King George County—William Willis (who died intestate before 5 December 1716), Henry Wood (who died intestate before 6 July 1722), and Rush Hudson (who died intestate before 7 November 1735).[16] Her last husband, Edward Turberville, died intestate in Orange County by September 1750.[17] While Sarah did not own any land when she died in 1761, she received dower rights in each of her husband's estates.

Sarah and William Willis had at least two sons—John (who was identified as their eldest son in his 1737 deed to the Church Wardens) and William. Sarah's daughter Sarah Hawkins, who was named in her mother's will, was probably also the daughter of Sarah and William Willis. There is always the possibility that they may have had other children who predeceased them or other children who were not named in Sarah's will.

Confusion remains regarding William's birthdate. The fact that his father deeded to him in 1701 suggests that William was born by 1680, and the deed indicates that William was unmarried at that time. Land could be deeded to minors, but it was customary for title to be acknowledged again when the minor became an adult, and this was apparently not the case as no such record was found.

Family historian George B. Loeffler estimated that William and Sarah's son John was

---

[15]Hudson Family Association *Bulletin* No. 81 (Slidell, LA: Hudson Family Association South, 1993).

[16]Sparacio, *King George County Deeds 1735–1752*, p. 133, and County Orders.

[17]Sparacio, *Digest of Orange County, Virginia, Will Books 1734–1838*, p. 114 (Will Book 2:153–154).

born *circa* 1709-10. Loeffler was a meticulous researcher and based his estimate on the fact that John married Elizabeth Plunkett in January 1734/35.[18] However, it is often difficult to distinguish between John (son of William) and his cousin John (son of Charles) in the records as both were born before 1715, both were orphaned as minors, and both became heirs of John Willis Sr. upon their fathers' deaths. To further confuse the issue, both married women by the name "Elizabeth."

However, the identity of our John Willis who sold his grandfather's patent to the Church Wardens and moved to Orange County is clearly established in the records. John, son of Charles, appears to have died intestate in King George County in 1753. Our John, son of William, died in Orange County in 1762. In addition, the name "Plunkett" was repeated by the descendants of William's son John of King George and Orange counties, but not in the lines of Charles Willis's son John.

More will be said about William and Sarah's children in Chapter IX, but a few comments are added here. Very little is known about William and Sarah's son William except that he accompanied the family to Orange County and was named in his mother's will. Sarah Hawkins, who was named in Sarah's will, appears to have been the wife of Benjamin Hawkins (son of John Hawkins who died in 1715/16 in Richmond County and wife Elizabeth). Benjamin Hawkins probably died *circa* 1770 and certainly before 1790 when his son William Hawkins deeded land which his father had willed to him to Lewis Willis, son of John Willis who died in 1762. Early deeds in both Orange and Culpeper counties contain many entries for the Willis, Hudson, and Hawkins families.

Because John Willis's land was entailed to his sons and William Willis died intestate, the tract automatically devolved to William's eldest son. However, Sarah had lifetime occupancy rights, so the family may have remained on the 161 acres in King George following William's death. Subsequent deeds show that her future husbands also owned land in the area and that they left a surprisingly good paper trail.

Sarah's name appears in the Richmond and King George records only when she and William Willis sold the 12 acres to John Hauxford, for the administrations of her first three husbands' estates, and for her release when her son John deeded to the Church Wardens, so it was crucial that the records of her other husbands (who were stepfathers of John and William Willis) be reviewed for additional clues about her maiden name and to learn more about John and William's early lives before migrating to Orange County.

Henry Wood was living in the Willis neighborhood prior to his marriage to Sarah and was called the brother of Susanna Butler, wife of Richard Butler, in a Power of Attorney (although the term could also have meant brother-in-law, stepbrother, or half-brother.[19] I once suspected that perhaps Susanna was the daughter named by John

---

[18] George H. S. King, *The Register of Saint Paul's Parish 1715–1798* (Easley: Southern Historical Press, 1960), p. 155.

[19] Sparacio, *Richmond County Deeds 1711–1714*, pp. 73–74.

Willis Sr. in his will, but no documents were found which identified Susannah beyond her father's will.

Henry Wood had a son William by a former marriage. If he had other children, their names are unknown to me. It is very possible that Henry's son William was related to John Marks or one of the other men who leased land on the Rapidan River from the Spotswood executors in December 1734 (see Chapter IX).

In March 1712/13 Henry Wood Sr. bought 40 acres from John Kendall and his wife Grace in St. Mary's Parish, Richmond County, the tract joining land owned by Ralph Wormley, Esq., deceased on a run of Bald Eagle Neck.[20] As given below, after Wood's death this tract became the property of his eldest son, William Wood, who then sold it to Rush Hudson Sr. with it later falling to Rush Hudson Jr. as his eldest son and heir-at-law. Consequently it could be assumed that Sarah may have lived on this tract at some time before moving to Orange County.

County Court Orders show that in April 1713 the Richmond County Court dismissed a suit which Wood brought against John Pittman (or Pitman), the plaintiff not prosecuting. On 2 May 1716 Wood was awarded judgment against William Pitman, administrator of Augustine Blake, deceased, in the amount of 415 pounds of tobacco, although the matter was later dropped. On the same date Wood's petition for "tuition of an orphan boy named Benjamin Hawkins" was rejected after Richard Butler stated that John Haskins [Hawkins] and his wife Elizabeth, both deceased, had left their two youngest sons, Benjamin and James, to James Butler (brother of the petitioner Richard Butler), that James Butler was now deceased, and that the children were to be bound to Richard Butler until they were twenty-one with John Willis (undoubtedly John Jr., Sarah's brother-in-law) as Butler's security. In his will John Hawkins requested that his son William, not Benjamin, was to be placed with Henry Wood[21]. Witnesses of Hawkins' will in March 1715/16 were Isaac Arnold (who was also named as Hawkins' executor), Rebecca Butler, and John Suttle (or Settle). Benjamin Hawkins later married Sarah (Willis), assumed daughter of William and Sarah. Mildred Hawkins, daughter of Benjamin Hawkins and Sarah Willis, married first John Plunkett Jr. (brother of her sister-in-law Elizabeth Plunkett Willis) and second Capt. Isaac Rucker of Orange and Amhurst counties.

Henry Wood's petition for the administration of William Gough's [Goff's] estate was rejected in Court on 5 April 1716 with Thomas and Margaret Gough [Goff] being granted administration. John Hauxford, George Green, Richard Butler, and John Tayler were ordered to appraise the estate.[22] It is unknown why Wood petitioned for administration, but he must have been either a relative or a creditor. In August 1717 Henry Wood's two actions of debt against Charles Willis and John Pitman were dismissed without explanation, the plaintiff not prosecuting.

[20]Ibid., pp. 74–75.

[21]Headley, op. cit., p. 31.

[22]Richmond County Orders.

In December 1717, probably after Wood had married Sarah, John Hauxford and wife Elizabeth sold 100 acres to Henry Wood, plaisterer (or planter?), which Hauxford had obtained by escheat in 1704. The tract lay on Poultridges (Portridges) Creek and joined Hauxford, Francis Thornton, John Willis, and Tippett.[23]

Henry Wood was appointed surveyor of the roads from Foxhall's Mill to Gingoteague (Chingoteague) Creek in August 1718. On the same day John Willis (*i.e.*, Jr.; Wood's brother-in-law) and Christopher Edrington were appointed surveyors from Gravelly Run to Crows Swamp. In 1719 and 1720 John Willis was made surveyor of roads from Chingoteague to the lower end of the parish, apparently replacing Wood.

Henry Wood's name is found in the Richmond County Orders several times as plaintiff in various suits. In November 1718 he sued Thomas James (husband of Mary Willis James) for 230 pounds of tobacco. James did not appear and judgment was granted to Wood. In 1719 Wood sued Mary Combs, executrix of the estate of William Combs, deceased, and was nonsuited when Wood failed to appear to prosecute. In 1719 the Court summoned Wood to answer charges that he sold liquor without a license. In March 1719/20 Wood dropped suits against Thomas James and Charles Willis, each for 773.5 pounds of tobacco "due by account."

Sarah and Henry Wood had a son, Henry, who was named in his mother's will in 1760 in Orange County although little is known about him. While a Henry Wood's name appears in several Orange County deeds, he seems to have lived in a different part of the county and I found no clues which prove that he was Sarah's son.

When Henry Wood Sr. died, his eldest son William (who was then underage) became his heir-at-law. In July 1722 Rush and Sarah Hudson appeared in King George County Court, stated that Henry Wood had died without making a will, and were granted administration of his estate with Rush Hudson, Neal McCormack, and William Strother Jr. giving security in the amount of 200 pounds sterling.[24] William Strother, Rowland Thornton, William Howard, and Richard Tankersly were ordered to inventory and appraise Wood's estate after being sworn before Joseph Strother, Gent., or another justice. On that date Rush and Sarah Hutson (Hudson) also presented inventories for the estate of William Willis, Sarah's first husband, and they were ordered to be recorded on 3 August 1722.[25] William's inventory was probably an accounting to the Court as his son and heir-at-law, John Willis, was still underage. At the time Sarah still had dower rights in the estates of both William Willis and Henry Wood. Dower rights which she had as the widow of William Willis became Henry Wood's upon her marriage to Wood, and dower rights which she had as Wood's widow became the property of Rush Hudson Sr. when they married. It is easy to see how complicated some of these estates were because of entailed land, lifetime occupancy rights, dower rights, legatees, heirs-at-law, and remarriages.

[23] Sparacio, *Richmond County Deeds 1714–1720*, p. 3 (Deed Book 7:278).

[24] King George County Order Book 1:52.

[25] King George County Inventories 1:15 and 1:17.

On 3 August 1722, the same date that Henry Wood's inventory was recorded, Rush and Sarah Hudson and Aaron Thornley were summoned to appear at the next Court to answer a petition of Richard Butler.[26] In January 1722/23 Rush Hutson [Hudson] and wife Sarah were again summoned to appear in Court on Butler's petition. Although the cause is not stated in the County Orders, it may have been related to the estate of Henry Wood and his heir-at-law, William Wood. At the same time Rush and Sarah Hudson, as administrators of Wood (who was the assignee of a David Dickey), sued Archibald Douglas (?) for 400 pounds of tobacco due by bill. When Douglas did not appear in Court, judgment with costs was granted against his security Martin Sheffler.[27]

Whatever the differences between Rush Hudson and Richard Butler were, they appear to have been resolved in March 1722/23 after the Court appointed Butler as guardian of William Wood with Isaac Arnold as Butler's security,[28] and followed by Butler's sale of 30 acres in Hanover Parish to Hudson.[29] The tract included the plantation where William Hawkins was living and was part of Washington's 1,700-acre patent on the lower side of Bald Eagle Run adjoining George Green, Wm. Tippett, and Rowland Thornton.

In 1724 George Green sold 65 acres to Rush Hudson adjoining Hudson's other land, Richard Butler, Rowland Thornton, and Bald Eagle.[30] This tract was part of an 885-acre grant which was given to Green in 1708. In 1734 William Wood, who had moved to Orange County, sold the tracts of 40 and 100 acres which his father bought from John Kendall in 1712/13 and John Hauxford in 1717 to Rush Hudson Sr. who had married William Wood's stepmother. As Rush Hudson Sr.'s heir-at-law, Rush Hudson Jr. of Orange County sold four tracts to Francis Thornton, son of Rowland of Crows Swamp in 1746.[31]

In March 1729/30, on the motion of John Willis, Rush Hudson was appointed his guardian.[32] Orphans fourteen years of age and older could petition the Court for a specific guardian, so this John was born after 1708 and before 1715. On the same day a suit which had been brought by John Willis against Thomas Goff was dismissed. The identity of this John is not clear. The first John could not have brought suit as he was still a minor. The second John could have been either John Jr. (who filed suit prior to his death with it not being dismissed until after his death) or it could have been his nephew John, son of William.

Also in March 1729/30 the administration of the estate of William Hudson, deceased, was granted to his widow, Sarah Hudson, who with Rush Hudson gave bond for her

[26]King George County Order Book 1:59 and 1:79.

[27]Ibid., pp. 89 and 99.

[28]Ibid., p. 104.

[29]Sparacio, *King George County Deeds 1721–1735*, p. 26 (Deed Book 1:175–179).

[30]Ibid., p. 29 (Deed Book 1:217–221).

[31]Sparacio, *King George County Deeds 1735–1752*, p. 86 (Deed Book 3:173).

[32]King George County Order Book 1:489.

administration.[33] This Sarah should not be confused with Rush Hudson's wife Sarah. The relationship between William and Rush Hudson is unknown to me.

Sometime in 1735 before his death (the pages of the Order Book being partially destroyed with the date missing) Rush Hudson, John Randall, Neal McCormack, and Maxfield Brown were appointed by the Court to appraise the estate of their neighbor John Green, deceased.[34] Green (son of the above George Green) had married Abigail Tippett, daughter of Thomas Tippett, and was the brother-in-law of Edmund Donahoe and William Tippett (see Chapter IV).

On 7 November 1735 Edward Turberville and his wife Sarah were granted letters of administration for Rush Hudson's estate. Benjamin Berryman, Gent., Thomas Thatcher, Isaac Arnold, and Neal McCormack provided bond in the amount of 600 pounds for administration of his estate.[35] John Wren, Thomas Bartlett, and William Marshall returned an inventory and appraisal on 5 December 1735 showing a total evaluation of 238 pounds 8 shillings 8 pence. The inventory included seven slaves, five beds, livestock, nearly 200 pounds of pot iron and 60 pounds "best pewter," cooper and carpenter tools, and other items commonly found in inventories at that time.[36]

The Court summoned Edward Turberville several times regarding the administration of Hudson's estate, and another inventory was recorded in April 1736.[37] The records suggest that probably embedded in Hudson's estate were pending settlements from the estates of John Willis Sr., William Willis, Charles Willis, John Willis Jr., Henry Wood, and John Jennings (who had all died within twenty years of each other), related guardianship accounts, and dower rights of Sarah (—) Willis Wood Hudson Turberville and Mary Coghill Willis Jennings.

In November 1736 Turberville's securities (Isaac Arnold, Neal McCormack, and Thomas Thatcher) petitioned the Court to be released from their bonds in Hudson's administration, and the Court appointed Capt. Joseph Strother, Samuel Skinner (Skinker?), and Thomas Turner to audit and settle the accounts and differences in the estates of John Jennings (who had married Mary Coghill Willis and died in Orange County) and Rush Hudson Sr.[38]

For the next two years there were a variety of actions recorded in the King George County Orders. John Willis sued Mary James and was awarded 910 pounds of tobacco. He also sued Mary Jennings, executrix of the will of John Willis (Jr.), deceased, and was awarded 3,288 pounds of tobacco from his uncle's estate. This may

---

[33] Ibid.

[34] King George County Order Book 2:4.

[35] Sparacio, *King George County Deeds 1735-1752*, p. 133; Order Book 2:4 and 2:36.

[36] King George County Order Book 2:39; Inventory Book 1:200.

[37] King George County Order Book 2:61.

[38] Ibid., p. 86.

have been Charles' son. In 1715 John Willis Sr. had willed adjoining parcels to his son Charles and his daughter Mary James. Charles (who was deceased by 1725) and his wife Matilda were to have a life interest in the land, and it was then to descend to Charles' son John who was also a legatee of his aunt, Mary Jennings.

In June 1737 John Willis, son of William and Sarah, and his wife Elizabeth (nee Plunkett) sold his grandfather's 1669 patent of 261 acres to the Church Wardens of Hanover Parish (see Chapter I). On June 4, 1737, John Willis, his wife Elizabeth, and his mother Sarah Turberville all appeared in Court to acknowledge their deeds of lease and release and to release dower rights, suggesting that they were still living in King George County on that date. However, this does not preclude the possibility that in 1737 some of the family had already moved to Orange County to prepare for the transition and that the family was in the process of settling their affairs in King George.

According to King George County Orders, Edward Turberville was still administering Hudson's estate in September 1737.[39] In October John and Elizabeth Willis acknowledged a deed for 60 acres to Isaac Pitman (this John probably being the son of Charles based upon the description of the land in the deed).[40] The following month the Court noted that Rush Hudson's estate had been settled with the auditors' report to be considered at the next session on the motion of Zachary Lewis, attorney for Edward and Sarah Turberville.[41] The fact that the Turbervilles appointed Lewis as their attorney may indicate that they had already moved to Orange County and were unable to attend Court.

In February 1737/38 the King George County Court ordered Hudson's remaining undivided estate amounting to 342 pounds 12 shillings 8 pence (after debts and charges of 111 pounds 6 shillings 6 pence) to be distributed and Sarah's dower to be set apart.[42] By law Hudson's land descended to his eldest son, Rush Hudson Jr. Sarah's one-third dower would have been approximately 114 pounds and was legally Turberville's property as no prenuptial agreement was found. On the following day the Court Orders noted that judgment was granted to Jeremiah Murdock against William Wood (who was already living in Orange County) or Wood's security, John Willis, unless Wood appeared at the next session to answer the suit. Later King George County Court Orders have not been reviewed as of this date.

Besides family members, other neighbors who are named frequently in the documents for Sarah (—) Willis Wood Hudson Turberville in King George are John Hauxford, Isaac Arnold, Richard Butler, the Pitmans, George Green (and his heir-at-law, John Green), and William Marshall.

John Hauxford owned land adjoining William and Sarah Willis, and he was the guardian of John Plunkett whose daughter Elizabeth married John Willis, the son of

---

[39] Ibid., p. 124.

[40] Sparacio, *King George County Deeds 1735–1752*, p. 15 (Deed Book 2:142–147).

[41] King George County Orders 2:132.

[42] Ibid., p. 140.

William and Sarah. A brief sketch of John and Saints Hauxford has been given in Chapter IV.

Isaac Arnold's name is found on many of the documents for William Willis and his wife Sarah from the will of John Willis Sr. to Turberville's administration of Rush Hudson's estate, but no direct relationship was found. It is known that Isaac and his wife Margaret were given 40 acres by her father Thomas Goff in 1707/08 (see Chapter IV). This tract was undoubtedly part of either the 403 acres which Goff and Kendall purchased jointly with John Willis Sr. in 1687/88 or Goff's 1696/97 grant of 105 acres which adjoined John Willis Sr.

In November 1758 William Willis (son of William and Sarah) placed an attachment on the estate of an Isaac Arnold in Orange County, and James Arnold paid the debt to Willis in 1759.[43] While Isaac Arnold Sr. of King George County wrote his will in September 1757 and it was proved the following May, Isaac did not have a known son named James, and it seems doubtful that this was the man whose estate was attached by William Willis. Review of the records for the Arnold family continues because of their proximity to the Willises in both Richmond/King George and Orange counties.

The Butler connection to the Willis family is elusive, but a Christopher Butler witnessed John Willis Sr.'s deed to his son William in 1701, and earlier references to the Butler family can be found in other parts of this manuscript. If or how Christopher was related to Richard Butler or Caleb Butler is unknown. What is clear from the records is that Richard Butler and wife Susanna were neighbors to the Woods and Hudsons, that Henry Wood was related to the Butlers, and that Richard acted as guardian to both William Wood and Benjamin Hawkins who migrated to Orange County with the extended Willis family.

The Pitmans were also close neighbors and probably lived near Pitman's Landing which was identified on the 1737 Northern Neck survey map reprinted in King's volume, *King George County Will Book A-1*. Pitman's Landing was in the same general area as Greenlaw's wharf which is shown on the 1968 USGS Rollins Fork map.

In 1708 George Green received a grant of 885 acres in Richmond County *(q.v.)*. The original grant indicated that this land was just west of Francis Thornton Sr. (*i.e.*, the 1,000 acres which Thornton purchased from the Wrights which was part of Washington's 1,700-acre patent) and John Hauxford, and just east of Francis Slaughter's land. Green leased 100 acres of this patent to John Willis Jr. in 1709 and 65 acres to Rush Hudson in 1724, as well as parts which he either sold or leased to other people before he died. In 1750 John Green was identified as George Green's heir-at-law. I do not know if George Green was related to Richard Green who died in 1705 in Richmond County or to William Duff who died in 1745 in King George County and who left much of his land to his Green relatives (see below).

---

[43] Orange County Orders.

The Marshall family has not been thoroughly reviewed. However, a Thomas Marshall of Washington Parish, Westmoreland County, died testate in 1704 leaving his estate to his wife Martha (nee Sherwood, daughter of Phillip Sherwood), his son William, other unnamed children, and Elizabeth Rosser (to whom he gave a heifer).[44] If his wife remarried, David Brown Sr. and John Brown were to assume guardianship of Marshall's children. Witnesses were Edward Taylor, John Hearford (also given as Oxford), and John Taylor. Marshall's inventory was returned in August 1705 by Joseph Hemings, Michael Halbert, and Anthony Rawlins which suggests that Marshall lived just over the ridge as he sold 50 acres to Halbert on 1714 at the head of Mattox Creek adjoining John Piper. By 1705 Marshall's wife Martha had married Alexander Thompson who, with Hemings/Hemmings, is named in documents with Robert Frank Sr. of Washington Parish (father of Frances Frank who married John Plunkett, the ward of John Hauxford and the presumed father of Elizabeth Plunkett who married John Willis, son of William and Sarah).

There is little doubt that William Marshall, who died testate in 1748, was related to the Hudsons. His will names sons William, George, Rush, Hudson, and Merryman Marshall.[45] Hudson family researcher Newman A. Hall has speculated that Marshall's wife, Ann, was the sister of Rush Hudson Sr., but no proofs have been found.[46] In 1753 William Marshall (son of William) and his mother Ann sold 123 acres, which had been bequeathed by his father, to Thomas Turner with Ann to retain lifetime occupancy rights.[47] Turner's will in 1757/58 mentioned the tract. Also in 1758 Walter Anderson of Washington Parish, Westmoreland County, left George Marshall of Hanover Parish, King George County, a tract of 90 acres "**excluding a burying place of half an acre excepted joining to the glebe land of Hanover Parish in said county.**"[48] In 1758 the Hanover Parish glebe was John Willis's 1669 patent. It appears then that the 90 acres which Anderson gave to George Marshall were probably part of the tract which Edwin Conway sold to John Anderson and which was part of Conway's resurvey which nullified much of John Willis Jr.'s and Walter Anderson's title to the 1690/91 Willis–Parsons grant as discussed in Chapters I–III.

In 1741 Newman Brown and wife Martha of Hanover Parish deeded 100 acres to William Marshall, the land having been given by deed of gift in Richmond County on 11 July 1711 by Francis Slaughter to Ann Hudson who was Slaughter's second wife and the mother of Martha, wife of Newman Brown.[49] Newman was the son of Maxfield Brown who died testate in 1745,[50] and the Browns were related to the Hudsons. In 1709 George Green leased 100 acres to John Willis Jr. adjoining Maxfield Brown who can be traced back to the will of Evan Morgan in 1684 in Old

[44] Dorman, *Westmoreland County Deeds & Wills No, 3, 1701–1707*, pp. 62 and 88.

[45] King, *King George County Will Book A-1*, pp. 162–163.

[46] Personal correspondence.

[47] King George County Deed Book 4:40–41, from microfilm.

[48] Ibid., p. 380.

[49] King George County Deed Book 2:389–393.

[50] King, *King George County Will Book A-1*, pp. 131–132.

Rappahannock County (see Chapter IV).

A few notes about the Hudson family will be given here before continuing with the records for Sarah and her last husband, Edward Turberville. Rush Hudson Sr. was the son of Joshua Hudson and Elizabeth Rush. Joshua Hudson died in 1704 in Westmoreland County, his will naming sons John, Joshua, Caleb, and Rush Hudson and his wife Elizabeth.[51] Soon after Joshua's death, Chap(man) Dark [sic] deeded certain personal property for love and affection to Joshua's daughters Sarah, Ann, Elizabeth, and Margaret Hudson with Caleb Hudson and Cossom Bennett witnessing the deed.[52]

Newman A. Hall estimates the birthdate of Rush Hudson Sr. as *circa* 1695. However, Caleb and Rush witnessed their brother John Hudson's will in Westmoreland County in 1708, so I believe that Rush may have been born between 1685 and 1690. While a minor could be a witness, it was usually indicated in the record, and nothing was given to show that Rush was underage at the time. Sarah (—) Willis Wood may have been Rush Hudson's second wife. Very little is known about Rush before he moved across the dividing ridge from Westmoreland County to Richmond/King George County, but the records suggest a family connection to the Duffs and Greens and to Ann Hudson who married (as his second wife) Francis Slaughter of Richmond County.

On 7 June 1723 the King George County Court dismissed charges against Rush Hudson (who was married to Sarah at the time) for not attending church after Hudson stated that he was a member of the Quaker Communion.[53] It appears that Sarah belonged to the established church because she bequeathed a book, *William Beverages's* (Beveridge's) *Sermons*, to her daughter, and Beveridge was an Anglican prelate and author.

In Chapter VII it will be shown that William Duff, a wealthy Quaker, purchased land from Charles Willis (William's brother) in 1714/15 and 1719 and operated an ordinary (inn) in King George County. Duff died in 1746 leaving a lengthy will and giving much of his land in several counties to his Green family relatives.[54] The Greens were neighbors to the Willises in King George, and Duff's nephew, Robert Green, moved to Orange County where he died testate in 1748. Green's will named his uncle William Duff, deceased, and Duff's wife, Elizabeth.[55] One of Robert Green's executors in Orange County was Francis Slaughter who may have been related to the Francis Slaughter who appraised the estate of John Willis Sr. of Richmond County in 1715.

In her will Elizabeth Duff (William's widow) named her son Benjamin Rush, a

[51] Dorman, *Westmoreland County Deeds & Wills No. 3*, p. 65.

[52] Ibid., p. 75.

[53] Sparacio, *King George County Orders 1721–1723*, p. 92.

[54] King, *King George County Will Book A-1*, pp. 133–136.

[55] Orange County Will Book 2:127–131.

William Rush (who was deceased), Rush grandchildren, and Green relatives.[56] George H. S. King does not identify Elizabeth (—) Rush Duff in either of his books, but I suspect that she could have been related to Rush Hudson Sr. whose mother was Elizabeth Rush.

Edward Turberville, Sarah's last husband, was the first Clerk of the King George County Court and served in that position until August 1723. He was followed as County Clerk by Thomas Turner.[57] According to King, Turberville married first by 1 November 1704 Anne Size, widow of John Size (of Sise), by whom he had one child, Elizabeth, who married St. John Shropshire.[58] By 7 November 1735 Turberville had married Sarah (the widow of William Willis, Henry Wood, and Rush Hudson) by whom he had no issue. I have not been able to identify the connection between Edmund Turberville and George Turberville, a Justice in Westmoreland County, or George Turberville (called Capt. in 1726, Maj. in 1741) of King George County, but one undoubtedly existed. Also a William Turberville who is named in King George deeds was probably related.[59]

Although the exact date of their migration to Orange County has not been found, it is assumed that Sarah and her family moved there sometime in the 1730s, perhaps shortly after Sarah's son John Willis deeded his grandfather's tract to the Church Wardens in 1737. Willis family researcher George B. Loeffler stated that Sarah, Edward Turberville, Sarah's sons John Willis (and wife Elizabeth Plunkett) and William Willis, Sarah's sons by Rush Hudson, her daughter Sarah Hawkins, a brother of Elizabeth Plunkett (*i.e.*, John Plunkett Jr. who married Mildred Hawkins, daughter of Sarah and Benjamin Hawkins), and the Shropshires moved to Orange County between 1734 and 1740.[60] Data in Chapter IX and related documents show that William Wood (Sarah's stepson) and John Jennings (second husband of Mary Coghill Willis) were in Orange County by 1734 where Jennings died in 1735.

Turberville died intestate in Orange County where his widow, Sarah, was granted letters of administration in November 1750 with Francis Moore, Gent., and William Willis (probably her son) as her securities in the amount of 600 pounds. An appraisal of Turberville's estate was taken on 6 October 1750 and returned on 28 February 1751/52 (total 334.14.11) with an additional inventory returned on 28 May 1752.[61]

On 15 March 1750/51 Walter Shropshire of Orange County deeded a slave named Winny, age about ten years, to Sarah Turberville in consideration of Sarah's relinquishing all right to the one-third or any part of the slaves belonging to the estate of her late husband Edmund [*sic*] Turberville. Witnesses were Alexander Waugh and

---

[56] King, *King George County Will Book A-1*, pp. 179–181.

[57] Dates taken from original Order Books.

[58] King, *Marriages of Richmond County, Virginia*, p. 219.

[59] Sparacio, *King George County Deeds 1721–1735.*

[60] George B. Loeffler, "Ancestry of the Willises of Locust Grove, Culpeper County, VA," Willis–Gordon–Garnett and Allied Families *Journal*, vol. I, no. 10 (1982).

[61] Orange County Will Book 2:153–154 and 2:165; Order Book 5:284.

George Gray. On the same day Walter gave Sarah a bond in the amount of 200 pounds for the above Winny.[62] In 1760 Sarah willed Winny to her son Rush Hudson and his children.

On 27 September 1751 Walter Shropshire executed a guardian bond for John and Ann Shropshire, orphans of John Shropshire, deceased, (probably Walter's younger brother and sister) with John Willis as his security.[63] An account of Turberville's estate was presented in 1752 with Walter Shropshire's guardian account settled on 17 March 1753.[64] In April 1753 William Taliaferro and Alex. Waugh, administrators, submitted a report of Turberville's estate which included money paid to Walter Shropshire as heir and guardian to the children.

Edward Turberville's grandson, Walter Shropshire, married Sarah (Willis), daughter of John Willis and granddaughter of Sarah (—) Willis Wood Hudson Turberville. Previous histories stating that Sarah Willis (daughter of John) married her "stepbrother" are incorrect. She married the grandson of her grandmother's fourth husband.

When John Willis, son of Sarah and William, wrote his will in 1761, he left Walter Shropshire one shilling and three pence and divided the rest of his estate between his other eleven children—William, Edmund Terrill (the husband of his daughter Margaret/Peggy Willis), John, Benjamin, Joshua, James, Reuben, Frances, Lewis, Moses, and Mary—with his wife Elizabeth to have a life interest in his estate.[65] Although Walter Shropshire and Margaret/Peggy Terrill were not specifically identified in his will, their names were confirmed with the other heirs in *Willis vs. Willis*, a suit involving the heirs of John's son Benjamin who died testate and without issue in 1810 in Orange County.[66] According to George H. S. King, Walter Shropshire and wife Sarah were both deceased by 1816.[67]

Finally, some comments will be offered regarding efforts to identify Sarah (—) Willis Wood Hudson Turberville. While the records provide ample identification of her four husbands, her date of death, and the names of her surviving children, unfortunately some vital information is missing, such as her date of birth, her parents, and the names of any siblings.

Dr. Newman A. Hall, with whom I have been privileged to share my research the past two years and who descends from Sarah and her third husband, Rush Hudson Sr., has developed an excellent kinship study which he calls "Ancestor Domains." Hall's findings, which I hope will be published someday, are too extensive to explore in this

---

[62]Orange County Deed Book 12:19–21.

[63]Orange County Will Book 2:163.

[64]Ibid., pp. 176–177.

[65]Orange County Will Book 2:323 and Deed Book 13:484.

[66]Orange County Will Book 4:372–373 and related loose suit papers.

[67]George H. S. King, "A Digest of the Suit Papers *Willis vs. Willis*," from the defunct Fredericksburg District Court (undated).

manuscript. However, he states that although each person's genealogy begins with a finite family element (mother, father, and child), the number of preceding ancestors is not always doubled because of certain factors such as marriages between cousins of different degrees or "within a community of families of limited size to which no external individuals are added."[68] Hall postulates that when such anomalies (my term) occur, then genealogical research "is essentially dependent on the history of groups of people rather than specific knowledge about individuals." I believe that Hall's theory reflects some of the problems we have seen in previous searches for the parents, siblings, and wife or wives of John Willis Sr., and for Sarah's maiden name. I also share his emphasis on the need to expand one's research to include the extended family or cluster (whatever one wishes to call it) because important strands are lost when research is limited to one individual. My emphasis on the extended family and community is obvious throughout this manuscript because I would not have found important new data without looking at collateral lines and neighboring land owners.

Based upon the premise that Sarah was the daughter of a neighbor, which is almost a certainty, I reviewed records for many of those neighbors. Fortunately, the computer facilitates such searches and makes it possible to focus on a specific time period. The years 1701 to 1710 are particularly important in identifying Sarah's family because it appears that William Willis was single in 1701, married soon after that, and was deceased by December, 1716.

By 1700 the Willis neighborhood was well-established. Adjacent or close neighbors or landowners included John Combs, Thomas Goff, Thomas Kendall, John Hauxford, Thomas Tippett, Isaac Arnold, William Underwood, and Nathaniel Pope. When records for each were reviewed and no primary evidence was found which identified Sarah, the search was expanded to a "second ring" of neighbors who were still close enough to be considered as possible candidates. Again, no proofs were found.

Based upon circumstantial evidence, Hall believes that Sarah was the daughter of David Rosser (who died by June 1698 in Richmond County) and Sarah Sherwood (daughter of Phillip Sherwood). Phillip Sherwood received a patent jointly with John Waight [*sic*] in 1666, and the following year Sherwood bought 300 acres from Peter Jett, the immigrant. Sherwood died by 4 September 1684 leaving four daughters: (1) Mary Sherwood who married Francis James before 1684; (2) Martha Sherwood who married Thomas Marshall before 1684 and secondly *ca.* 1705 Alexander Thompson; (3) Sarah Sherwood who married David Rosser after 1684 and before 1689; and (4) Ann Sherwood who married James Dabney after 1684 and before 1690. Phillip Sherwood's land was in Sittenburne Parish.[69]

Sarah (Sherwood) Rosser predeceased her husband, David Rosser, who was dead by 1 June 1698 when his widow, Margaret, was granted administration of his estate.[70] David Rosser left orphans Elizabeth, Sarah, David, and Mary who were placed under

---

[68] Personal correspondence.

[69] Rappahannock County Court Orders and later deeds.

[70] Richmond County Orders.

the guardianship of Francis and Mary James (their father's sister and brother-in-law).[71] Francis James died in 1721. His will names his wife Margaret, son Sherwood James, daughter Jane James, and his sister-in-law Martha Marshall.[72] Court Orders show that Francis James had another son, Francis Jr., who petitioned the Court for his filial share of his father's estate (which the Court dismissed based upon the father's will). Apparently Francis Jr. had been given land previously or was a younger son because under the laws of primogeniture the eldest son could not be disinherited. George H. S. King stated that Margaret, the second wife of David Rosser, and Margaret, the second wife of Francis James, were probably the same person.[73] However, no direct proofs have been found.

Whether Francis James was related to Thomas James (husband of Mary Willis) is unknown. To my knowledge none of the descendants in Sarah's line (with the exception of her youngest son, David Hudson) used the Christian name "David," and none used the names "Phillip" or "Sherwood" which is surprising because Sarah and her children seemed to follow traditional naming patterns.

Also little is known about David and Sarah (Sherwood) Rosser's daughters Elizabeth and Mary. David Rosser Jr., is believed to have married Ellenor Field, daughter of Abraham Field (Jr.) of Westmoreland County. Although there were connections between the Field and Hudson families in early Westmoreland County, those records will not be included in this manuscript except for a few selected items in Chapter X. Also not included are the records which Newman A. Hall and I found for Phillip Sherwood and David Rosser because of the inconclusiveness of the findings and the fact that my focus here is the Willis family.

My own personal journey with Sarah has been both exhilarating and sfrustrating—exhilarating because during the process she ceased to be a statistic on a lineage chart and became a very real person and a "usable memory" as described in the Introduction, but frustrating because of my failure to find proofs of the names of her parents. Hall's thesis that Sarah was the daughter of David Rosser and Sarah Sherwood may indeed be valid, but at this point any assumptions regarding Sarah's identity are based upon circumstantial evidence and are still open to examination.

As I imagined Sarah and tried to see life through her eyes, she became a symbol for me in many ways. Widowed as a young woman, twice again as a woman with small children, and finally as a grandmother, she endured with perseverance and grace, daring to move to a new area and to begin life again in a strange place in her later years. Her Christian faith sustained her, and she was wise enough in her old age to write a will—something which all of her husbands, including Edward Turberville who was once a Clerk of Court, failed to do. Although she did not have a lot of property or money to give her children and grandchildren, she left beloved treasures—a book of sermons, a chest, and a trunk. I will always wonder what was in the trunk; but

---

[71] Richmond County Orders, 5 July 1698.

[72] King, *King George County Will Book A-1*, pp. 4–5; King George County Deed Book 1:6.

[73] King, *Marriages of Richmond County*, p. 173.

perhaps I know because I keep a trunk for my grandchildren, too.

Since Sarah is such a fascinating person, I am confident that someone else will be motivated to continue the search to find her family so that her identity can eventually be known. My only advice to future historians is that they do not ignore Sarah's children by Henry Wood and Rush Hudson or the rich and complex relationships between this family and their neighbors in Old Rappahannock, Richmond, King George, Westmoreland, Orange, and Culpeper counties.

Chapter VII

Charles Willis

Charles Willis, the younger brother of John Willis Jr. and William Willis, is something of a mystery. He is identified in his father's will, but beyond that his name appears only a few times in the records. Based on what clues are available, Charles was probably born between 1680 and 1690. He died after May 1719 and before 6 August 1725, but no records were found for his estate in either Richmond/King George or Westmoreland counties. Consequently, the data reported below is fragmented and incomplete.

Charles appears to have been the third son of John Willis Sr. and may have been a half-brother to John Jr. and William. To my knowledge the Christian name "Charles" was never used in the families who descended from William and Sarah Willis.

The earliest record I found for Charles was recorded in Westmoreland County and dated 1712 when Garrett Welch and wife Rebecca and Caleb Smith and wife Elizabeth, all of Washington Parish, sold 248 acres to William Duff. The land being deeded was "commonly called Hawkins old plantation" and was part of a patent to Robert Alexander, John Alexander, and Christopher Lunn (or Lund) on the south side of Rosier's dam between the land late belonging to David Rowland, deceased, the land now belonging to Charles Willis, and the land of Edward Taylor.[1] Another reference to this patent is found in the early Westmoreland County deeds when George Campden (or Campion/Campian) sold 244 acres to Thomas Rowland in 1672, it being one-sixth part of 1,464 acres to Alexander, Alexander, and Lund at the head of Attopin Creek dam.[2]

According to Eaton, Attopin was an earlier Indian name for the creek which was later called Rozier's (or Rosier's) Creek and that Attopin Creek dam became Rozier's dam although I have not verified that information. Eaton also stated that John Washington built a mill at the head of Attopin (Rozier's) Creek in 1662. The records suggest that this tract of Washington's was north of the dividing ridge in Westmoreland County, and the tract which Charles owned in 1712 was on the ridge. This land was not part of Charles' inheritance from his father because John Willis Sr. was still living in 1712 and the tracts which John Sr. willed to Charles were in Hanover Parish on the south side of the ridge.

On 19 January 1714/15 Charles Willis and wife Matildee [*sic*] of Hanover Parish,

---

[1] Dorman, Westmoreland County Deeds & Wills 1712–1716, pp. 5–6. For the Alexander-Lund patent, see Nugent I:447 dated 23 March 1664.

[2] Dorman, *Westmoreland County Deeds, Patents, etc., 1665–1677*, Part two, p. 35. Garrett Welch died testate in Westmoreland County in 1715/16 (Fothergill, op. cit., p. 61). Caleb Smith, who was called "my son-in-law" by Basil Bayley in his 1694 will, died testate in 1725 in Westmoreland County (Fothergill, op. cit., pp. 9 and 81).

Richmond County, deeded 170 acres to William Duff of Washington Parish, Westmoreland County, for 8,000 pounds of tobacco.[3] Review of the original document from microfilm indicated that the tract lay partly in Westmoreland and partly in Richmond and was known as Hawkins (not Hackers as reported on one source) Old Plantation. It was part of the above patent of 1,428 [*sic*] acres granted to Alexander, Alexander, and Lunn (Lund). The parcel adjoined Edward Tayler, Joshua Davis (deceased), a branch which led into Roazers (Roziers, Rosiers) dam, Catherine Davis, and land of Charles Willis then occupied by Stephen Sabastine (probably as a tenant). Witnesses on the deeds of lease and release and on Charles' and Matilda's bond were Isaac Arnold and Tho. Parker, probably the same Thomas Parker who witnessed John Willis Sr.'s will in 1715.

No record was found showing how or when Charles obtained this 170 acres. Matilda may have received it by inheritance. Previous researchers have assumed that Matilda was the daughter of Henry Thacker (who was deceased in 1693) and his wife, Matilda, who married John Willis Sr. as the widow Thacker. Henry Thacker's will of 1693, which was proved by Joshua Davis, is missing and only the name of his widow, Matilda, survives in the Richmond County Orders. Joshua Davis is named in John Willis Sr.'s deed of gift to Matilda in 1693 (see Chapter I). If Matilda was the daughter of Henry Thacker, a search of earlier deeds might shed light on the descent of this tract because the Alexander-Lund patent might be mentioned. Another factor which makes tracing this tract difficult is that Westmoreland County County deeds which might clarify the issue are missing.

The next record I found for Charles was in his father's will dated 7 June 1715 which identifies Charles, his wife Matilda (Mattildoe), and their son John. In addition to land and other bequests, John Sr. left certain personal property to Charles and Matilda, "it being the will of my late wife Mattildoe Willis."

Besides Charles' son John, who is specifically named in John's will, Charles probably had other children whose names are unknown to me. Of particular interest is the Settle or Suttle(s) family whose name is also found in records with the Butlers and Hudsons.

Some former researchers stated that John Willis Sr. left certain legacies to his son Charles in accordance with John's prenuptial agreement with Matilda Thacker in 1693, but review of that deed of gift does not support this claim because neither Charles nor his wife Matilda is mentioned (see Chapter I). In his will in 1715 John said that the specific legacies which he was giving to Charles and Matilda was "his [John Sr.'s] wife Matilda's desire." While it is entirely possible that Charles wife, Matilda, was the daughter of Henry and Matilda Thacker, other possibilities should not be ignored until a document is found which directly proves that assumption. The name "Matilda" was not found in any of the neighboring families or descendant Willis lines.

John Willis Sr. left Charles two plantations—the one where John Sr. lived plus the tract where Charles was living except for those parts which John willed to Charles'

---

[3]Sparacio, *Richmond County Deeds 1714–1720*, pp. 68–70 (Deed Book 7:20–23).

sister Mary Willis James and to Mary Cullins. Both tracts which John left to Charles, including the one where Charles as living, can be traced in later records, and both were south of the ridge in Richmond (later King George) County. Charles and Matilda had only lifetime occupancy rights with the tracts to descend at their deaths to their son John in fee simple. This effectively entailed the tracts during Charles' and Matilda's lives and would have prevented Charles from selling them, but allowed their son John to sell them later.

On 15 July 1715 Francis Slaughter, Richard Tutt, and Combs made an inventory and appraisal of John Willis's estate and transferred certain articles to Mary Cullins, Charles Willis, and Thomas James. Charles received an old cow, two yearlings and two young calves, one young shoat and two heifers, four sheep, sixteen hogs, twelve small pigs, and a young cow. According to the terms of the will, Charles was also to receive a feather bed, furniture, curtains, a Vallins rug, blankets, boulster, pillows, John's entire stock of hogs and sheep (except one ewe and lamb devised to Mary Cullins), an iron pot, a brass kettle, John's crop of Indian corn and a share of his crop of tobacco, 3,000 nails, powder, and shot.

In December 1716 Charles and his brother John posted bond of 100 pounds sterling with Sarah Willis, widow of their deceased brother William, for her administration of William's estate.[4]

Charles Willis, his sister Mary (Willis) James, and Isaac Arnold witnessed John Combes' will on 11 December 1716 (see Chapter IV).

In February 1716/17 the names of Charles Willis, William Kendall, and Isaac Arnold appear on deeds of lease and release from Thomas Kendall and on a Power of Attorney from Kendall to Isaac Arnold when Kendall deeded fifty acres of land in Hanover Parish on a branch of Poultridges (Portridges) Creek adjoining Thomas Goff, Edwin Conway's land, and John Green.[5] As shown elsewhere in this manuscript, Thomas Goff's daughter Margaret married Isaac Arnold, and William Kendall married Elizabeth Combs who was the daughter of John Combs. John Green and Edmond Donahoe married daughters of Thomas Tippett.

In May 1719 Charles Willis again deeded to William Duff. This tract contained 78 acres and lay in both Westmoreland and Richmond counties. The lease and release state that it was part of the same patent of 1,428 acres granted to Robert Alexander, John Alexander, and Christopher Lunn (Lund) by Sir William Barkley (Berkeley), late Governor of Virginia, and adjoined lands of William Duff and Joshua Davis near Reazors (Roziers) Dam, and that it was the tract where Steven Sabastine, deceased, formerly lived as a tenant of Charles Willis.[6] Witnesses were Isaac Arnold, Henry Wood, and Neal McCormack. At that time Henry Wood was married to Sarah, the widow of William Willis, and was Charles' brother-in-law. As John Sr. entailed his

---

[4]Sparacio, *Richmond County Deeds 1714–1720*, pp. 54–55 (Deed Book 7:173–174).

[5]Ibid., pp. 76–77 (Deed Book 7:207–209).

[6]Ibid., pp. 87–88 (Deed Book 7:403–405).

land to Charles in 1715 and that land can be traced later, this 78 acres was not John's land but was part of the tract which Charles sold to Duff in 1714/15.

Neal McCormack's name is found on several documents with this group. He died testate in King George in 1743 leaving his land in King George to his son John.[7] This son, John McCormic(k), witnessed the will of Mary Coghill Willis Jennings in 1745.

As given above, William Duff, a wealthy Quaker, died testate in King George County in 1745. He was survived by his widow Elizabeth (—) Rush Duff, but no children, and left his large holdings in Westmoreland, King George, Orange, and Culpeper counties to relatives including the Green family. A considerable amount of time was spent researching William Duff and his wife Elizabeth with inconclusive results. However, there seems to have been a family connection between them and Rush Hudson, the third husband of Sarah (—) Willis Wood Hudson Turberville.

No record of a will, estate inventory or appraisal, or administration was found for Charles Willis, but he was deceased by 6 August 1725 when the following entry was made in the King George County Orders:

> On the petition of John Willis Junr., son of Charles Willis deced. [deceased],
> it is ordered that John Willis, Unckle to ye Petitioner, be appointed his
> Guardian.

As orphans over the age of fourteen could petition the Court to choose their guardian, this indicated that Charles' son John was born after 1704 and before 1711.

John's uncle and guardian, John Willis Jr., died by 3 May 1728 when his will was presented for probate. On 7 March 1728/29 this entry is found in the King George County Orders:

> On the Petition of John Willis, it is ordered that Thomas Goff be admitted his
> Guardian, the said Goff and Neal McCormack acknowledged their bond for
> fifty pounds to save the Court harmless.

As John was under twenty-one in March 1728/29 and over fourteen in 1725, he was born sometime between 1708/09 and 1711. These entries suggest that John probably lived with his uncle John (Jr.) and wife, Mary Coghill Willis, after his father, Charles', death. John Willis Jr. did not mention his nephew John Willis in his will, but Mary willed the 12-acre tract where she was living in 1745 to John (the son of Charles) during his lifetime. At John's death it was to descend to her nephew, Frederick Coghill Jr. In 1761 Frederick Coghill sold this parcel to Francis Thornton.[8] The deed fully describes the descent of the land from John Hauxford to John Willis Jr. to his wife Mary to Frederick Coghill. According to the 1709 deed from Hauxford to John Willis Jr., it was part of Washington's 1664 patent and was part of the 300 acres which

---

[7] King, *King George County Will Book A-1*, pp. 120–121.

[8] King George County Deed Book 4:460 from microfilm.

Washington sold to William Freake and which Freake's widow Martha (who had married Robert Vincent) sold to Hauxford in 1691.

In March 1729/30 the Court dismissed a suit brought by John Willis against Thomas Goff, and upon John's motion Rush Hudson was appointed as his guardian. Consequently, this John would have been born between 1709/10 and 1715. While it might appear that the John named in these guardianship petitions was the son of William and Sarah, especially because the last one involved Rush Hudson who in 1729/30 was married to Sarah, the first record implies that it pertained to Charles' son. The fact that both William and Charles had sons named John has caused confusion for family researchers who estimated the birthdate of William's son John as 1709 or 1710.

Between John Willis Sr.'s death in 1715 and John Willis Jr.'s death in 1728 there were three by the name John Willis in King George County—John Jr. (son of John Sr.); John (son of William); and John (son of Charles), the last two being nephews of John Willis Jr.

The Court Orders in 1725 explicitly identify John as both "Jr." (literally meaning the younger) and as the son of Charles. His uncle, who was called "Jr." while his father was still living, was identified as the boy's uncle rather than as "Sr." As William and Sarah's son John was also living in the county in 1725 and was underage, it appears that the Court was careful to identify both men so that no ambiguity was created. Another reason why Charles' son John was called "Jr." in 1725 was probably because he had an elder cousin named John. One of the problems in tracing this family is due to the fact that the Christian names "William" and "John" were repeated in every generation, so careful examination of the records for age, place of residence, and other clues is crucial.

Confusion between the two younger men named John is further intensified because both married women by the name of "Elizabeth." The maiden name of the wife of John, son of Charles, is unknown to me.

The question as to which John was the oldest (William's son or Charles' son) can be determined by the deeds from John Sr. to his sons John Jr. and William in 1694 and 1701, the deeds from John Willis to the Church Wardens in 1737, and the law of primogeniture. John Willis Sr. deeded land to his second eldest son William in 1701 which suggests that William was born by 1680. I believe that William married shortly after his father deeded to him and that his eldest son, John, was older than Charles' son John. This conclusion appears to be valid because John Willis Jr.'s entailed land which he had received from his father in 1694 descended to John, son of William, according to the law of primogeniture. If Charles' son John had been older than William's son John, the entailed tract which John Sr. deeded to his son John Jr. (who died without issue) would have descended by law to Charles' son. This means that William's son John was older than Charles' son John. John Sr. specifically names his grandsons John Willis (son of Charles and Matilda) and David James (son of Mary Willis and Thomas James) in his will, but not his grandson John Willis (son of William and Sarah). However, John Sr. had given William's son John land by entailing the tract which he deeded to William in 1701. The fact that Charles' son John had no interest in the entailed tract is proved by the deeds to the Church Wardens in 1737 as he was still living but was never mentioned in those records. Other records for William's son John will be discussed in Chapter IX.

An entry in King George County Deed Book 1-A indicates that in 1729 John Willis was awarded 53 pounds 14 shillings in General Court in a judgment against John Jennings who, with William Grant, posted bond in the amount of 100 pounds and was appealing.[9] This may have been John (son of Charles) who sued Jennings (then married to Mary Coghill Willis) over something relating to his uncle's guardianship, or it may have been John (son of William) who sued Jennings for some other reason. The issue is unclear.

On 16 and 17 January 1732/33 John Willis deeded (through a lease and release) 78 acres of land in Westmoreland County to William Duff. The deed states that both of the men lived in Hanover Parish, King George County, but that the tract was in Westmoreland joining the lands of William Duff and Joshua Davis and near Rozier's Dam. It was all of John's interest in a patent for 1,428 acres which was granted to Robert Alexander, John Alexander, and Christopher Lund (see above). William Marders and William Sarjant witnessed the deed, and John's wife, Elizabeth Willis, released her dower on 29 May 1733.[10] This would seem to be the same 78 acres which Charles Willis deeded to Duff in 1719. Probably Duff was perfecting his title by getting John's release and bond because John was his father's heir-at-law. It is noted that Charles Willis (later John), the Welchs and Smiths, and George Campden (Campion/Campian) each seemed to own approximately a one-fourth share in the Alexander, Alexander, and Lund patent. I do not know who owned the other fourth.[11]

In 1736 a John Willis brought suits against Mary (Willis) James and Mary (Coghill Willis) Jennings for unspecified reasons. In April 1737 the Court ruled for John Willis, plaintiff, against Mary Jennings, executrix of the last will of John Willis, deceased, and ordered that Capt. Joseph Strother, Samuel Skinner (Skinker?), and Thomas Turner be appointed to audit and settle and accounts and differences and make their report to the next Court. In addition it was ordered that the auditors settle the estate of John Jennings, deceased.[12] This information suggests that the man bringing suit was probably the son of Charles and that the suit stemmed from John Willis's guardianship. The suit was continued until the Court ruled that Mary Jennings, executrix of John Willis Jr., was to pay John 3,288 pounds of tobacco.

---

[9] Sparacio, *King George County Deeds 1721–1735*, p. 116.

[10] Dorman, *Westmoreland County Deeds & Wills 1723–1738*, pp. 20–21.

[11] William Marders was one of the witnesses to William Duff's will in 1741 (King, *King George Will Book A-1*, pp. 133–136). Rowley Marders, Francis Willis, and Jane Willis witnessed Daniel White's will in 1770 (Sparacio, *King George County Will Book A*, p. 96). William Rowley's 1774 will names his sister Ann Marders and Jane Willis among others (ibid., p. 107).

[12] King George County Orders 2:105.

In 1736/37 John Willis and wife Elizabeth sold 60 acres to Isaac Pitman.[13] Both John Willises (cousins) were adults and living in King George at the time. Consequently, it is difficult to distinguish which John is involved in this deed until one looks at the descriptors in the deed and the names of adjacent landowners. Based on those clues, this parcel appears to have part of one of the plantations which John Willis Sr. willed to Charles and Matilda for their lifetimes and then descended to their son John.

Court Orders show that on January 1737/38 John Willis was appointed as constable in the room of Thomas Goff. (William and Sarah's son John had probably migrated to Orange County by then.)

In 1742 William James, the son of Mary Willis and Thomas James and grandson of John Willis Sr., sold 20 acres which had been bequeathed to his parents and his brother David, all of who were deceased, to Jeremiah Murdock.[14] The deed states that the tract adjoined Isaac Arnold, Wormley's line now Jeremiah Murdock's, and the lines of Isaac Pitman and John Willis. As this tract was originally part of one of the tracts which John Willis Sr. had left to Charles, this John can be identified as the son of Charles and not the son of William.

In 1745 Mary Coghill Willis Jennings, the widow of John Willis Jr. and John Jennings, left her home tract to John Willis, the son of Charles, deceased, and three slaves for his lifetime, with the property to revert to her nephew Frederick Coghill at John's death (see Chapter V).

John Willis of Hanover Parish, King George County, mortgaged 170 acres plus three slaves to the executors of Harry Turner, deceased, it "being the land where said John Willis now lives," in 1752. His note in the amount of 69 pounds 2 pence 10 shillings was due on 30 January 1753.[15] It appears that John died intestate in 1753.[16]

In 1761 Frederick Coghill sold 12 acres (the home tract which Mary Coghill Willis Jennings had willed to John Willis, son of Charles, during his lifetime) to Francis Thornton indicating that John Willis had died by then. As shown above, the 1761 deed traced the parcel by stating that John's uncle, John Willis Jr., had purchased it from John Hauxford in 1709 and that it was part of Washington's 1664 patent of 1,400 acres.[17]

Elizabeth Willis, who died testate in King George County in 1767, was probably the widow of John (son of Charles). Her will names grandchildren William, Elizabeth, Willis, and Younger Johnson, her son Francis Willis, and Francis's daughter Jane

[13]Sparacio, *King George County Deeds 1735-1752*, pp. 15-16 (Deed Book 2:142–147).

[14]Ibid., p. 41 (Deed Book 2:398–402).

[15]Ibid., p. 130 (Deed Book 3:499–502).

[16]Clayton Torrence, *Virginia Wills and Administrations 1632-1800* (Greenville, SC: Southern Historical Press, 1985, 1996), p. 462.

[17]King George County Deed Book 4:460 (microfilm).

Willis.[18] If this Elizabeth was the widow of John, son of Charles, then they probably had a daughter who married a Johnson because one of the grandchildren was named Willis Johnson. I have not reviewed the records for the Johnson family, but the King George County deed index contains many references to Younger Johnson.

Immediately following Elizabeth's will in King George County Will Book A is the 1766/67 will of Francis Thornton, son of Rowland and grandson of Francis Thornton Sr. The testator mentions his land below Crows Swamp, George Reading (Riding), and a Francis Willis who was living on his property. Thornton also bequeathed to Judith and Nanny Settle, daughters of Emma and William Settle (also seen as Suttle, Suttles, or Settles), who may connect to the Willis-Settle families in the early 1800's in Barren County, Kentucky, and thought by some researchers to have been the descendants of Charles Willis.

In the early 1960's Elizabeth W. DeHuff published a manuscript, *Descendants of John Willis of Richmond Co., Virginia, 1715*, which includes some of the records for Charles Willis's family. According to her research, Francis Willis (son of John and Elizabeth and grandson of Charles) married Jane Marders and moved to Culpeper where he died intestate in 1789. I do not know if this is correct or not, but a review of the Culpeper records does not indicate that this Francis Willis lived in the same part of the county as William Willis, son of John and Elizabeth (Plunkett) Willis, or that either was ever named in the other's records. This may, of course, reinforce the suspicion that William and Charles Willis of King George were half-brothers and that the descendants of each did not remain close.

Charles may have also had a son named Charles Jr., but the records are very confusing. With due respect to DeHuff's study, it should be used with caution because it contains significant errors and repeats unreliable information from earlier, undocumented studies.

While many questions remain regarding Charles and Matilda Willis, perhaps the above will provide some new information for those who are researching this line.

---

[18] Sparacio, *King George County Will Book A*, p. 89.

Chapter VIII

Mary Willis James

In 1715 Mary Willis James, daughter of John Willis Sr., was married to Thomas James, living on her father's land in Richmond County, and had at least one son named David. As will be shown, their second son was William.

John Willis Sr. willed Mary and Thomas James the parcel of land where they were living which, based upon a later deed, was twenty acres. Her father stipulated that they were to have a life interest in the tract and that after their deaths it would descend to their son David in fee simple. The tract adjoined land owned by John Wormley and Isaac Arnold, and this tract and Arnold's land were separated by a fence—probably an unusual sight at the time. John's will says that this tract was part of a larger one, some of which he left to Mary Cullins with the balance going to his son Charles, and that John held a patent for it. John also gave Mary and Thomas a cow named Browney. In John's estate inventory the cow (valued at two pounds) was listed under articles given to Charles Willis (Mary's brother) as "one young kow [*sic*] to Tho. James."

Little is known about Thomas James or his family. Two references were found in the Westmoreland County records for a man by that name who may or may not be the same person. In 1696 John Washington, Gent., of Westmoreland County (probably the son of John the immigrant) deeded 119.5 acres in Richmond County to Thomas James, planter, of Richmond County for 6,000 pounds of tobacco. The land was in a great swamp on a branch of Rappahannock (*i.e.*, Cat Point) Creek adjoining James and was part of a dividend of 400 acres.[1] The second was in 1709 when George Brown of Cople Parish, Westmoreland County, deeded all of his interest in the above 119.5 acres to Thomas James of Richmond County.[2] Descriptors in the deeds place this tract on Rappahannock (Cat Point) Creek, not to be confused with the Rappahannock River, which suggests that it may have been on the dividing line between Westmoreland and Richmond counties but at some distance from John Willis's tracts in Richmond (later King George) County.

The names of Thomas James' parents are not known, and his name is seldom found in the records. No references to this James family are found in any wills or estates in King George County Will Book A-1 which covers the years 1721–1752, and the family is not mentioned in the wills of Mary's brother John Willis Jr. in 1727 or her sister-in-law Mary Coghill Willis Jennings in 1745 (unless an unidentified daughter was among Mary Jennings' legatees).

I do not know if Thomas James was related to Francis James who died testate in 1721 in Richmond/King George County (see Chapter VI). However, an interesting item is

---

[1] Dorman, *Westmoreland County Deeds & Wills No. 2*, p. 26.

[2] Westmoreland County Deeds & Wills 5:352 from microfilm.

found in the Richmond County Orders dated 4 November 1698 as part of a complaint by Francis James against Margaret Rosser in which Joshua Davice [Davis] and Nathaniel Pope were ordered tomeet at the house of Francis James to settle "all manner of differences between the said parties concerning the estate and orphans of David Rosser, deceased." On 1 March 1698/99 the Court ordered that a report made by the auditors (Davis and Pope) regarding a suit between Francis James and Margaret Rosser, administratrix of John (or David?) Rosser, deceased, be entered and recorded. Nathaniel Pope has been discussed above. No direct relationship has been found between John Rozier of Rozier's Dam/Creek and the David Rosser family however.

In December 1716 Mary James, her brother Charles Willis, and Isaac Arnold witnessed the will of their neighbor John Combs. Charles Willis and his brother John Jr. provided bond for Sarah Willis's administration of William Willis's estate in 1717, but Thomas James was never mentioned and did not take part in the inventory and appraisal of either John Willis Sr.'s or William Willis's estates.

In *Marriages of Richmond County* George H. S. King states that Thomas and Mary (Willis) James later separated, and an entry in the King George County Orders on 6 October 1721 confirms the fact that they were living separately at that time.[3] James is named infrequently in the Court Orders for a few years and then seems to disappear from the records.

When John Willis, son of Charles, and his wife Elizabeth sold 60 acres to Isaac Pitman in 1737/8, the deed described the land as adjoining the land of Archdell Combs, deceased (the son of the above John Combs), near the road which led from Maj. Jeremiah Murdock to the Bristol Iron Works, and next to the lands of Isaac Pitman and Ralph Wormley, deceased, and land formerly belonging to Thomas James. From this and the deed given below, it is assumed that Thomas James may have been deceased in 1737/8. One entry was found in the King George County Orders in 1736 when John Willis sued Mary James (assumed to be his aunt) for 910 pounds of tobacco, so she apparently died between 1736 and 1742.

William James, son of Thomas and Mary (Willis) James, was living in Spotsylvania County in 1742 when he deeded a tract in King George County to Jeremiah Murdock. Records show that the Murdocks bought several tracts and were involved with the iron works on Bristol Mines Run. The deed to Murdock was for 20 acres which William's grandfather Willis had willed to his mother and father, which after their deaths was to descend to their eldest son David, and is abstracted from a copy of the original on microfilm as follows:

> *1 April 1742, William James of St. George's Parish, Spotsylvania County, planter, to Jeremiah Murdock of Hanover Parish, King George County, Gentleman, deeds of lease and release for 20 acres which was given and bequeathed by the last will and testament of John Willis the Elder bearing date 7 June 1715 to Thomas James and Mary his wife during their natural*

---

[3] Order Book 1:16.

lives and after their decease to descend to David James, son of the said Thomas James, which on the death of the said David James the same land became vested in the said William James, party to these presents, who was the next brother and heir-at-law to the said David James, deceased; beginning in the line of Isaac Arnold, then southwestwardly to Wormley's line now Jeremiah Murdock's, then along Murdock's line southeast to line of Isaac Pitman, then northeast to land of John Willis and along said Willis's line northwest to the beginning.

Signed: William James

Witnesses: M[oseley] Battaley, Ja[mes] Strother, Harry Turner, and Jos[eph] Strother.[4]

Consequently, Mary Willis James, Thomas James, and their son David were all deceased by 1742 and their son William died sometime after that. I have been unable to find the names of their other children and the date and place of Mary Willis James' death.

However, an interesting entry was found in the Spotsylvania County records. While it does not *prove* that the person named was the daughter of John Willis Sr., there could have been some unknown connection. On 5 May 1733 Robert Spotswood (who was a single person and whose identity and any relationship to Governor Alexander Spotswood are unknowns) wrote his will leaving personal items to Col. Edmund Boggs [or Bagge?], Col. Henry Willis, Mary James (to whom he left twenty shillings), and Thomas Barnett. Spotswood left the bulk of his estate including his land to a John Willis, the son of Henry and Mildred Willis.[5] Robert Spotswood's will is given in full in Chapter XIII where this John Willis is discussed in more detail.

There are other records in Spotsylvania County during this time for a James family, but none of them which I reviewed can positively be identified as pertaining to the descendants of Mary Willis James. With the knowledge that John Willis Sr.'s grandson William James was living in Spotsylvania County in 1742 and an unknown Mary James was living there in 1733, further research may be warranted.

---

[4] Sparacio, *King George County Deeds 1735–1752*, p. 41 (Deed Book 2:398).

[5] Spotsylvania County Will Book A:190 from microfilm; abstracted by Crozier, op. cit, p. 4.

Descendants of William Willis and wife Sarah (—)
and the children of Sarah (—) Willis by subsequent marriages

William Willis (son of John Willis Sr. who d.t. 1715 Richmond County and (—?—)
  born by 1680(?) in Old Rappahannock County, Virginia
  died intestate 1716 Richmond County, Virginia
  married (after 1701?)
Sarah (—?—) who married 2nd Henry Wood, 3rd Rush Hudson, 4th Edward Turberville
  died testate 1760–1761 Orange County, Virginia

Children of William Willis and Sarah:

I. **John Willis** who died testate 1761–1762 in Orange County, Virginia
  married Elizabeth Plunkett 1734/35 King George County, Virginia; issue:
  A. Sarah Willis married Walter Shropshire
  B. Margaret "Peggy" Willis married Edmund Terrill
  C. William Willis married Elizabeth "Betsy" Garnett
    (parents of Capt. Isaac Willis of "Locust Grove" in Culpeper County, Virginia)
  D. John Willis married Sarah (Porter? per Loeffler)[1]
  E. Benjamin Willis *d.s.p.* 1810 Orange County, Virginia
  F. Joshua Willis married Sarah (Thomas? per Loeffler)
  G. James Willis married 1st Ann (—?—); married 2nd Judith (—?—)
  H. Reuben Willis married Ann "Nancy" Garnett
  I. Frances Willis married William Camp
  J. Lewis Willis married Edna Tilman
  K. Moses Willis married 1st Elizabeth Thomas; married 2nd Susan White
  L. Mary Willis married Richard Price
II. **William Willis** (named in mother's will); no further record of marriage or children
III. **Sarah Willis**[2] married (Benjamin) Hawkins; seven children

Sarah (—?—) Willis, widow of William, married 2nd Henry Wood who died intestate before July 1722 in King George County, Virginia. Sarah and Henry Wood had son:

I. **Henry Wood** (named in mother's will); no further record of marriage or children

Sarah (—?—) Willis Wood married 3rd Rush Hudson who died intestate before November 1735 in King George County, Virginia. Sarah and Rush Hudson had the following sons who are named in her will:

I. **Rush Hudson Jr.** (whose wife in 1746 was Sarah). Rush Hudson Jr. had the following known children who were named in Sarah (—?—) Willis Wood Hudson Turberville's will:
  A. Mary Hudson
  B. Elizabeth Hudson
  C. Rush Hudson
II. **Joshua Hudson** married Mary Terrill
III. **David Hudson** married Keziah Plunkett

Sarah (—?—) Willis Wood Hudson married 4th Edward Turberville who died intestate in 1750 in Orange County, Virginia; no issue.

---

[1] George B. Loeffler, "Ancestry of the Willises of Locust Grove, Culpeper County, Virginia," Willis–Gordon–Garnett and Allied Families *Journal*, vol. I, no. 10, 1982.

[2] Named in her mother's will as Sarah Hawkins; see Chapter VI.

Chapter IX

Transition from
King George County to Orange County, Virginia

The descendants of William Willis (son of John Willis Sr.) and his wife, Sarah, moved from King George County to Orange County, Virginia. This chapter will discuss the last records found for them in King George, early records found in Orange and Culpeper counties, and other members of the extended family who migrated with them.

As shown in Chapters I and VI, William died intestate in 1716 in that part of Richmond County which became King George. He was survived by his wife (Sarah), two underage sons (John and William), and an assumed underage daughter (Sarah, who later married Benjamin Hawkins).

After William's death, his widow Sarah married Henry Wood, Sr. (by whom she had a son, Henry). After Wood's death Sarah married Rush Hudson Sr. (by whom she had sons Rush Jr., Joshua, and David). Rush Hudson Sr. died in 1735, and Sarah married Edward Turberville (by whom she had no issue). Also prior to their migration John Willis (the eldest son of William and Sarah) married Elizabeth Plunkett, and Sarah (Willis?) married Benjamin Hawkins.

Throughout this chapter the name "John Willis" will refer to the son of William (d. 1716) and Sarah Willis and the grandson of John Willis Sr. (d. 1715) unless otherwise noted. This John was the grandfather of Capt. Isaac Willis whose descendants founded the Willis–Gordon–Garnett and Allied Families Association.

The actual date of the family's migration is unknown. In May and June of 1737 when John and Elizabeth (Plunkett) Willis deeded to the Church Wardens of Hanover Parish and when Edward Turberville released his wife's (John Willis's mother) dower rights, their place of residence was not mentioned. However, the Court Orders state that John, his wife Elizabeth, and his mother Sarah Turberville, personally appeared in King George County Court to acknowledge their deeds and relinquishment of dower rights. Sarah and Edward Turberville were still settling the estate of Rush Hudson Sr. in King George County in January 1738/39 through their attorney Zachary Lewis. The fact that they were working through an attorney could indicate that they had already moved out of the county.[1] As discussed in Chapter VI, Edward Turberville died in Orange County in 1750, and Sarah Turberville died there in 1760–1761.

John Willis died in Orange County between 25 November 1761 when he wrote his will and 25 March 1762 when it was presented in Court. John's will and a related deed are

---

[1] See Chapters I and VI.

given here in their entirety as transcribed from the original records on microfilm.[2]

> *In the name of God, Amen, I John Willis doe constitute and ordain this as my*
> *last will and testament in the manner and form following: Imprimis, To my*
> *son William I give negroes Thom and Judith and the lot in Culpeper to*
> *belong to the aforesaid William after my decease. The negroes Daniel and*
> *Millie I give to Edmund Terrill. To Walter Shropshire— I allow him one*
> *shilling and three pence. And to every child viz: John, Benjamin, Joshua,*
> *James, Rhewben, Francis [sic], Lewis, Moses and Mary, The rest of my*
> *estate to be equally divided among them. My beloved wife shall keep in her*
> *possession the aforesaid estate during her life. The place formerly belonging*
> *to Mr. Marks belongs to Benjamin. This place where I live belongs to John.*
> *Signed: John Willis*

> *N.B. My son William and Edmund Terrill to be Executors.*
> *Witnesses: Arch. Campbell, Elizabeth Willis.*

John's will was produced in Court on 25 March 1762 by William Willis, one of the executors, and was certified with Rush Hudson and Joshua Hudson (John's half-brothers) as his securities in the sum of 2,000 pounds.[3] An inventory of his estate was made on 22 May 1762 and recorded on 27 May 1762.[4]

Archibald Campbell, one of the witnesses, was a doctor and may have been treating him at the time John wrote his will.[5] According to Hurst, Doctor's Run was named for Dr. Archibald Campbell and was a later name for Petty's Mill Run. Campbell died intestate in 1786.[6] The other witness was probably John's wife, Elizabeth. While a wife did not usually witness her husband's will, she may have been the only other person present when it was written. John may have died of smallpox as there was an epidemic in the area at the time according to several accounts.

John Willis married Elizabeth Plunkett of Hanover Parish on 17 January 1734/35 at St. Paul's Parish,[7] so they had been married twenty-seven years when he died and had twelve children. Elizabeth Plunkett was the daughter of John Plunkett, Sr. Willis family historian George B. Loeffler, now deceased, summarized John's family in his article, "Ancestry of the Willises of Locust Grove, Culpeper County, Virginia."[8] John's widow, Elizabeth (Plunkett) Willis, made the following indenture (deed of gift) on 19 November 1762.[9]

---

[2] Orange County Will Book 2:323.

[3] Orange County Order Book 6:615.

[4] Orange County Will Book 2:327–329 from microfilm.

[5] No documents were found which linked the Willis and Campbell families in King George.

[6] Orange County Will Book 3:109.

[7] King, *The Register of Saint Paul's Parish 1715–1798*, p. 155.

[8] Willis-Gordon-Garnett and Allied Families *Journal*, vol. I, no. 10, 1982.

[9] Orange County Deed Book 13:484 from microfilm.

To all to whom these presents shall come Know ye that I, Elizabeth Willis, Relict of John Willis of the County of Orange Dec'd send greeting—Whereas the said John Willis did by his last will and testament in writing bearing date the () of November 1761 after giving some legacies to his children did leave the rest of the estate to be in my possession during my life and at my decease to be divided equally among my nine youngest children viz: John, Benjamin, Joshua, James, Reuben, Frances, Lewis, Moses, and Mary—and I, being willing that they should be assured of their parts of the estate of my late husband and for the natural love and affection which I bear them do of my own free will give and confirm unto the before mentioned children all the slaves and personal estate left to me by my late husband John Willis Dec'd provided nevertheless that I shall keep possession of the same during my widowhood and no longer. In witness whereof I have hereunto set my hand and seal this nineteenth day of November 1762. Signed: Elizabeth (mark) Willis. Witnesses: James Pollard, William Willis, Edmund Terrill, David Hudson.

At a Court for Orange County on Thursday 22 day of November 1764 this Deed of Gift was proved by the oaths of James Pollard, Edmund Terrill, Wm. Willis, and David Hudson Witnesses thereto and ordered to be recorded. Teste: Geo. Taylor COC

According to the following information which was found in "British Mercantile Claims 1775-1803," Elizabeth (Plunkett) Willis died in 1798:[10]

Elizabeth Willis of Culpeper died in Madison County on 3 March 1798 possessed a life estate in shares more than sufficient to have paid the claim from 1760 (the time of her husband's death) [sic] until her own death in 1798. In 1790 an account of 160 and some odd pounds due to John Glassell [i.e., agent of creditor] was first presented to William Willis, son and agent for Elizabeth Willis, who paid in part 76 pounds 11 shillings 8 pence by Law. [Lawrence] Taliaferro's, John Waugh's and Reubin Willis' bonds. Since the death of Mrs. Willis five shares valued at 431 pounds 8 shillings have been divided among her nine children and their representatives agreeably to her husband's will.

In an attempt to bridge the gap between the time that the family was living in King George County and the time that William's son John died, various records in early Spotsylvania, Orange, and Culpeper counties were reviewed. No documents were found in Spotsylvania County for John, his brother William, or his mother and stepfather. This suggests that they probably moved directly to Orange County which was created from Spotsylvania in 1734. Culpeper County was formed from Orange in 1748/49. Madison County (where Elizabeth Plunkett Willis and her son Joshua both died) was created from Culpeper in 1792. Consequently, researchers working in the records are faced with some of the same problems of changing county and parish

---

[10] *Virginia Genealogist*, vol. 27–2, April–June 1983, p. 111.

lines that are encountered earlier in Old Rappahannock, Richmond, and King George counties.

I have not been able to find documents which state when the three tracts which John willed to his sons William, John, and Benjamin in 1761 were acquired. When John wrote his will, he had a *lot* (a term commonly used for a leasehold) in Culpeper County, a tract formerly belonging to Mr. Marks, and his home tract which was presumably in Orange County where John was living. Records suggest that John Willis, his brother William, Joshua Hudson, and Benjamin Hawkins lived in the area of Petty's Mill Run which was south of the Rapidan River near the present junction of highways 627 and 636.

The names of John Willis, his brother William Willis, his Wood and Hudson half-brothers, and Edward Turberville do not appear on a 1742 petition for improvement of a rolling road in Orange County although other known residents (John Marks, Thomas Petty, Tavernor Beale, Harbin Moore, and several Thorntons) are given. The petition describes the road as being along the ridge of the mountain (*i.e.*, Little Mountains or Chestnut Mountains, later called Clark's Mountain) and going by John Taliaferro's Quarter to Fredericksburg. However, Benjamin Hawkins (probably the husband of Sarah, daughter of Sarah Willis) is named as one of several men who were to maintain the old road in September 1742.[11] In 1751 the Court found the overseer of the road guilty of not keeping the upper bridge over Petty's Mill Run from Benjamin Hawkins' to a place opposite Benjamin Porter's in repair.[12]

The first record which I found naming John Willis in Orange was dated February 1747 when he, Rush Hudson, and Elijah Morton witnessed a deed and a bond between William Henderson and Charles Walker, both of St. Thomas Parish, Orange County.[13] In September 1751 following Edward Turberville's death, John Willis provided security for Walter Shropshire (who would marry John's daughter Sarah) as guardian of John and Ann Shropshire, orphans of John Shropshire, deceased (who had married Edward Turberville's daughter Ann, then deceased).[14] John Willis served on a jury in 1758, and in 1760 he was named by his mother in her will. These entries can be assumed to be for John, son of William and Sarah. However, some records in Orange County are problematic.

In June 1749 a committee of men including John Willis, Benjamin Cave, George Taylor, Taverner Beale, and others was instructed to determine the most convenient location for a new courthouse and to arrange for its construction. Court sessions were held in homes until about 1738 when the first courthouse was built south of the Rapidan River near Governor's (later Somerville's) Ford which is four miles downstream from "Locust Grove," the Willis family home on the north side of the Rapidan River. When Culpeper County was cut off from Orange County, the old

---

[11] Orange County Order Book 4:249.

[12] Hurst, op. cit., p. 18.

[13] Orange County Deed Book 11:35–37.

[14] Orange County Will Book 2:163.

courthouse was at the far end of the county and a new courthouse was built at Orange.

While it would be tempting to identify this John Willis as our ancestor, another John Willis was living in the area at the time. The second John was the son of Col. Henry Willis of Fredericksburg and his first wife Anne Alexander according to published histories. This John Willis was born in 1724, married Elizabeth Madison (daughter of Ambrose Madison) and died intestate in February 1750 in Orange County.[15] John Willis and Elizabeth Madison had one child (Mary) who married William Daingerfield Jr. By 1753 Elizabeth Madison Willis married secondly Richard Beale, brother of the above Taverner Beale. Consequently, for a short period of time there were two men by the name of John Willis (both with wives named Elizabeth) in Orange County, and it is not known which John was on the 1749 committee.

To further complicate research, a third John Willis (born in 1728 and called "the younger son of that name of Col. Henry Willis of Fredericksburg and his second wife Mildred") and his wife Nanny were living in Culpeper County during the same period and were selling land which he inherited from Robert Spotswood in both Culpeper and Orange counties. These sons of Col. Henry Willis are discussed in more detail in Chapter XIII.

The first mention of our John Willis's brother William in Orange County was in 1750 when he and Francis Moore, Gent., provided security in the amount of 600 pounds for the administration of Edward Turberville's estate by his mother, Sarah Turberville. On the same date William was appointed surveyor of the highway. In a deed for 275 acres from John Spotswood to Benjamin Porter in 1751, William Willis was described as living on a lot (leasehold) formerly belonging to Sims near Petty's Mill Run.[16] In 1752 Spotswood sold Benjamin Porter two additional tracts of 120 and 7 acres at the mouth of Petty's Mill Run on the south side of the Rapidan and joining William Willis.[17] This William could not have been the son of John who died in 1762 and no other William Willis was known to be in the area, so it is assumed that he was the son of Sarah and William and the younger brother of John.

According to Hurst, Petty's Mill Run was part of a tract which Spotswood leased to the Pettys on 23 October 1734 which was the same date that Spotswood leased to Thomas Sims.[18] From later deeds it is known that our Willises owned land on or near Petty's Mill Run for several generations. Benjamin Willis (son of John and Elizabeth) willed his land there to his nephew Isaac Willis in 1810.

In 1751 an Isaac Arnold was granted a license to keep an ordinary (inn) in Orange County where John Ingham [Ingram] lately lived.[19] George Wells and John Goff were Arnold's securities. Arnold renewed his license the following year with William

---

[15] See Sparacio, *Digest of Orange County, Virginia, Will Book 1734–1838*, p. 122.

[16] Orange County Deed Book 12:21–25.

[17] Ibid., pp. 112–117.

[18] Hurst, op. cit., p. 47, and below.

[19] Orange County Orders.

Willis and Joseph Williams as his securities. Isaac Arnold was also one of the securities for the executors of the estate of George Petty that year, and by 1755 a James Arnold had married George Petty's widow, Jemima.[20]

In 1758 William Willis filed an attachment against the estate of Isaac Arnold, and James Arnold was ordered to pay damages in 1759. The reason for the attachment is unknown.[21]

Newman A. Hall, an Arnold family researcher, believes that this Isaac Arnold was the son of Thomas Arnold (son of Isaac Arnold and Margaret Goff) of King George County.[22] The identity of James Arnold is still being researched as there were more than one by that name. While this does not prove any direct relationship to the Willis family, it shows that descendants of at least two of John Willis's neighbors in King George County (Arnold and Goff) were also neighbors in Orange County.

Based on these and other documents which have been found, John and Elizabeth Willis moved to Orange County permanently between circa 1737/38 and 1747. The family was probably settled in Orange County before 1746 when Rush Hudson Jr. deeded his land in King George to Francis Thornton (see below).

Considering that the migration involved a large contingent of several related families, some questions come to mind. Why did John and his mother's extended family sell their lands in King George and move? What factors contributed to their decision to settle in Orange County? Did they follow relatives who had already migrated there?

The records indicate that three generations of Willises had been landowners in King George County and that the Woods and Hudsons were also landowners. However, the family had changed dramatically since the death of John Willis Sr. in 1715. William Willis died in 1716, and his widow Sarah married Henry Wood. In 1722 Henry Wood died, and Sarah married Rush Hudson Sr. By 1725 Charles Willis had died, and in 1728 John Willis Jr. died. In 1735 Rush Hudson Sr. died, and Sarah married Edward Turberville. William James, son of Mary (Willis) James, was living in Spotsylvania County in 1742 when he stated that his parents and brother David were deceased. Consequently, there were few family connections in King George by the time John Willis sold his grandfather's patent to the Church Wardens.

Almost seventy years of usage may have impoverished the land that John Willis Sr. and his sons farmed in King George, and the valuable timber was disappearing, as was available land for expanding families. However, the law had prohibited John from selling the entailed portion of the lands which he received upon his father's and uncle's deaths. In 1734 two events took place which may have significantly influenced the family's decision to move to Orange County. First, the Virginia Assembly passed an Act which allowed entailed lands of less than 200 pounds in value and not part of, or

[20] Sparacio, *Digest of Orange County, Virginia, Will Books 1734–1838*, p. 84.

[21] Orange County Orders.

[22] Personal correspondence.

contiguous to, other entailed lands to be sold if, after being appraised, a writ of *ad quod damnum* was filed with the sheriff.[23] With this Act John was able to sell his grandfather's 1669 patent.

The second event concerned Gov. Alexander Spotswood's leases along the Rapidan River. In the fall of 1734 Spotswood issued at least fourteen leases for 1,862 acres, the tracts ranging in size from 100 to 200 acres, in his large Spotsylvania Tract which lay on both sides of the Rapidan River. The following is a summary of those leases as reported by Crozier,[24] all of which are found in Spotsylvania County Deed Book C.

> *23 October 1734 to William Wood, planter, 110 acres in St. Mark's Parish, Spotsylvania County, on the south side of the Rapidan, etc., for the lives of William Wood and Isabel, his wife; witnesses John Grame, Tho. Sims, William Morton.*

> *23 October 1734 to John Marks, planter, 100 acres on the south side of the Rapidan, etc., for the lives of John Marks, Mary his wife, and Mary his daughter; same witnesses as above.*

> *23 October 1734 to Thomas Sims, planter, 108 acres on the south side of the Rapidan, etc., for the lives of Thomas Sims, Rebecca his wife, and Thomas his son; witnesses John Grame, John Pattey [Petty], William Morton.*

> *23 October 1734 to James Jones Sr., 200 acres on the south side of the Rapidan, etc., for the lives of Thomas Jones and James Jones, sons of said James Jones Sr.; witnesses John Grame, Tho. Sims, William Morton.*

> *23 October 1734 to William Croucher, planter, 100 acres on the south side of the Rapidan, etc., for the lives of William Croucher, Anne his wife, and Priscilla his daughter; same witnesses.*

> *23 October 1734 to Thomas Pettey [Petty], planter, 100 acres on the south side of the Rapidan, etc., for the lives of Thomas Pettey, Katherine his wife, and Christopher Pettey his son; same witnesses.*

> *23 October 1734 to John Pettey [Petty], planter, 100 acres on the north side of the Rapidan for the lives of John Petty, Rebecca his wife, and Thomas Petty his son; same witnesses.*

> *2 November 1734 to Robert Allistone, planter, 100 acres on the south side of the Rapidan for the lives of Robert Allistone and his son Jacob Allistone; witnesses Joseph Delaney, William Bunting, Thomas Lewis.*

---

[23] John Frederick Dorman, *Colonial Laws of Primogeniture* (a paper read at the World Conference on Records and Genealogical Seminar at Salt Lake City, Utah, in August 1969).

[24] William Armstrong Crozier, *Virginia County Records, vol. I, Spotsylvania County 1721–1800* (Baltimore: Genealogical Publishing Co., 1990), pp. 136–137, 139–140.

25 October 1734 to Simon Miller, planter, 100 acres on the north side of the Rapidan for the lives of Simon Miller and John Allistone, son of Robert Allistone; witnesses Thomas Lewis, Simon Miller, John Blackeley.

23 October 1734 to William Morton, 200 acres on the south side of the Rapidan for the lives of William Morton, Jeremiah Morton, and Elijah Morton; witnesses John Grame, Tho. Sims, John Pettey.

28 October 1734 to Elias Smith, planter, 100 acres on the south side of the Rapidan for the lives of Elias Smith and sons Elias Smith Jr., and William Smith; witnesses Elliott Benger, John Blackaby, Thomas Pitcher.

31 December 1734 to William Pannell, planter, 172 acres on the south side of the Rapidan for the lives of William Pannell and Sarah his wife; witnessed John Lightfoot, Elliott Benger, Abraham Chambers.

30 November 1734 to John Ingram, planter, 172 acres on the south side of the Rapidan for the lives of John Ingram, Hannah his wife, and John Ingram Jr. his son; witnesses And. Landale, James Gibbs, Luke Thornton.

30 November 1734 to Luke Thornton, planter, 200 acres on the south side of the Rapidan for the lives of Luke Thornton and John Randell, his brother-in-law; witnesses And. Landale, James Gibbs, John Ingram.

The above William Wood was undoubtedly the eldest son of Henry Wood Sr., deceased, and the stepson of Sarah (—) Willis Wood Hudson Turberville. On 5 March 1734/35 William Wood of St. Mark's Parish, Orange County, deeded two parcels of land in King George County to Rush Hudson Sr (who was married to William's stepmother, Sarah). One tract of 40 acres was the land "whereon Rush Hudson now dwells and whereon Henry Wood formerly lived." The other tract of 100 acres was "the land where George Parsons dwells adjacent to the land of Mr. Rowland Thornton, John Willis, and Edward Dunnahoe (Donahoe), being formerly purchased by Henry Wood, father to the said William Wood."[25] Both tracts were on branches of Portrages (Portridges) Creek. So in 1734 the Willises of King George County had at least one family connection, William Wood, who was living in Orange County. Some of the other recipients of the Spotswood leases can also be identified as former residents of Westmoreland, Richmond, and King George counties, but those findings will not be included in this manuscript.

By 4 February 1746 Rush Hudson Jr. (the half-brother of John Willis) and his wife Sarah (not to be confused with Rush Hudson Jr.'s mother, Sarah) had moved to St. Mark's Parish, Orange County, when they sold four tracts in King George to Francis

---

[25] King George County Deed Book 1A:324; also see Orange County Order Book 1:392 dated 26 October 1738 when John Hawkins was ordered to clear the road from William Wood(s) to the courthouse according to instructions of Benjamin Porter..

Thornton of Hanover Parish, including the above tracts.[26] Whether this was the son or grandson of Francis Thornton Sr. who died in 1726 is unknown to me.

In 1761 John Willis of Orange left his son Benjamin a tract which he (John) had bought from Mr. Marks. Although no lease or deed was found for this transaction, Marks probably assigned the above 1734 Spotswood lease to John. (This may even be the 100 acres which Benjamin's heirs divided after Benjamin's death.[27])

John Marks is of interest for another reason. From information given by King in *Marriages of Richmond County* and the Culpeper County records, it appears that Ann (Harbin?) married first Francis Moore of Ireland and Old Rappahannock counties and second John Naylor of Richmond and King George counties.[28] Ann died in 1744 in Orange County where she and some of her family had moved.[29] Harbin Moore, son of Ann and Francis, married the daughter of John Marks who died testate in 1759 in Culpeper County.[30] A daughter of Ann and Francis Moore married Thomas Pattey [Petty] Jr. In 1793 Harbin Moore (Jr.) married Ann Tutt in Culpeper County.[31] It is not known if Ann Tutt was related to the descendants of Richard Tutt and wife Mary Underwood (daughter of William Underwood who died in 1717 in Richmond County), but it was possible and would have been another connection from King George.

John Willis left his *lot* or leasehold in Culpeper County to his son William, and again no initial lease or deed was found. Ann Miller, Orange County historian, stated that Spotswood was not always careful about recording leases and that the tract which later became "Locust Grove" on the north side of the Rapidan was probably a lease and incorporated into William Willis's (son of John) purchase from the Spotswood executors in 1767.[32] Family historians claim that William married Elizabeth Garnett, daughter of Anthony Garnett, in 1760 and was probably living on his father's Culpeper tract when John died. In any event William Willis was living in Culpeper County by May 1766 when he and his brother-in-law Edmund Terrill witnessed John Hill's will.[33]

The above Sims' lease from Spotswood was probably the tract where William Willis, son of William and Sarah, was living in 1751. No records were found to explain what happened to this tract. It may have eventually reverted to Spotswood's heirs at the end of the term of the lease and was sold.

Others who received early patents in Orange County adjoining the Spotswood tract included several families whose names were familiar in King George

---

[26]Sparacio, *King George County Deed Book 3*, p.173 and microfilm .

[27]See Culpeper County Deed Book HH:423 dated 14 October 1816.

[28]See King, *Marriages of Richmond County 1668–1853.*

[29]Sparacio, *Digest of Orange County, Virginia, Will Books 1734–1838*, p. 77.

[30]Dorman, *Culpeper County, Virginia, Will Book A, 1749–1770*, pp. 51 and 59.

[31]John Vogt and T. William Kethley, Jr., *Culpeper County Marriages 1780–1853* (Athens, GA: Iberian Pub. Co., 1986), p. 80.

[32]Culpeper County Deed Book E:271, and personal correspondence with Ann Miller.

[33]Culpeper County Will Book A:442–443.

County—Thornton, Conway, Taliaferro, Gibson, and Catlett. Deeds and wills confirm the fact that John Willis Sr.'s land in King George County adjoined the Thorntons who were related to the others by marriage. It certainly appears that the Willises moved to an area where they had several previous associations.

By 1800 several children of John and Elizabeth (Plunkett) Willis had acquired land in Orange County and those parts of Orange which had become Culpeper and Madison counties. Their eldest son, William, (who married Elizabeth Garnett) eventually owned a total of 2,277 acres on the north side of the Rapidan including the home place which was named "Locust Grove." The original 16 foot by 20 foot portion of "Locust Grove" is believed to be the oldest building in Culpeper County.[34] It was meticulously restored by John and Elizabeth Womeldorph in the 1970s and has been admitted to the National Register of Historic Places (DHL File #23-49).

Before moving to Adair County, Kentucky, William and Elizabeth (Garnett) Willis gave two tracts to sons Isaac and Sandy (Alexander) Willis and sold 1,408 acres to Robert Patton of Fredericksburg.[35] After finally settling in Boone County, Kentucky, William and Elizabeth sold their last remaining tract in Culpeper to their son Isaac.[36] William and Elizabeth had eleven children and died in Boone County, Kentucky, at advanced ages.[37] Their son Isaac Willis married Anne Garnett and lived at "Locust Grove" until his death in 1867. The descendants of Isaac Willis and Anne Garnett established the Willis–Gordon–Garnett and Allied Families Association in 1935.

Joshua Willis, son of John and Elizabeth (Plunkett) Willis, died testate in 1820 in that part of Culpeper which became Madison leaving a widow and fourteen children. He willed land in both Madison County, Virginia, and in Grayson County, Kentucky, to his children.

Benjamin Willis, son of John and Elizabeth (Plunkett) Willis, never married and spent his entire life on the Rapidan River. When he died in 1810, he left a considerable estate to several of his siblings and his lands to his nephew Isaac Willis (son of William and Elizabeth).[38] One brother and one sister brought suit against Benjamin's executors in Fredericksburg, but the suit was discontinued in 1816.

Margaret (Peggy) Willis, daughter of John and Elizabeth, married Edmund Terrill, son of Robert Terrill, in 1760[39] and had eleven children, many who later moved to

---

[34] Mary Stevens Jones, *An 18th Century Perspective: Culpeper County* (Culpeper: Culpeper Historical Society, 1976), p. 114.

[35] Culpeper County Deed Books X:98, X:100, and AA:265.

[36] Culpeper County Deed Book FF:464.

[37] George B. Loeffler and Elizabeth L. Loeffler, "William Willis (1739–1833) of Virginia and Kentucky," Willis–Gordon–Garnett and Allied Families Association *Journal*, vol. I, no. 10, 1982; also see J. A. Kirtley, *History of Bullittsburg Church* (Boone County, Kentucky, pub. 1872), p. 25, and various Boone County, Kentucky, records.

[38] Sparacio, *Digest of Orange County, Virginia, Will Books 1734–1838*, p.121.

[39] John Vogt and T. William Kethley, Jr., *Orange County Marriages 1747–1850* (Athens, GA: Iberian Publ Co., 1984), p. 123, and related deeds and family bible records.

Albemarle County and then to Kentucky. Edmund Terrill, who fought in the Revolutionary War, died testate in Culpeper County in 1784-85.[40] He owned land on both sides of the Rapidan and was often mentioned in the deeds as neighbor of his brother-in-law William Willis who bought a large tract from the heirs of Edmund Terrill in 1795.[41]

The other children of John and Elizabeth (Plunkett) Willis were Sarah (who married Walter Shropshire), John (who married Sarah, perhaps Porter, and died in Kentucky), James and Lewis (who both died testate in Wilkes County, Georgia), Reuben (who married Ann/Nancy Garnett and died in Todd County, Kentucky), Moses (who married twice, first to Elizabeth Thomas and second to Susan White, and died intestate in Orange County, Virginia, in 1805), and Mary (who married Richard Price and moved to Kentucky). These descendants are discussed by George B. Loeffler in the *Journal* of the Willis–Gordon–Garnett and Allied Families Association, and specific lines have been researched by this author and others, but that data is beyond the scope of this manuscript.

Benjamin Hawkins and wife Sarah (Willis?) were married when the family moved to Orange County. Benjamin Hawkins purchased 370 acres on the Rapidan from the Spotswood executors in 1767.[42] Newman A. Hall has researched this family and has identified seven children.[43] Their eldest daughter, Mildred Hawkins, married first John Plunkett Jr. (brother of Elizabeth Plunkett who married John Willis) and second Isaac Rucker.[44] The other children of Benjamin and Sarah Hawkins will not be discussed here because that research was done primarily by others. However, their descendants married into many of the established families in the area, and some of them migrated to Kentucky.

No records were found to show if either William Willis (son of William and Sarah) or Henry Wood (son of Henry and Sarah) ever married or left children.

The children of Sarah and Rush Hudson Sr. are still being researched. Rush Hudson Jr. (Sarah's eldest son by Rush Hudson Sr.) and his wife Sarah were living in St. Mark's Parish, Orange County in 1746/47 when they deeded his land in King George County to Francis Thornton.[45] In 1751 he and his brother David Hudson appraised John Stapp's estate in Culpeper County, and Rush was named executor of his mother's estate in Orange County in 1762. It is known from his mother's will that in 1760 Rush Jr. had daughters Mary and Elizabeth and a son named Rush. The maiden name of Sarah, wife of Rush Hudson Jr. is unknown to me, but she was probably related to one of the neighboring families in King George County.

---

[40]Culpeper County Will Book C:92.

[41]Culpeper County Deed Book S:397 ff. and Z:76.

[42]Orange County Deed Book 14:142.

[43]Personal correspondence.

[44]See King George County Deed Book 3:393 and Orange County Will Book 2:273.

[45]King George County Deed Book 3:173.

Joshua Hudson purchased 175 acres at the head of Petty's Mill Pond from Spotswood's executors in 1767.[46] In 1769 he was married to Mary Terrill who was the sister of Edmund Terrill (John Willis's son-in-law). Mary (Terrill) Hudson was named in her father, Robert Terrill's, will in 1786.[47] Also named in Robert Terrill's will was his grandson, Rush Hudson. Joshua Hudson moved to Amherst County where he died between 5 January 1799 and 20 April 1801.[48]

According to Newman A. Hall, David Hudson married Keziah Plunkett and had eleven children. David died in 1811 in Culpeper County on a tract which he purchased from John Spotswood in 1771 and which joined the Garnett family.[49]

My own research indicates that David was living in Culpeper County in by 1748 when he and John Stapp witnessed the will of Thomas Salmon. David then became the guardian of Salmon's children.[50] In 1751 David Hudson, Rush Hudson, and Anthony Garnett appraised John Stapp's estate.[51] In November 1771 the Spotswood executors deeded 400 acres in Culpeper County to David Hudson[52] and 700 acres in St. Mark's Parish, Culpeper County, to Anthony Garnett, the father of Elizabeth Garnett who married William Willis. The land joined Thomas Gaines, Cedar Run, Sutton's lot line, Hudson's line, and Garnett's old line.[53] In 1789 Anthony Garnett deeded 245 acres on Cedar Mountain Run joining David Hutson [Hudson] to Edmund Willis and 182 acres adjoining this tract to Jeremiah Ingram, son and son-in-law of William Willis and wife Elizabeth Garnett.[54] Edmund Willis and wife Fanny [Frances Towles] deeded the 245 acres to his brother-in-law Jeremiah Ingram in 1794, the deed again citing David Hudson's line.[55] In 1804 and just prior to migrating to Kentucky, Jeremiah and Sarah (Willis) Ingram sold these tracts plus a third parcel to Reuben Garnett, son of Anthony, with the deed mentioning David Hudson's line.[56] Several of David's descendants moved to Kentucky, and his land was eventually acquired by the Garnett family.

Numerous later records have been found in Orange and Culpeper counties, but they are beyond the focus of this manuscript. However, it is obvious that many descendants of these families from Orange, Culpeper, and Madison counties can trace their lineage back to Sarah (—) Willis Wood Hudson Turberville.

---

[46] Orange County Deed Book 14:142.

[47] Ruth and Sam Sparacio, *Digest of Orange County, Virginia, Will Book 1734–1838* (McLean, VA: The Antient Press, 1987), p. 111, and microfilm.

[48] Amherst County Will Book 4:6 (per Newman A. Hall).

[49] Culpeper County Deed Book F:379 and DD:36 (per Newman A. Hall).

[50] Culpeper County Will Book A:46 and A:95.

[51] Ibid., p. 62.

[52] Culpeper County Deed Book F:379.

[53] Ibid., pp. 361–363.

[54] Culpeper County Deed Book P:61 and P:63.

[55] Culpeper County Deed Book S:159; Frances Towles was the daughter of Joseph Towles and Sarah Terrill, sister to Edmund Terrill who married Margaret/Peggy Willis, daughter of John and Elizabeth (Plunkett) Willis.

[56] Culpeper County Deed Book Z:250.

Chapter X

Early Westmoreland County Records

John Willis Sr.'s 1669 patent implied that his land was in Westmoreland County or that he was a resident of that county. However, later deeds clearly show that his land was on the south side of the ridge line in Old Rappahannock (later Richmond, then King George) County.

Records for eight men with the name "Willis" were found in the Westmoreland County between 1668 and 1720. This chapter will review the documents which were found for six of them because the information may be helpful to other family researchers. Any relationship between these men or between them and John Willis Sr. who died in 1715 in Richmond County is unproven at this time. Those six men were:

1. John Willis, born *circa* 1617; died testate before 26 July 1682.
2. William Willis, m. Mary, widow of William Offile, and died intestate in 1720.
3. William Willis, m. Bridgett (Robinson?) and died intestate in 1713.
4. John Willis, died intestate by March 1717 (probably related to #3).
5. William Willis, m. Mary Kirke, daughter of Thomas Kirke, by 1711/12.
6. Thomas Willis, mentioned in records in 1669 and 1674.

Documents for these men will be summarized in the above order. My emphasis on dates is intentional because dates are so important in sorting these men to determine if any of them were related to John Willis Sr.

Names in Old Rappahannock and Richmond records which were found in the Westmoreland County records with one or more of the above Willis men included the Washingtons, Nathaniel Pope, Christopher Butler, John Parsons, and John Foxhall.

An aside is given here regarding the spelling of names. For several years names such as Pierce and Field were commonly seen as Peirce and Feild, so researchers must search indexes for both. Read was also seen as Reid, Reed, and Reade or Reads, and Kirk was also given as Kerke or Kirke and in one instance, probably by clerk's error, as Clark. Place names such as Potomac, Nomini, and Cos Cos are also found with different spellings. The old records are full of similar examples and probably reflected both cultural spelling patterns brought by the immigrants from their native countries and the individual spelling habits of County Clerks.

John Frederick Dorman's published abstracts of Westmoreland County records were used in the initial stages of my research, followed by a review of microfilmed copies of the original documents in order to read the most important ones in their entirety. Other primary sources included Nugent, Fleet, Norris, Eaton, and Fothergill (see bibliography). As many of the records are specific to this chapter, sources will be given below and will not be summarized in Chapter XIV.

John Willis (#1)

John Willis #1 died testate in 1682. His will is among the missing Westmoreland records, so the names of his heirs are unknown. Extant documents show that the executor of his estate was John Crabb(e).[1] I suspect that he was the father of John Willis Sr., but no proofs have been discovered as yet. It appears that this John Willis was born by 1617 because he was relieved of paying levies in 1677 due to his age which, according to Merrill Hill Mosher, C.G., indicated that he was probably sixty years old in 1677.[2] By comparison, John Willis Sr., the subject of this manuscript, was born by 1648 if he was an adult when he received his 1669 patent.

In 1668 John Willis #1 purchased land from Andrew Read(e).[3] In 1668/69 John sold half of it to Phillip White, and in 1675 he sold the other half to Henry Kirke (see below). The tract was described as being on Herring Creek, a branch of Nomony [Nomini], and near Col. William Peirce (Pierce) who married Sarah Underwood.

The date of this John's arrival in Virginia is unknown. On 18 October 1650 George Read, Gentleman, submitted the names of 40 headrights for a patent of 2,000 acres dated 2 November 1648. The headrights included the names of John Fryer and John Willis which was given as "Wilks" by Dorman but as "Willis" in the original.[4] On the same date Reade was granted 500 acres in Northumberland County on the south side of Potomeck [Potomac] River and south side of Herrin[g] Cr., next adjoining land of Mr. Robert Yoe, "the rights to be taken out of the first patent given above."[5] The second tract was described as being at the mouth of Coss Coss [Cos Cos] Creek. Both parcels fell into Westmoreland County when it was created from Northumberland County in 1653. Andrew Read's relationship, if any, to George Read(e) is unknown to me.

It cannot be said with certainty that this John Willis of Read's headrights was the same man whose name appears in the Westmoreland County records beginning in 1668, but it is a definite possibility based upon later documents. Neither can it be assumed that Willis's name as a headright meant that he was indentured. Many headrights were for family or relatives who came from England, and headright system was widely abused. The same headrights were often claimed by two or three different men—once for the person who actually paid for the immigrants' passage, once for the captain of the ship, and again by someone who had bought the headrights which could be assigned.

The following entries were found on microfilm in Westmoreland County Deeds & Wills, vol.1 (1653–1671), pp. 329–330.

I the said William Berkley, Lt. Gov., do with the counsul of the state

---

[1] Dorman, *Westmoreland County Order Book 1675/6–1688/9*, Part three, p. 4.

[2] Ibid., Part one, p. 49.

[3] See below.

[4] Nugent, 1:180, Patent Book 2:165, and below.

[5] Nugent, I:201 and Patent Book 2:260.

*accordingly give and grant unto Andrew Read 400 acres of land in
Westmoreland County near the head of Nomony River on the eastermost side
of the westermost Herring Creek beginning at a white oak standing on the
eastward side of the main branch of the said Herring Creek extending W.S.W.
to a point westerly 320 perches to a white oak which divides this land and the
land of Anne Hutt S 220 perches to a red oak S.E. 180 perches to a red oak
standing near the said main branch which divides this land and the land of
Mr. Richard Sturman finally down the said main branch (N?)E. Northerly to
the first white oak which branch divides this land and a tract of land surveyed
for Thomas Dyas [Dyos] the said land being due unto the said Andrew Read
by and for the transportation of eight persons into this colony whose names
are on the record mentioned under this patent. To have and to hold, given
under my hand and seal of the colony this 6th day of June 1666. Recorded on
28th October 1668. (See note below.)*

*Read to Willis. For a valuable consideration in hand received have assigned
the contents of the above patent unto John Willis, () my hand this (28th) of
October 1668. Signed: Andrew Read. Teste: Morris Veale, John Nolan.
28th of October 1668. This assignment of land was ack. in court by the said
Read and recorded.*

*Willis to White. Know all men by these presents that I John Willis do assign
over one hundred acres of land within mentioned unto Philip White which
land the said Andrew Read sold to me and I do bind myself to make good sale
to the said Phillip White and to record it as witnesseth my hand the 1st day of
January 1668 [1669]. Signed: John Willis. Teste: Thomas Burrell, Henry
Kirk.
24th of February 1668 [1669]. This sale of land was acknowledged in court
by John Willis and there recorded.*

The first part of this entry is somewhat misleading. Often when a man sold part of a
patent, the entire patent would be mentioned or re-entered in the record. I found
instances in the Westmoreland records when the same patent was entered several times
as the tract or parts of it were sold. As will be shown, Andrew Read actually sold only
200 of the above 400 acres to Willis with Willis then selling 100 acres to White and
100 acres to Kirk(e).

Andrew Read received two patents in the same general area on 6 June 1666. The
second patent, also for 400 acres, adjoined Randolph Kirke and the land of Col. Payton
[Peyton], deceased.[6]

Other patents and deeds show that by the 1660s Thomas Dyos, Daniel Hutt (who was
a merchant), Richard Sturman, William Overett (or Overed), and John Crabb (who was
also a merchant) all lived on or near Cos Cos Creek, a branch of Herring Creek which

---

[6]Nugent, I:563 and Virginia Land Grants 5:527; also Dorman, op. cit., Part one, p. 33.

was a branch of the Nomony River and a few miles east of present Montross.[7] On 15 June 1666 Richard Sturman deeded 500 acres out of a 2,000-acre patent to Robert Cooper and Agnes [Mase? Moss?], widow, at the head of Nomony on the back side of the land of Daniel Hutt on Cosh Cosh [Cos Cos] Creek.[8]

On 11 July 1666 Andrew Read deeded to Robert Cooper and Richard Clouther jointly "all right, title, and interest of ½ of tract of 350 acres of which I am now seated."[9] The deed mentioned Mr. Sturman's line. Witnesses were Wm. Overed (Overett) and Wm. Bailey. In 1677 Andrew Read re-deeded to correct the acreage.[10] Dorman also gives these related entries:

> *Westmoreland County Deeds, Patents, etc., 1665–1677, Part 1, p. 34:*
> *Page 20 (D&W 1, p. 330). 22 Oct. 16(). Andrew Read of (), planter, to John Willis, planter. 400 acres, excepting 200 acres being the one halfe which I formerly (sold) to Richard Clouther and Robert Cooper 11 July 16(). [Signed]: Andrew Read. Wit: Lestrange Mordaunt, Morris Veale.*
> *28 Oct. 1668. Acknowledged by Andrew Reade.*
> *1 Feb. 1668 [1669]. John Willis to Phillip White. 100 acres which Andrew Reade sould [sic] me. [Signed]: John (X) Willis. Wit: Thomas Burrell, Henry Kirke.*
> *24 Feb. 1668 [1669)]. Acknowledged by John Willis.*
> (This is the same tract which was given on the previous page.)

> *Op. cit., Part III, pp. 18–19.*
> *Page 212–212a. Jno. Wilks [sic] assignment of land to Phillip White, recorded in foll. (folio) 20 (which was an older, now extinct book).*
> *28 8ber [Oct.] 1674. Phillip White to Mr. Jno. Foxhall. All my right of 100 acres. [Signed]: Phillip (X) White. Wit. Jno: Crabb, Corderoy Ironmonger.*
> *28 8ber. Acknowledged by Phillip White*
> (Review of the original record indicates that this was Willis and not Willks.)

> *Op. cit., Part III, p. 45:*
> *Pages 246a–247. 24 Aug. 1675. Jno. Willis of Westmoreland County, planter, to Hen: Kirke of same, cooper. For a valuable summ [sic]. 100 acres whereon Willis is not seated upon the south west branch of Nomminy and bounding upon the land of Coll: Nicho: Spencer. [Signed] John Willis Wit. Ollivar Griffinn, Robt Willice)*
> *Acknowledged by Jno. Willis*
> (Original on microfilm is poor, and "robt. will..." may or may not be Willis. No other references were found for a Robert Willis or Willice in the records.)

---

[7] Nugent, I:201, I:499, I:522, I:563, and others.

[8] Dorman, *Westmoreland County Deeds, Patents, etc., 1665–1677*, Part one, p. 26, and microfilm.

[9] Ibid., p. 21, and microfilm.

[10] Dorman, op. cit., Part four, pp. 9–10, and microfilm.

Op. cit., Part III, p. 66:
Pages 277–277a.   27 April 1677.   A survey made by Randolph Kerke
[Kirke/Kirk] of 100 acres by the request and order of John Willis and Henry
Kerke which land is sold unto Kerke by Willis, being part of 200 acres which
Willis bought of Andrew Read lying on the head of the branches of Nomeny
... side of a marsh ... and land formerly belonging to William Overett,
deceased ... on great branch in Nomeny. [Signed] John (X) Willis
Wit. James Harwich, Joseph Hardwich
16 May 1677. Recorded.

Other documents which were found for this John Willis will be reviewed before
continuing with his land records, but the reader is warned that sometimes it is not clear
as to which John Willis they refer.

The first record found for this John Willis in Westmoreland County was the above
deed from Andrew Read in October 1668. The next reference was Willis's assignment
of 100 acres to White on 1 February 1668/69. On 15 February 1668/69 Phillip
Silvester's estate inventory was presented in Court and included a calf "about John
Willis's."[11] Analysis of the early records suggests that a man by the name of Phillip
Silvester was living next to James Willis on Yeocomoco Neck in 1650 (see Chapter
XI), but that he may have migrated to the Mattox or Popes Creek area where he died.
This information placed him several miles north of John Willis of Cos Cos Creek, so
the John named in Silvester's estate may have been John Willis Sr. To place these
documents in perspective, it is noted that John Willis Sr. received his patent for 261
acres on "the falling branches of Appomattox [Mattox] Creek" on 21 October 1669
(see Chapters I and II).

On 2 March 1670/71 John Willis, John Parker, George Browne, and others were on
a jury to determine the cause of death of Martin Cole who accidentally drowned. This
John has not been identified.[12]

In 1674 Phillip White sold (assigned) the 100 acres which he bought from John Willis
in 1668/69 to John Foxhall Sr. with John Crabb and Corderoy Ironmonger as witnesses
(see above), and in 1697 John Foxhall Jr. sold it to Charles Smith.[13]

23 and 24 November 1697.   John Foxhall of Washington Parish,
Westmoreland County, planter, to Charles Smith of Nomony in Cople Parish
in said county, locksmith. Lease and release for 12,000 pounds of tobacco.
200 acres in the forest of Nomony now in occupation of Charles Smith and
Henry Asbury or one of them, bounded with the lands of Mr. James
Hardwick, Richard White, Thomas Robinson, and land late of Elizabeth
Broadhurst, part of 560 acres granted by patent dated 22 October 1666 by
Sir William Berkley unto Henry Durent [Durrant], which said 200 acres was

---

[11]Dorman, op. cit., Part one, p. 45.

[12]Ibid., p. 73.

[13]Dorman, *Westmoreland County Deeds & Wills No. 2, 1691–1699*, p. 49.

assigned unto William Harris and by Harris assigned to John Foxhall, deceased, father of the said John Foxhall. And 100 acres in Nomony Forest bounded with the land now of William Carr, James Hardwick, Henry Kirk, and John Dowsett, part of 400 acres granted unto Andrew Read, 200 acres whereof was sold by Read to John Willis, 100 acres of which 200 acres was sold by Willis to Phillip White and by White sold to John Foxhall, deceased, father of the said John Foxhall.

The deed from White to John Foxhall Sr. was probably recorded in the missing records. This was the last record which was found for John Foxhall Jr. who wrote his will on 15 March 1697/98 and died by 30 March 1698.[14]

In January 1697/98 Charles Smith, smith [blacksmith], sold 100 acres to Henry Asbury. The deed called the tract "Tarbutt's" and said that it was between the land which Smith had bought from Mr. John Foxhall and was adjacent to Henry Kirke, William Carr, James Hardwick, and John Dowsett[15]. Henry Asbury died testate in Westmoreland County 1706–1707 and left this 100 acres which he called "Talbott's" land to his son Benjamin who was underage. Asbury also willed land which he bought from Francis Wright, Gent., at the head of Mattox Creek to his sons Henry and Thomas.[16] Charles Smith died in 1714 leaving a different 100 acres to his daughter Mary and son William with the tract to go to his son Francis if Mary and William died without heirs.[17] Nathaniel Pope Sr. (alias Bridges) and Mr. Joseph Bayly were named as trustees in Smith's will. This Charles Smith was also named with a William Willis (see below). The duplication of names in these Westmoreland County with those in Richmond County is obvious.

A few additional records will be given here. In the spring of 1675 the County Court ordered that John Willis pay 973 pounds of tobacco due by bill to John Foxhall and that John Willis and Thomas Blundall pay 900 pounds of tobacco to Mr. Stephen Manwering.[18]

On 5 June 1675 the inventory of Corderoy Ironmonger, deceased, as taken by Stephen Manwering, John Butler, and Humphrey Pope was presented in Court by his widow Mary.[19] Several disbursements were allowed including 15,000 pounds of tobacco to the orphans of Abram Feild/Field (Mary's previous husband), 490 pounds of tobacco to Col. John Washington for corn, 600 pounds of tobacco to John Willis for corn, 400 pounds of tobacco to Mr. William Butler (per judgment?), and 500 pounds of tobacco to Mr. Bridges, trustee.

---

[14] See Chapter IV.

[15] Dorman, op. cit., p. 61.

[16] Dorman, *Westmoreland County Deeds, Patents, etc., 1665–1677*, Part four, pp. 38–39.

[17] Dorman, *Westmoreland County Deeds & Wills No. 5, 1712–1716*, pp. 65–66.

[18] Dorman, *Westmoreland County Order Book 1675/6–1688/9*, Part one, p. 3.

[19] Dorman, *Westmoreland County Deeds, Patents, etc., 1665–1667*, Part three, p. 41, and microfilm.

Corderoy Ironmonger, whose name was found in both the Old Rappahannock and Westmoreland records, married the widow of Abram Feild/Field who died testate in 1674. Ironmonger gave bond to John Foxhall and Patrick Spence, trustees of the estate of Field's orphans, in February 1674/75. William Butler was probably the minister who married Joan/Jane Brooks (the widow of Daniel Lisson who died in 1679) and the brother of Caleb Butler who married (as her fourth husband) Mary Foxhall (see Chapter IV). Later marriages between the descendants of Abram Field and the Hudsons were found, but will not be discussed in this manuscript. John Washington, Mr. Bridges, William Butler, and Daniel Lisson were all part of the early Mattox Creek group (see Pope sketch in Chapter IV).

In August 1675 John Willis deeded 100 acres to Henry Kirke as given above. On 9 January 1677/78 John Willis was released from levy, "being by adge past labour." It was customary for men to be released from taxes at age 60, so it is assumed that he was born around 1617.

On 27 April 1677 Willis and Kirke requested that Randolph Kirke survey the tract which John Willis had sold to Henry Kirke.[20] On 11 December 1678 the Court found Henry Kirk indebted to John Willis for 1,000 pounds of tobacco and ordered Kirk to make payment. County Orders on 11 December 1678 reported (without further explanation): "Mr. Taylor vs. John Willis. Order vs. Sherriffe. Attachment."[21]

On 5 November 1679 the Court Orders noted: "John Willis vs. Abram Blagg. Mr. Abram Blagg confessed judgment out of the estate of Mr. John Watts, deceased, for 450 pounds tobacco."[22] Based on the fact that John Watts bought Nathaniel Pope's patent on Mattox and that both Watts and Blagg(e) were living on Mattox in 1679, this may have been John Willis Sr. (see Chapter IV).

On 26 July 1683 the following entry was made in the Westmoreland County Orders:[23]

> *Upon a scire facias John Crabb claymes as executor of John Willis 1000 pounds of tobacco from Henry Kirk and Kirk makeing plainely appeare the payment thereof, the Court order that John Crabb pay Henry Kirk 50 pounds of tobacco for a nonsuite.*

Consequently, John Willis, presumably the man who was past age of labor in 1677, died testate before July 1682 at which time John Crabb was his executor. As this John Willis's will is among the missing records, it is unknown if or how he was related to Crabb, why Crabb was his executor, or if he left heirs. The loss of those records is very unfortunate because John was the correct age to have been the father of our John Willis Sr. and several clues suggest that he probably was. Without documented proof, however, any such assumption must be based on circumstantial evidence.

---

[20]Ibid., p. 66.

[21]Dorman, *Westmoreland County Order Book 1675/6–1688/9*, Part one, pp. 78–79.

[22]Ibid., Part two, p. 14.

[23]Ibid., Part three, p. 4.

John Crabb(e) married Temperance Gerrard Hutt, the widow of Daniel Hutt.[24] Apparently she was the sister of John Washington's second and third wives (Anne and Frances Gerrard, daughters of Thomas Gerrard and both widows when they married Washington).

Daniel Hutt and John Crabb were both early merchants, and an entry was found in the Westmoreland County Orders dated 26 May 1687 which suggests that perhaps John Willis who died in 1682 was also a merchant.

> *Lewis Markham, attorney of Richard Gotley, vs. John Crabb. The plaintiff demanding 6000 pounds of tobacco due by bond and the defendant (Crabb) producing a letter from Gotley whereby Gotley hath ordered the said tobacco to John Wills [Willis], the Court dismis [sic] the cause.*[25]

Richard Gotley was a merchant in Bristol, England, and one of the executors of the 1684 will of Thomas Pope Sr. (eldest son of Nathaniel Pope Sr. and uncle of Nathaniel Pope alias Bridges).[26] This entry implies that prior to his death John Willis had placed an order for goods with Gotley or Pope (who was also a merchant and died in 1685) and that Willis died in 1682 before receiving or paying for the goods.

In *Marriages of Richmond County* George H. S. King states that in 1663 Thomas Pope married Jane (rendered Joanna in some records) Dowle alias Gatly [Gotley] in Bristol. These entries suggest that the John Willis who died in 1682 had some type of business relationship with Pope and Gotley, both merchants who lived in St. Philip & Jacob Parish in Bristol, England. Willis and Crabb may have been partners which would explain Crabb's being Willis's executor.

Another intriguing entry was found in the Westmoreland County Orders dated 10 January 1682/83 when "John Crabb complains that Wm. Wells [Willis?] did oblige himself to work on his plantation which he () and praying the order of this Court against Wells and obligation past by Wells to Crabb, and Wells pleading that he was forced to pass the obligation but desiring time to prove the same, the Court refer the cause till the next Court."[27] On 28 February 1682/83 (probably the next session of Court) Joseph Beale confessed judgment to John Crabb, attorney of William Wills [sic], for 500 pounds of tobacco.[28] I believe that this William Wells/Wills/Willis may have been a son of John who died in 1682 and a brother to John Willis Sr. of

---

[24] Ibid., p. 321; For additional information see Dorman, *Westmoreland County Deeds, Patents, etc., 1665–1677*, Part three, pp. 3, 9, 52, and 57; and Dorman, *Westmoreland County Order Book 1690-1698*, Part two, p. 30. It should be noted that Eaton's statement on p. 22 of *Historical Atlas of Westmoreland County, Virginia*, that John Waugh married Temperance Gerrard is incorrect. Eaton may have meant that John Waugh, clerk, *officiated* at the wedding of Mrs. Temperance Crabb and Benjamin Blanchflower in 1692. Eaton later says (p. 36) that John Crabb married Temperance Gerrard, the daughter of Thomas Gerrard, as the widow of Daniel Hutt.

[25] Dorman, *Westmoreland County Order Book 1688/9–1689*, Part three, pp. 67-68.

[26] See Withington and Chapter XII.

[27] Dorman, *Westmoreland County Order Book 1675/6–1688/9*, Part three, p. 13.

[28] Ibid., p. 17.

Richmond County. These Westmoreland County Orders imply that William had promised or contracted with Crabb to work on Crabb's plantation (in what capacity is unknown) and had changed his mind for some reason, causing Crabb to sue for breach of contract.

Crabb was deceased by 25 February 1690/91 when James Hardwick was appointed surveyor of the highways in Copley [Cople] Parish where Crabb had served.[29] Crabb's will, which is among the missing records, was proved in Court on 24 June 1691 by Capt. Wm. Hardidge, one of the trustees.[30] Consequently, both John Willis's will and John Crabb's will are not available to researchers which makes existing deeds and County Orders very important in determining what relationship there was between the two men.

Temperance then married Benjamin Blanchflower, and the Westmoreland County records show that litigation and settlement of Crabb's estate spanned several years.[31] The Blanchflowers lived in Cople Parish, and in 1695 Benjamin Blachflower and Charles Smith (very likely the same man who bought the above Willis tract from Foxhall) witnessed a deed from William Smith to William Carr.[32] Temperance (Gerrard Hutt Crabbe Blanchflower) died in Westmoreland County in 1711–1712.[33] Maj. Francis Wright, who married Ann Washington and later sold land inherited from her father John Washington in Richmond County, also lived in Cople Parish. The Crabb family connects in some way to the William Willis who married Bridgett (Robinson?) in records which are discussed below.

Other deeds were found which may be important in connecting these early Westmoreland people with those later named in Old Rappahannock and Richmond County documents. In particular are the records regarding the 1690/91 Willis–Parson grant. As given in Chapter III in 1696 Thomas Crane sued John Willis Jr. and Walter Anderson over their claim to a tract in Richmond County which Crane alleged had been patented by Phillip Brown. Brown defaulted, and the tract was then granted to Randolph Kirke and John Fryer of Westmoreland County in 1680. Kirke died, and the land became Fryer's by right of survivorship. Frye and his wife Rosamond sold the land (125 acres) to Crane in 1689,[34] and Crane received a certificate from the County Clerk in 1694. There seems to be only one man named John Fryer in the records, and he may be the same person who was listed as a headright on George Read(e)'s patent in 1650 with John Willis, the same man mentioned by John Washington in his 1777 will, and the man who sold to Crane in 1689.

---

[29]Dorman, *Westmoreland County Order Book 1690–1698*, Part one, p. 53.

[30]Ibid., p. 37.

[31]See Dorman, *Westmoreland County Order Book 1690–1698*, Part three, pp. 23–24, and other entries which show that Robert Carter and Henry Rosse, Gent., were trustees of the estate of John Crabb.

[32]Dorman, *Westmoreland County Deeds & Wills No. 2*, p. 20.

[33]Dorman, *Westmoreland County Deeds & Wills No. 5*, 1712–1716, p. 22.

[34]Sparacio, *Deed Abstracts of (Old) Rappahannock County, Virginia, 1688–1692*, p. 55.

A deed was found in Westmoreland County involving Henry Kerke/Kirk, John Fryer, and John Foxhall. The following is an abstract of the deed as taken from the original document.

> *Know all men by these presents that I Henry Kerke for a valuable consideration to me in hand paid ... have bargained ... and sold to Jno. Fryer of Rappa. one hundred acres of land which I bought of Rand. Kirke bounding upon Jno. Spencer [given as Carpenter by Dorman] ... and my wife will acknowledge same unto Jno. Fryer at the next court held at Nominy ... witness my hand and seal this 8th of March 1674 [1675]. Signed: Henry Kerke. Wit. Jno. Foxhall, John (Paine?)*
>
> *28 April 75 this sale of land acknowledged in Ct by Hen. Kerke & his wife and Jno. Fryer.*
>
> *Mr. Jno. Fryer does hereby authorize & appoint good friend Mr. Jno. Foxhall lawful attorney for me (to acknowledge), etc. Signed: Jno. Fryer (mark). Wit. Jno. (mark) Paine*
>
> *28 April 75 recorded.*

Since one of the first entries found for John Willis Sr. in Old Rappahannock County was his appointment as surveyor of roads from Foxhall's Mill to Keyes Swamp in 1687, these documents may be important in connecting him to the John Willis who died in Westmoreland County in 1682.

To summarize the Westmoreland County records for John Willis #1, he was probably born by 1617 and died in 1682. He lived on Cos Cos, a branch of Herring Creek, bought land from Andrew Read, and sold half of it to Henry Kirk(e) and half of it to Phillip White. This John's will is among the missing records, but his executor was John Crabb(e) who died in 1691. While the dates for this John and other clues strongly suggest a relationship to John Willis Sr. of Old Rappahannock and Richmond counties, no proofs were found and such a claim would have to be based upon circumstantial evidence. While that type of evidence is acceptable, it should be used with care. If incorrect, the validity of subsequent conclusions becomes questionable. It is hoped that eventually those missing wills and deeds will be found so that the problem can be resolved.

William Willis (#2)

At least two different men by the name of William Willis were found in the Westmoreland records between 1712 and 1720 and had to be sorted according to dates, the names of their wives, and other men who were mentioned in the documents with them as indicators of the area where they lived.

The first William Willis appears to have lived in the Popes Creek area in Washington Parish. His name was found in the County Order Book on 25 June 1712 when Mary Willis, relict of William Offile, made oath that William Offile departed without making a will.[35] On the petition of William Willis and said Mary, his wife, a certificate was granted to them for obtaining letters of administration. Nathaniel Pope, Gent., and Charles Smith were their securities. The appraisers (John Higdon/Higden, John Steele, Charles Goddard, and Christopher Butler) were sworn in by Joseph Bayly. Offile's inventory was returned on 27 August 1712 by William and Mary Willis.[36] I suspect that this was the same Charles Smith who bought land from John Foxhall in 1697 and sold it to Asbury in 1697/98 and the same person who died testate in 1714 naming Nathaniel Pope and Joseph Bayly as trustees of his estate.[37]

On 2 May 1713 William Willis, John Parsons, and others served on a jury before Joseph Bayly, Gentleman, to determine the cause of death of a man found in Pope's Creek. This John Parsons was deceased by 1715 when an inventory of his estate was returned to Joseph Bayly in Court by Nathaniel Washington, Anthony Baxter, John Higdon/Higden, and James Creed.[38] This probably was John Parsons Jr. whose father received the 1690/91 grant with John Willis Sr. in Old Rappahannock County.

On 1 June 1716 the County Orders reported that John Bagge (the clergyman?) brought suit against William Willis for 1,536 pounds of tobacco due by bill.[39] The defendant failed to appear, and it was ordered that his security, Nathaniel Pope, pay. The Orders do not indicate what the suit was about, although it may have been for William's tithables for the church glebe. The fact that Pope was his security suggests a connection between the two men. Nathaniel Pope married Jane Brown and was a neighboring landholder to John Willis Sr. (see Chapter IV). Nathaniel Pope (alias Bridges) was also the nephew of Jane (or Joanna) Gotley Pope, widow of Thomas Pope of Bristol, England.

Jane Brown Pope had a sister named Mary who would have been the correct age to have married William Offile and William Willis. As given in Chapter IV, John Bagge married Mary Foxhall who was the sister of John Foxhall Jr. and the widow of Robert Vaulx, Alexander Gorge, Edward Duddleston, and Caleb Butler. Jane Butler, daughter of Caleb Butler and Mary Foxhall, was the first wife of Augustine Washington, father of the President.

In January 1716/17 the Court ordered Benjamin Berryman, sheriff, to attach John Jett to answer William Willis's plea, and the sheriff returned *cepi corpus*. A conditional order was then passed against Jett's security, John Cooper.[40] In 1717 the Court ordered the sheriff to summon Charles Locker to answer Wm. Willis on a plea of debt. Again the defendant failed to appear and conditional order was passed against his security, Wantsford Arrington.[41]

---

[35] Dorman, *Westmoreland County Order Book 1705–1721*, Part four, p. 34.

[36] Dorman, *Westmoreland County Deeds & Wills No. 5, 1712–1716*, p. 11.

[37] Ibid., pp. 65–66.

[38] Ibid., p. 117.

[39] Dorman, *Westmoreland County Order Book 1705–1721*, Part six, p. 32.

[40] Ibid., Part seven, p. 72.

[41] Ibid., pp. 17-18 and p. 32.

William Willis, Charles Lohier [sic] Wansford Arrington, Daniel Higdon/Higden, James Creed, Isaac Whitliff (Wickliffe?), and others were on a jury before Nathaniel Pope on 10 February 1718/19 to determine the cause of death of John Seamour who died on the road near Augustine Washington's plantation in Washington Parish. In August 1719 William and many of the same men were on another coroner's jury before Nathaniel Pope to rule on the cause of death of a Joseph Baker who was killed by lightning.[42] Washington Parish in Westmoreland County abutted Hanover Parish in Richmond/King George County.

Other entries were found in the County Orders for this William Willis until 31 August 1720 when an inventory of his estate was presented by his widow Mary and the appraisers R. V. Vaulx, Mark Cullum (a relative of Nathaniel Pope's wife), and John Gammon.[43] In Chapter IV it is noted that Nathaniel Pope died by 17 March 1719/20 when his inventory was presented in Court by Robert Vaulx, Augustine Washington (who married Jane Butler), and John Elliot.

I have identified this William Willis as the husband of Mary, the widow Offile, on the basis of the names of his appraisers and probably area of residence given in other clues in the records. The probability of some type of relationship between this William and John Willis Sr. seems extremely high. Although he could not have been John Sr.'s son William who died intestate in 1716, the time frame would be appropriate for William being a younger brother, a cousin, or a nephew of John Sr. He could also have been the William who with Nathaniel Pope witnessed John Willis Sr.'s deed to his son John Jr. in 1694.

William Willis (#3) and John Willis (#4)

While the above William lived in Washington Parish, the second unidentified William Willis (#3) lived in Cople Parish in the Yeocomoco Neck area of lower Westmoreland County. His name was found in County Orders on 24 February 1713/14 when Bridgett Willis, relict of William Willis, made oath that he departed without making a will and obtained letters of administration with Stephen Selfe and William Garland as her securities.[44] The Court ordered that James Johnson, Thomas Newton, Henry Netherton, and Richard Hopwood appraise the estate with the appraisers being sworn before Col. Allerton. William's estate inventory, which totaled 30,400 pounds of tobacco, was returned on 31 March 1714.[45]

Bridgett Willis was deceased by 27 March 1717 when Henry Lee made an oath at the County Court that Bridgett Willis, John Willis (another unknown, but possibly a son), and William Willis departed this life without making any will.[46] Letters of administration for their estates was granted to Lee with George Eskridge as his

---

[42] Dorman, *Westmoreland County Deeds & Wills No. 6, 1716–1720*, pp. 74 and 87.

[43] Westmoreland County Deeds & Wills 7:50.

[44] Dorman, *Westmoreland County Order Book 1705–1721*, Part five, p. 21.

[45] Dorman, *Westmoreland County Deeds & Wills No. 5*, p. 62.

[46] Dorman, *Westmoreland County Order Book 1705–1721*, Part six, p. 74.

security. Daniel Tebbs, Thomas Newton, William Wigginton, and Osman Crabb were ordered to appraise the estate; an inventory was taken and returned the following month.[47] Perhaps the above John Willis was "John Willee," who was deceased by 1 June 1699 and identified as the later overseer to Gawin Corbin, Gent.[48]

The most obvious clue here is the name of Osman Crabb. Osman, the son of John Crabb(e) and Temperance (Gerrard Hutt) died in Westmoreland County in 1719. Daniel Tebbs was one of the appraisers of his estate.[49]

William and Bridgett Willis may have been the same people who are named in the Christ Church Parish Register in Middlesex County.[50]

William Willis and Bridgett Robinson m. 23 June 1685
Isabella Willis, daughter of Wm. & Bridgett Willis, bap. 21 March 1685 [1686]
William Willis, son of William and Bridgett Willis, bap. 4 January 1693 [1694]

Although Maud Potter in *The Willises of Virginia* (1964) claimed that this William was a brother to John Willis Sr. who died in 1715 and to Thomas Willis who had a wife Mary in Middlesex County, I have been unable to find proofs for those assumptions. Many records were found in Middlesex County for Thomas Willis's descendants and a few were found for a William Willis, but they will not be included here because the findings are still inconclusive at this point.

The John Willis who was mentioned in Lee's petition in 1717 in Westmoreland County could not have been the John Willis who died in 1682 in Westmoreland or John Willis Sr. who died in 1715 in Richmond. It appears that the three intestate estates—William's, Bridgett's, and John's—were intermingled and that the three people were closely related. No other record was found for this John in Westmoreland, so he may have died elsewhere.

William Willis (#5)

A third William Willis was found in Essex County Deeds & Wills (Book 14:23) when William Willis of Westmoreland and Mary his wife and daughter and heir apparent of Thomas Kirk, deceased, deeded a tract in Essex County to Charles Brown in January 1711/12.[51] The tract was part of a patent to James Coghill on 24 March 1664/65 and was assigned by Coghill to Thomas Kirk, Mary's father. Witnesses on the deed in 1711/12 were Arthur Gowers and Richard Good. From these records it is not possible to determine if this Mary was the same as the Mary Offile, widow of William Offile,

---

[47] Dorman, *Westmoreland County Deeds & Wills No. 6*, p. 25.

[48] Dorman, *Westmoreland County Order Book 1698–1705*, Part one, p. 52.

[49] Ibid., p. 94, and Dorman, *Westmoreland County Deeds & Wills No. 6*, p. 50.

[50] *The Parish Register of Christ Church, Middlesex County, Va., from 1653 to 1812* (National Society of the Colonial Dames of America: Southern Historical Press, 1988), pp. 23, 30, 52.

[51] Beverly Fleet, *Virginia Colonial Abstracts*, vol. VIII, Essex County Wills & Deeds 1711–1714, p. 10.

but they appear to be different people. Neither is it known if Thomas Kirk(e) was related to Henry Kirk of Westmoreland County or how this entry might connect to John Willis Jr. and his wife Mary Coghill who was James Coghill's daughter. A prior connection between these families is certainly possible.

In summary, there were at least two and probably three men named William Willis who could not have been our William who died intestate in Richmond County in 1716. One lived in Washington Parish, married Mary (Brown?) as the widow of William Offile; this William Willis died in 1720 in Westmoreland County. Another William Willis was married to Bridgett (Robinson?), lived in Cople Parish, Westmoreland County, and died in 1717; they may have had a son named John who also was deceased by 1717. The third William Willis was married to Mary, the daughter of Thomas Kirke, in 1712; no estate records were found for him, and the records suggest that he was still living after 1720. Various other references in the County Court Orders for men named William Willis were too vague to be of help.

Thomas Willis (#6)

Three entries were found in Westmoreland and Old Rappahannock counties for a Thomas Willis between 1669 and 1674 although they may have referred to two different men. Thomas was mentioned in 1669 in Westmoreland County on a coroner's jury with Thomas Pope, Edmund Goddard, and others before John Washington, Justice.[52] In 1674 a Thomas Willis witnessed two documents in Old Rappahannock County.[53] The first was a Power of Attorney from Cuthbert Potter to John Appleton and was witnessed by Richard Robinson. Cuthbert Potter's name appears frequently in the Middlesex County records. The second was a deed from Samuel Ward to Nicholas Coplin, both of Rappahannock County, for 145 acres which was patented by David Faulkner in 1670 and purchased by Ward.[54]

In 1710/11 Johanna Pope of Bristol, England, widow of Thomas Pope who died in 1685 (the brother of Ann Pope Washington and uncle of Nathaniel Pope alias Bridges), gave her Power of Attorney to Thomas Wills (perhaps Willis) of Bristol, merchant, and Nathaniel Pope of Pope's Creek in Virginia to recover debts and to sell a plantation called "Cliffs" in Westmoreland County on the Potomac River and all of her land and stock.[55] The document was recorded in Essex County. I do not know how this relates to the other data, but it is included here as an informational item, especially as the Popes were merchants, John Willis of Cos Cos Creek seems to have been a merchant, and both John Willis Sr. (d. 1715) and William Willis (#2 above) were found in the records with Nathaniel Pope.

Finally, a few brief notes will be offered regarding three men by the name of Richard Willis because the records are confusing. The Middlesex County *Christ Church*

---

[52] Dorman, *Westmoreland County Deeds, Patents, etc., 1665–1677*, Part one, p. 52.

[53] Sparacio, *(Old) Rappahannock Deed Book 1656–1664*, Part II, p. 61.

[54] Sparacio, *(Old) Rappahannock County Deed Book 1672–1676*, Part II, p. 35.

[55] See Chapter XII for the wills of Thomas Pope and his son John Pope of Bristol, England.

Register states that Richard Willis, son of Thomas and Mary Willis, was born in 1656. In 1688 his brother John, who apparently died as a single man, wrote his will naming his sister Eleanor (Alden/Adkin) and others. Richard Willis, his brother, was executor and was granted probate on 3 July 1688.

Published histories claim that a Richard Willis was the first husband of Betty Landon who married secondly in 1702 Robert Carter (1663–1732) who owned land in Westmoreland County. Based upon the records, the Richard Willis who married Betty Landon does not appear to have been the son of Thomas and Mary Willis.

Another Richard Willis was identified in the Rappahannock County records as "Richard Willis of Willis Landing in Middlesex County." An Order Book entry in Rappahannock County dated 1691 states that a Richard Willis married the executrix (not the *widow* as reported in Withington) of Richard Bray. Withington[56] stated that Richard Bray was the uncle of Edward Bray of Bray's Wharf who sold his Leedstown property to John King of Bristol, England, in 1699.[57]

I have reviewed many of the early Middlesex County records for the Willis, Jenkinson, Vallott, and Towles families. Those records will not be discussed here except to say that connections are circuitous and inconclusive, although perhaps important to future researchers. It time permits, the results of that research will be compiled at a later date. At this point it seems that there were at least two, and perhaps three, different men named Richard Willis, but none of them has been proved as being related to John Willis Sr. who died in 1715 in Richmond County.

In conclusion, existing Westmoreland County records suggest a connection between John Willis who died there in 1682, William Willis who died there in 1720, and John Willis Sr. who died in Richmond County in 1715 because of the overlapping references to the Crabb, Foxhall, and Pope families. The abundance of clues indicates that the records should be examined more closely, especially for John Willis who died in 1682 and his executor, John Crabb(e).

It is very unfortunate that the Westmoreland County wills during that period have been lost because, based upon circumstantial evidences, I believe there is a good likelihood that John Willis Sr. who died in 1715 was the son of John Willis who died in 1682 in Westmoreland County. It may be that the answer could be found hidden in the fine print of a later deed and unindexed.

When John Willis Sr. received his 1669 patent, the document inferred that either the land was located in Westmoreland County (which was not the case as shown above) or that he was a resident of Westmoreland. Other records indicate that prior to the 1680s John Willis Sr. was more closely allied to the Mattox Creek families on the north side of the dividing ridge in Westmoreland than he was to the Old Rappahannock group on the south side of the ridge.

---

[56] Withington, op. cit., p. 15.

[57] See Sparacio, *Richmond County Deeds 1695–1701*, pp. 73–74.

Because the exact connection between John Willis who died in 1682 and his executor, John Crabb(e) is unclear, it might be productive to research the records in Bristol and Somerset, England, where Osmond Crabbe wrote his will in 1684 leaving most of his estate to his brother John.[58]

Chapter XI will discuss documents which were found for James Willis who died in 1655 on Yeocomoco Neck in that part of Northumberland County which became Westmoreland County and who may have been related to John Willis (d. 1682) of Westmoreland County.

---

[58]Osmond Crabbe's will is abstracted in Chapter XII.

Chapter XI

Early Records for James Willis (d. 1655) in Northumberland and Westmoreland Counties

In 1645 the Chickacoan Indian District was formed, encompassing a large area with undefined western boundaries. In her article, "Corrections to Published Maps of County Boundaries of the Northern Neck," Merrill Hill Mosher, C.G., stated that Northumberland was the first county on the Northern Neck and the "parent" of Westmoreland County.[1] Northumberland was created from the Chickocoan District in 1645 (or 1648) and included the entire peninsula. In 1651 Lancaster County was formed from that part of Northumberland which was in the Rappahannock watershed and from portions of York County. Two years later Westmoreland County was created from the western part of Northumberland in the Potomac watershed.

Because John Willis Sr.'s 1669 patent implied that either his tract was located in or that he was a resident of Westmoreland County, records in that county were reviewed first. The next logical step was to look at the early Northumberland County records in an attempt to identify the John Willis who died in 1682 in Westmoreland County or other Willises who lived in that locale when it was still part of Northumberland.

My initial research began with Nugent's *Cavaliers and Pioneers,*[2] published abstracts of county records by Beverly Fleet,[3] Ruth and Sam Sparacio,[4] and John Frederick Dorman,[5] and Norris's *Westmoreland County, Virginia 1653–1983.*[6] Selected items were then reviewed from microfilm of the originals through the LDS Family History Center.

While spellings of names and places vary widely in the documents, and although some of the old records have been lost and others are in poor condition, we are very fortunate to have the remaining ones which are almost 350 years old and which give us valuable insights into the lives of the colonists in the 1600s. Not all available sources were reviewed, but those which I did read will be noted within the text below and are included in the bibliography.

---

[1] *Virginia Genealogist,* vol. 37, no. 4 (1994).

[2] Nell Marion Nugent, *Cavaliers and Pioneers. Abstracts of Virginia Land Patents and Grants,* vol. I (Baltimore: Genealogical Publishing Co., 1963); see selected entries below.

[3] Beverly Fleet, *Virginia Colonial Abstracts,* vol. II, Northumberland County Records 1652–1655 with Order Book 2 and Record Book 14 (Baltimore: Genealogical Publishing Co., 1971).

[4] Ruth Sparacio and Sam Sparacio, *Northumberland County Deeds & Orders 1650–1652,* Record Book 1652–1658, and Record Book 1658–1662 (McLean, VA: The Antient Press).

[5] John Frederick Dorman, selected early Westmoreland County abstracts as given here and elsewhere in this manuscript. (Washington, D. C.: author, various dates).

[6] Walter Biscoe Norris, Jr. (Montross, VA, 1983).

Several references were found for a James Willis who was living in Northumberland County by 1650 and perhaps as early as 1648. He died in 1655 on Yeocomoco Neck in what is now Westmoreland County and was survived by his widow, Rachel(I), who then married Thomas Phillpot(t). James and Rachel Willis appear to have been related to the family of immigrant John Earle, so a few of his records were also reviewed. Rachel Willis was named as a headright on one of John Earle's patents, and James Willis's land joined Earle's land. It is said that the Earles, like the Popes and others, came to the Northern Neck with the Kent Island group which fled to Virginia during the 1640s.

Documents for James Willis will be given in chronological order beginning with the "First Northumberland Index 1648–1652."[7] The original book to which the index referred has not been found, but it is presumed to have been an index for an Order Book beginning 20 January 1648/49. The only Willis on the list was a Ja. (James?) Willis. While no Washingtons were given, other names included John Earle, William Freake, Thomas Garrard (Gerrard), John Hollis (Hallowes), Hany (or Haney), Nathaniel Pope, William Presley, and Phillip Silvester.

A copy of the original Parliament Oath of Allegiance in 1652, which was required by Cromwell's government, contained James Willis's name next to the names of Edw. Hudson, Hen. Barnes (or Barnet), Tho. Sheapard, Hen. Mosley, Luke Dyne, Rob. Newman, Rich. Walker, John Ingram, John Hallowes, John Rosier, etc. John Earle, William Vincent, and John Waddy were also on the list.[8] Early patents for these people in Nugent's *Cavaliers and Pioneers* and the Virginia Land Patent Books are too numerous to include here, but those which seem to be the most significant to our research are noted at the end of the chapter.

One problem was obvious from the first land records which were found for James Willis when a patent to John Hany stated that James owned a tract on Dividing Creek in 1650/51.

> *John Hany 950 acs. Northumberland Co., 30 Jan. 1650 [1651], p. 281. Upon the N. side of the Dividing Cr., abutting Wly [westerly] thereon, continued with a swamp at the head of land of George Waterman & James Willis. Note: the uppermost 500 acs. of this patent lying next to the High Ponds is relinquished by the said John Hany as appeareth from under his hand the 23 Aug. 1651 & the said rights to make good another patent for the said Hany. Test: R. Huberd.[9]*

It is not known when or how James Willis acquired this tract, how large it was, or exactly where it was located. At first I assumed that it referred to the Dividing Creek on Chesapeake Bay at the eastern end of Northumberland County. However, James

[7] Ibid., pp. 4–9.

[8] Ibid., pp. 12–13 and Sparacio, *Northumberland County Deeds & Orders 1650–1652*, pp. 46–47.

[9] Nugent, op. cit., I:207.

seems to have been living on Yeocomoco Neck with the same group of men from 1650/51 until his death in 1655, so I suspect that there may have been another creek with that name.

The patent books show that James Willis's other neighbors included William Vincent and John Waddy.

> *William Vincent, 640 acs. Northumberland Co., 3 Apr. 1651, p. 303. Upon the N. side of Dividing Cr., abutting Ely. [easterly] upon the Bay, S. upon sd. Cr. & Wly. [westerly] upon a small Cr. which towards the head divideth itself into two branches & divides this & the land of James Willis, and Nly [northerly] upon the land of John Waddy.[10]*

According to Fleet's transcription of Record Book #14, Vincent assigned this patent to John Ingram on 27 September 1651. It was witnessed by Peter Knight and John Dennis and recorded on 20 September 1653.[11] This was followed by an agreement between Vincent and Ingram with Vincent assigning one-half "of a patent lying on Dividing Creek in Fleets bay" with Vincent to have the neck where he was seated and Ingram to have Cockorowes(?) Neck, the balance to be equally divided. The agreement was dated 16 July 1651, witnessed by W. Clairborne and David Spiller, and recorded on 20 September 1652. Early maps show an Ingram's Bay on the eastern shore of Northumberland County which may or may not have been related to this patent.

James Willis and George Waterman still owned adjoining tracts in 1652 when John Haney renewed a patent for 500 acres (probably Hany's other patent which he reserved rights for in 1650/51). However, George Waterman and *John* Willis, rather than James Willis, are given as Peter Ranson's neighbors on Dividing Creek in Ranson's 1656 patent, by which time James Willis had died.[12]

William Vincent had died by 1660 when his widow, Elizabeth, of London, England, wrote her will stating that her legacy from her deceased husband was still in the hands of Thomas Edmunds of Virginia.[13]

In 1651 John Ingram and Richard Flint (Flynt) received a patent of 406 acres in Northumberland County on Dividing Creek adjoining William Vincent and John Waddy.[14] Vincent, Willis, Waddy, Ingram, and Flynt all signed the 1652 Loyalty Oath, and Richard Flynt's name appeared in other records as a resident of Yeocomoco Neck.

---

[10]Ibid., 1:210. Sparacio and Fleet both give this tract as 600 acres. See Sparacio, *Northumberland County Record Book 1652–1658*, p. 92, and Fleet, *Virginia Colonial Abstracts*, vol. II, Northumberland County Records 1652–1655, p. 109.

[11]Fleet, op. cit, p. 109.

[12]Nugent, op. cit., 1:336.

[13]Lothrop Withington, *Virginia Gleanings in England* (Baltimore: Genealogical Publishing Co., 1980), pp. 181–182.

[14]Nugent, op. cit., 1:215.

At least two possible answers to the location of Dividing Creek are that (1) James Willis had tracts both on the Bay and on Yeocomoco Neck, or that (2) Dividing Creek was an older name of another creek upstream in the Potomac watershed. A third possibility—that there were two different men by the name of James Willis—has been discounted because of the duplication of names on Yeocomoco. After reviewing the records, I believe that the second alternative is probably the most correct and that Dividing Creak may have been a previous name for the Yeocomoco River which later became the boundary between Westmoreland and Northumberland counties as that is the area where these men were living in 1652.

On 20 July 1650 William Presley, Gentleman, received a patent for 100 acres in Northumberland County butting eastwardly upon the Potomac and southerly upon the land of John Earle for the transportation of two persons.[15] Original records show that a patent was issued to Presley on 29 July 1650. He assigned it to James Willis on 11 February 1650/51. After Willis's death, Thomas Philpott and his wife Rachell (widow of James Willis) assigned it to John Howell.[16]

> *Wm. Berkeley patent to Wm. Presley, Gent., 100 acres in Northumberland abutting easterly upon Potomac River, southerly upon land of John Earle, westerly & northerly upon the main woods, the said land being due the said Wm. Presley by & for the trans. of 2 persons into this Colony whose names are in the records mentioned under this patent; 29 July 1650.*

> *I, Wm. Presley, Gent., do assign over all my right title & interest of the within mentioned patent of land with every part parcel or member of the same unto James Willis his heirs executors admrs or assigns for ever he the said James Willis yielding & paying twelve pence for every fifty acres unto his maties [majesties] or his successors according to the within mentioned patent; in witness whereof I have set my hand this 11th day of Feb. 1650 [1651].*

> *Thomas Philpott assigns to John Howell: I do assign this patent & the land within mentioned unto John Howell or his admrs or assignees for ever with the consent of my wife Rachell Philpott dated 20 January 1656 [1657]; witnesses Samll Smyth, Jno. Haynie. 20 Jan 1656 [1657] this assignment of Thomas Philpott to John Howell was acknowledged.* (Note: This tract escheated and was granted to Charles Lee in 1713.)

On 15 August 1650 William Presley Sr. wrote his will leaving his lands to sons William and Peter. It was proved in Court on 20 January 1656/57. One tract of 100 acres was above the Yeocomoco River between John Earle and Phillip Silvester; another 100 acres were due for his transportation of Anne Gibbert and a Jonathan Persons [sic]. His bequests included certain articles of clothing and a cloak "after Henry Rocke and James Willis is [sic] paid for his cloth either in porke or corne."[17]

---

[15]Ibid., I:198.

[16]LDS film #0032638.

[17]Ibid.

Presley's will and Col. John Mottrom's estate accounting below imply that James Willis was a merchant. As there was very little hard currency in the colonies, tobacco, corn, pork, and land certificates were often used to pay bills, fines or judgments, tithes, and for necessities.

Phillip Silvester's name was found in several documents, and he connect to the Phillip Silvester (or Sylvester) whose name appears with the Mattox group in later Westmoreland County records. Silvester died by February 1668/69 leaving a daughter Margaret and placing Daniel Liston [Lisson] in charge of her inheritance. His inventory included a calf which was "about John Willis's." While I first assumed that this was the John who died in 1682 in Westmoreland, other clues now lead me to suspect that it was John Willis Sr. who died in 1715. Either option implies that there might have been a link between James Willis, Phillip Silvester, and other Willises on the Northern Neck. The fact that Silvester owned a calf which was at John Willis's strongly suggests a connection. This possibility is even more credible because of the numerous records found for John Willis Sr. in which Nathaniel Pope als. Bridges was named. Pope seems to have been the grandson of Daniel Lisson (see Chapter IV).

From microfilm which was in extremely poor condition the following entry was found in Northumberland County Orders 1650–1652 (p. 77)[18] and indicates that James Willis received another patent for 50 acres, probably in 1651:

> James Willis   *According to () sufficient proufe made to this Court*
> cert for land   *there is due unto James (hole) Willis fifty acres of land*
>   *for the transportacon of (Jacke Willis) to this Colony.*

James assigned this tract to John Earle who included it in a 1652 patent.[19]

> *To all &c., Whereas &c., Now know ye &c., that I the sd. Richard Bennett Esqr., &c, give & grant unto John Earle two hundred acres of land scituate lyeing and being in ye County of Northumberland abuttinge Easterly upon Potomake River, southerly upon the land of Thomas Hayles, westerly & northerly upon ye maine woods, the sd. two hundred acres of land one hundred & fifty acres thereof being granted unto him the sd. John Earle for his transportacon of three p:sons into this collony & the other fifty acres as assignment. from James Willis for the transportacon of one p:son; all which names are in the records menconed under this pattent. To have & to hold &c., dated ye 16th of November 1652.*

An entry in Nugent (I:266) indicates that Earle received another patent in November 1652 in which Rachell Willis, wife of James, was listed as a headright.

---

[18] LDS film #0032648; also see Sparacio, *Northumberland County Deeds & Orders 1650–1652*, p. 51.

[19] Record Book 1652–1658, LDS film #0032648; also see Sparacio, *Northumberland County Record Book 1652–1658*, p, 12.

John Earle, 200 ac. Northumberland Co., __ Nov. 1652, p. 134. Ely. upon Potomeck Riv. & Sly. upon land of Thomas Hayles. Trans. of 4 pers: Mary Earle Sr., Mary Earle Junr., Mary Holder, Rachell Willis.

On 19 January 1651/52 James Willis gave Mary Earle the younger a heifer as recorded in Sparacios' Northumberland County Deeds & Orders 1650–1652 and reviewed on microfilm.[20] Original spelling and punctuation have been retained.

Know all men to these presents that I James Willis have given to Mary Earle the younger a Blacke yeareling heifer marked on the right eare with a peece taken out before & a peece taken out beehinde & a peece taken out of the left eare before & goes by the name of Blacke Bess's Calfe wch calfe I James Willis doe give from me my executors assigns or administrators unto Mary Earle her heirs or assignes with all her increase for ever wch calfe I James Willis doe __ from any pson or psons In witnes whereof I havee hereunto set my hand & seale the nineteenth day of January 1651 [1652]. The marke of James Willis. Witness: John Earle, Edward Hudson. 22 Janu: 1651 [1652] recorded this gift.

Other entries which were found for James Willis in 1652 as taken from Fleet's and Sparacios' transcriptions will be noted briefly. An undated entry in Northumberland County Deeds & Orders 1650–1652 shows "Willis, Ja: Cert."[21] It was probably a recording of his certificate for 50 acres. James Willis and Hen. Hailes were shown as witnesses on an assignment of an indenture from Everard Roberts to Rich Holden on 14 May 1652 and recorded on 20 September 1653.[22] An entry dated 25 November 1652 was found in Order Book #2: "— Trussell agt [against] — ames Willis, referred till the next Court in Chancery at Mr. Trussell's motion."[23] This was probably John Trussell and James Willis. Nothing further was found regarding this suit.

In September and November 1652 these entries were found in Order Book #2 and show how valuable nails were in the colonies and the method by which the Court attached a person's estate for unpaid debts.

Whereas Edward Hudson did receive a keg and a bag of nailes of [from] John Waltons wife to be delivered to John Walton the Court doth therefore order that James Willis security for the said Hudson (who has secretly departed this country) shall pay unto the said Walton 350 lbs. tobo. And cask in full satisfaction of the goods aforesaid by the 10th of Novem[ber] next with charges of Court ... and the Court doth further order that the said Willis shall take soe much of the estate of the said Hudsons (if he can find any after John

---

[20] LDS film #0032648; Orders, p. 71; Sparacio, op. cit., p. 42..

[21] Microfilm.

[22] Fleet, op. cit., p. 112 (Record Book #2, p. 34).

[23] Ibid., p. 9 (Order Book #2, p. 5).

Powell is satisfied) as will satisfy the said 350 lb. tobo...; dated 20 September 1652.[24]

Thomas Hailes agt. [against] Edward Hudsons. Whereas it doth appear unto the Court by the deposition of James Willis and by the oath of Thomas Hailes that Edward Hudson doth owe unto the said Hailes 150 lb. of tobo. And that the said Hudson secretly departed this County without satisfying the said ... the Court doth therefore () that the said Hailes ... have an attachment agt. The estate of the said Hudson ... if ever he can find any after John Powell ... for the payment of the said debt with charges of Court. 25 November 1652.[25]

In 1653 and 1654 James Willis witnessed one document and served on three juries according to the Order Book. The jury lists basically confirm the names of James' neighbors whose names are consistent with the other records. The most interesting entry was the following which was dated 13 May 1653 and recorded in Court on 20 March 1653/54 with Willis and Holden noted as witnesses.

Be it knowne unto all men by these presents that I Edward Roberts doe quite [quit] & discharge Henry Hayler from all dues debts & demands & bills that wee was ingaged or bound with to any man as Mr. Jones bill & Mr. Lewis his bill from ye beginning of ye world to this prst. day; as Witness my hand this 13th of May 1653.[26]

In May 1655 James Willis wrote his will which is given below in its entirely as transcribed from the original on microfilm.[27] His will was also transcribed by Sparacio in Northumberland County Record Book 1652–1658 (p. 19).

Will of James Willis, written 25 May 1655, proved 20 January 1655 [1656]: In the name of God Amen I James Willis of Yeocomoco planter being in p(er)fect memory thank be to God though sick and weake in body have made this to be my last will and testament being followeth In that I committ & yield my Soule unto the hande of God __ hopeing and trusting that hee will receive it into his glory Itm [Item] I committ my body to the earth to be decently buried and leaveth unto my loving wife Rachell all my lands and p(er)sonall estate whatsoever It hath pleased God to possess me of excepting one gunn which is at Richard Holdeirs [Holders] the which I give & Bequeath unto Roger Stone & I make my loving wife Rachell sole executrix of this my last will & testament as witness my hand and seale upon Yeocomoco Neck this 25th day of May Anno Dei 1655, the marke of James Willis

---

[24] Ibid, p. 2 (Order Book #2, p. 1).

[25] Ibid., p. 10 (Order Book #2, p. 5); no connection was found between Edward Hudson and the later Hudson family in Richmond/King George County.

[26] Ibid., p. 122 (Record Book #14, p. 45).

[27] LDS Film #0032638.

Witnes Everard Roberts the mark of Luke Dyne Daniell Roberts. 20th January 1655 [1656] This will was proved in open Court by the oathes of Luke Dyne and Daniell Roberts.

Richard Holden (or Holder) was identified as a blacksmith living on Yeocomoco Neck and Potomac River when he gave his land and personal property as collateral on a performance bond to Henry Vincent, planter of York County, to secure "certain commodities bought from him by me."[28]

James Willis was deceased by 19 November 1655 according to a Power of Attorney which was recorded in the County Record Book 1652–1685, page 59 (original spelling and punctuation retained):

> *Know all men by these presents that I George Nott doe hereby authorize nominate & appoint my loveing friend, Anthony Lenton my true & lawfull Atturney for me & in my name as the Adtr. of ye Estate of John Kaye deced., to sue implead or otherwise compound a difference betweene Tho: Philpott, who marryed ye Widd: & Relict of James Willis, deced, & my selfe as Adtr. aforesd. & what my sd. Attur. Shall doe or cause to be done therein it being for & conserning a Cowe due from James Willis deced. Unto the sd. John Kaye, I doe hereby ratifie & confirme as if I my selfe were p:sonally pr:sent; Wittness my hand this 19th Novemb: 1655. Signed: Geo: Nott. Witness: Seth Foster, Rich: Flynt. 20 Novemb: 1655: This Lre. Of Attor: was recorded.[29]*

On the following day George Nott (or Knott) brought action against Thomas Phillpott who had married Rachel Willis, widow of James:

> *George Nott v. Thomas Phillpott. Wee being impannelled upon a jury in a difference depending between George Nott pltf and Thomas Philpott defent concerning a cowe delivered to John Kaye decd from James Willis decd the delivery of the sd cowe being confest by the defdt—and the said Kaye dying before he had performed more than halfe his service all the wages of the sd Kaye considered wee do awarde ... the defendt ... deliver to ... the pltf the cowe the pltf to pay dfdt 170 lb tobo and all charges of court ... 20 November 1655.[30]*

Members of the jury were John Haynie, Ralph Horsley, Abraham Byram, Tho Broughton, Henry Rocke, Will Spycer, Symon Richardson, John Parso [*sic*, perhaps Parson], Edward Coles, Geo Countnell, Robert Such, and Dan Holland.

On 15 May 1658 Martin Cole of Northumberland County and his wife Alice sold 200 (or 290?) acres in that county to Jonathan Jadwyn of Nansamund County. The tract was on Yeocomoco Neck upon the Potomac River between the lands of John Trussel

---

[28]Sparacio, p. 92.

[29]Sparacio, p. 12.

[30]Fleet, op. cit., p. 72 (Order Book #2, p. 36).

on one side and James Willis, deceased, on the other side.[31] In 1660 Jonathan Jadwyn of Rappahannock, Lancaster County, assigned his interest in the tract to Robert Jadwyn; witnesses were Henry Clark and Thomas Web(b).

James Willis is mentioned twice in the estate papers of Col. John Mottrom, deceased. In 1655 an inventory of Mottrom's estate contained various bills and receipts including one to James Willis "p(er) bill & caske," and to George Knott, Richard Flynt, Thomas Hayles, John Waddy, John Key (Kaye?), Anthony Lenton, Edward Henley, Hugh Lee, John Ingram, Mr. Henry Rocke, Capt. Fleet (*i.e.*, Henry Fleet Sr.), and others.[32] William Presley was one of the overseers of Mottrom's estate.

On 20 July 1658 William Presley (apparently the son of William Sr. who died by 20 January, 1656/57) submitted an accounting for Mottrom's estate which included the following entries:

> To Squire Rocke, to Mr. Henry Vincent "for sayleing ye sloop," to Col. Trussell "for a pair of oares," to Mr. Richard Flynt ... and receipts of Squire Rocke, John Earle, Hugh Lee, Mr. Vincent "for the fraught [freight] of ye sloope," to James Willis [probably a reference to a receipt for the above bill], Anthony Lenton, etc.[33]

The last reference to James Willis was found in Northern Neck Land Grants 1694–1742 by Gertrude E. Gray (p. 64):

> 5–139 James Willis died seized of 100 acres in Westmoreland, formerly Northumberland, granted to William Presley 29 July 1650 and assigned to Willis 11 February 1650 [1651]. Land escheats. George Eskridge presented on behalf of Charles Lee and Mary his wife of Westmoreland County who obtained grant ... on Yeocomocoe Neck, Potomac River, adj. John Earle, 13 September 1713.

This indicates that the tract which Presley assigned to James Willis was probably never seated and was forfeited by escheat. It was likely part of the lands which James willed to his wife, Rachell, and may have been the tract which her second husband, Thomas Philpot, sold to John Howell in 1656/57.

It is noted that after alterations were made in the boundary between Northumberland and Westmoreland counties the Yeocomoco River became the dividing line and Yeocomoco Neck fell into Westmoreland County. Data on this area can be found in Eaton's *Historical Atlas of Westmoreland County, Virginia*, including maps of early patents although it should be used with some caution. Maps 13, 14, and 15 in Eaton show the patents for many of these people and the area which later became part of Cople Parish. Eaton's Map 12 shows the area ten miles or so west of James Willis's

[31]Sparacio, Record Book 1652–1658, p. 123.

[32]Ibid., p. 96.

[33]Sparacio, Record Book 1658–1662, p. 1.

location where John Willis of Westmoreland County lived on Cos Cos, a branch of Herring which was a branch of the Nomony/Nomini River.

James Willis's will does not mention any children, and he left everything to his wife, Rachel, except for a gun which he willed to an unidentified Roger Stone. This would imply that he was not the father of John Willis who died in 1682, although it is possible that James did have children, but chose to leave his land to Rachel instead (as was seen in Chapter IV when William Freake left his estate to his wife Martha when he had a known daughter Ann). When Rachel remarried, her land automatically became Philpott's in the same manner that William Freake's land became Robert Vincent's when Vincent married Martha Freake. If James had died intestate, his land would have fallen automatically to his eldest son (if he had a son), and it might be easier to trace his family. As it is, the closest connection we can find to James and Rachel is John Earle's family and perhaps the "Jack" Willis who was a headright in James' 1651 patent.

If James Willis was not the father of John of Westmoreland County, he could have been related in another way depending upon his age. James may have been a young man when he died, or he could have been a grandfather. The records do not provide any clues.

Capt. Thomas Philpott was deceased by 26 August 1674 when Justinian Gerrard of Maryland sold a tract near Yeocomoco to Robert Gibbs.[34] I found no information regarding Rachel's death.

The William Willis and wife Bridgett who may have moved from Middlesex County to the Yeocomoco Neck by 1713/14 and James Willis may have had a common ancestor, especially as a previously cited record mentions William Willis, John Willis, and Bridgett Willis (see Chapter X). Also it could be significant that the 100 acres which Presley assigned to James Willis escheated and was granted to Charles Lee in 1713, that a Henry Lee petitioned the Court for administration of the estates of William Willis, his wife Bridgett, and John Willis in 1717, and that George Eskridge was involved in both documents. Eskridge, who owned land on the Yeocomoco, was named in other records with Osmond Crabb, son of John Crabb who was the executor of John Willis's will in Westmoreland in 1682.

The Earle family remained in the Yeocomoco Neck. Several unsuccessful attempts were made to learn more about their family. The records show that John Earle Sr. and his son John Earle Jr. were both deceased by May 1666 and were survived by Samuel Earle, son of John Sr.[35]

The general westering pattern of these various families is evident, as well as the many clues which seem to tie them to common groups. What is lacking, of course, is a document which proves a direct relationship.

---

[34]Dorman, *Westmoreland County, Virginia, Deeds, Patents, etc. 1665-1677*, Part three, p. 6.

[35]Dorman, op. cit., Part one, p.20.

Readers will notice that very little emphasis has been placed on names found on immigration lists. The surname "Willis" was fairly common in those lists from the 1640s onward, and accurate identification is problematic unless they can be tied to other documents.

Some of the earliest extant records which confirm the names of neighboring landowners as they settled on the Northern Neck were the land patents. Because I believe that those patents may contain clues which are important in attempting to trace John Willis Sr.'s ancestors, selected patents from Nugent's *Cavaliers and Pioneers* have been briefly abstracted below.

The location for all of the following patents was given as Northumberland County unless otherwise noted. These tracts later fell into Westmoreland County after its creation and adjustments were made to the county lines. Some of the later patents were renewals. The patents given below have been abstracted and briefly summarized. If researchers want more detailed information about these patents, they are referred to Nugent and the original patent books which are available on microfilm.

When a waterway is named (*e.g.*, Potomac, Nomony/Nomini), it often refers to that river's watershed unless specifically given as abutting the river. Names are found with a wide variety of spellings. It is not possible to tell when people named as headrights actually arrived in the colonies from the dates when the patents were issued, and the same names often appear on more than one list.

> 1648 George Read, 2,000 ac., given in Chapter X; headrights include John Willis.
> 1649 William Peirce (Pierce) & Francis Symons, 200 ac. adj. Horsley, John Earle.
> 1650 John Hany, 950 ac. on north side of Dividing Creek adj. land of George Waterman, James Willis.
> 1650 John Hallowes, 1,600 ac.; headrights include several Butlers, Wm. Freake.
> 1650 Wm. Presley, 100 ac. on Potomac adj. John Earle; assigned to James Willis.
> 1650 John Hallowes, 600 ac.; headrights include Richard Willis, Wm. Freake; assigned to John King 1651 who assigned to Wm. Dodman, atty for Heyward, in 1653; assigned to Col. Nathaniel Pope who willed to daughter Ann Pope Washington who repatented in 1661; on Hallowes/Mattox Creek.
> 1650 Thomas Gerrard, 1,000 ac. at mouth of Herring Creek of Potomac River; headrights include several family members including his daughter Temperance Gerrard who married Daniel Hutt, John Crabbe, and Benjamin Blanchflower.
> 1650 George Read, 500 ac., ss Herring Creek adj. Robert Yeo.
> 1651 William Vincent, 640 ac., ns Dividing Creek adj. James Willis, John Waddy.
> 1651 Mrs. Anna Bernard, 1,000 ac. ss Potomac; headrights include several

members of the Ironmonger family.

1651 John Ingram & Richard Flint (Flynt), 406 ac. on Dividing Creek adj. Wm. Vincent, John Waddy.

1652 Mr. Broadhurst, certificate for 100 ac.; headrights included Francis Willis, Patrick Potts. (This certificate was found in Northumberland County Order Book #2).

1652 John Haney, 500 ac. ss Dividing Creek adj. George Waterman, James Willis. (Renewal?)

1652 John Shepperd, 1,000 ac. at head of Jernews Creek adj. John Powell, Nicho. Jernew.

1652 John Earle, 200 ac. on Potomac adj. Thomas Hayles; 4 headrights: Mary Earle Sr., Mary Earle Jr., Mary Holder, Rachel Willis.

1653 Francis Symons, 224 ac. Mattapony River adj. John Chambers, John Earle.

1653 Richard Holden, 600 ac. nw side of Yeocomoco adj. Wm. Walker, Jon. Shakly; assigned to Richard Bennett & Vincent Cook who renewed in 1662.

1653 Thomas Philpot, 100 ac. Yeocomico Neck adj. Wm. Reynolds, Nicholas Jernew.

1653 Francis Symons, 91 ac. branch of Mattapony adj. Thomas Wilsford & land surveyed for John Earle.

1653 John Earle, 1,000 ac. Yeocomoco Riv. adj. Bloyce, Cooper, George Knott.

1653 Thomas Keene, 527 ac. adj. Ralph Horsley, Coppedge, Cherry Point; headrights include John Earle.

1654? Nich. Jernew, 200 ac. ss Potomac adj. Wm. Rennolls, John Earle.

1654 Robert Newman, 650 ac. assigned by John Branch; headrights include John Willis and some of the same people on Richard Gibble's 1656 patent. (Northumberland County Order Book.[36])

1655 William Walker, 839 ac. Yeocomoco Riv. adj. Richard Holden, John Earle, Bloyse.

1656 Peter Ranson, 950 ac. ns Dividing Creek adj. George Waterman, John Willis.

1656 Richard Gible (Gibble), 800 ac. adj. Hull, Souch, Magregor, Robert Newman, Mr. Presley; headrights include several Branches, David Griffin, John Willis (see Newman's patent in 1654).

1658 Richard Flinte (Flynt), 394 ac. on Potomac and little Wiccocomocie Cr.; granted to John Hany in 1654 and assigned by him to Flinte.

1658 John Earle, 1,100 ac. adj. Bloyce, Cooper, Yeocomoco Riv., George Knott, and his own land; renewal of 1653 patent and 100 ac. by patent 1655; renewed 12 Feb 1662 by John Earle, his son.

1658 Wm. Heaberd & John Heaberd, 300 ac.; headrights include Rachell Willis, Jno. Haies [sic].

1662 Robt. Jadwin, 200 ac. adj. Thomas Hayles; John Earle patented in 1652 and assigned to Wm. Thomas who assigned to Jadwin.

---

[36]Fleet, op. cit., p. 56.

1662 Nich. Jernew, 200 ac. ss Potomac adj. Wm. Renolls, land of John Earle; renewal of 1654 patent.

1662 Wm. Peirce (Pierce), 1,200 ac. Nomeny Riv. adj. Lewis Burwell, Odier, Rosier.

1663 Thomas Dios (Dyos), 450 ac. ss Potomac near Nomeny, adj. Daniel Hutt, Wm. Overred.

1664 Daniel Hutt, merchant, 250 ac. on Nomony and Cos Cos Creek, part of 500 ac. formerly George Reeds (Read).

1666 Daniel Hutt, 875 ac. Westmoreland County on Nomenie at mouth of Cos Cos Creek adj. Wm. Robertson, Wm. Overett; renewal of 1662 patent for 850 ac. plus 1 headright.

The last four patents are known to have been in the same area as the land of John Willis who died in 1682 in Westmoreland County and near Col. William Peirce (Pierce) who married Sarah Underwood (see Chapter IV). In 1669 John Willis Sr. received his patent of 261 acres as discussed in Chapters I and II. Circumstantially then, members of the Underwood family lived near a Willis family both on Cos Cos Creek in Westmoreland County and in that part of Old Rappahannock which became Richmond (later King George) County.

Some miscellaneous, possibly related items will be included here. In 1670 John Alexander surveyed 1,177 acres on the branches of Nomony in Westmoreland County for William Pierce and Randolph Kirke adjacent to Mr. Daniel Hutt, Mr. William Loyden, Mr. Rich. Sutten, and the heirs of William Robertson, deceased, on the main branch of Cos Cos. Pierce assigned all of his interest to Randel/Randolph Kirke.[37] I do not know what the relationship was between Randolph Kirke, Andrew Kirk, Henry Kirke, or Thomas Kirk who are named elsewhere in this manuscript.

None of the patents for Francis Willis in Gloucester/York County have been given above, but Francis Symons was included because of possible connections to Francis Willis (see Chapter XII). This Mattapony River/Creek was an earlier name for Machodoc, the first boundary between Northumberland and Westmoreland counties.

Other early patents not cited here are those of Thomas Willis and Robert Middleton of Lancaster County and John Willis and Richard Willis of Middlesex County. The latter two men seem to have been the sons of Thomas Willis who lived in Middlesex County and who was deceased by October 1684. My review of those records did not disclose any relationship between the Thomas Willis family and John Willis Sr.

In summary, the above James Willis was probably born by 1620, making him within the same generation as John Willis who was born *circa* 1617 and died in Westmoreland County in 1682. It is possible that John Willis was *Jacke* Willis for whom James received a headright of fifty acres in 1651, although no proofs were found. James appears to have been a merchant and landowner on Yeocomoco Neck.

---

[37]This may be the same John Alexander whose patent with Robert Alexander and Christopher Lund on Attopin Creek was mentioned in Chapter VII.

James Willis was probably related to John Earle because he executed a deed of gift to Mary Earle "the younger" for a heifer in 1651/52 with Earle as one of the witnesses. In addition, James assigned the fifty acres he received as a headright for *Jacke* Willis to John Earle, and Rachell Willis was named as a headright on Earle's patent in 1652. James died testate in 1655 and was survived by his wife, Rachell, who then married Thomas Phillpott. One hundred acres which James willed to his wife eventually escheated and was granted to Charles and Mary Lee in 1713.

The reader should be aware that not all of the Northumberland or early Westmoreland County records were reviewed. If new evidence is found suggesting a connection between James and John Willis of Westmoreland or between John Willis of Westmoreland and John Willis Sr. of Old Rappahannock and Richmond counties, these records should be revisited.

Chapter XII

Francis Willis (d. 1689–1691)

S everal articles have been written about Col. Francis Willis who was Clerk of the Charles River County Court, Justice of York County, and a member of the House of Burgesses for Gloucester County before returning to England in 1675/76 where he died in 1691. Unfortunately, the accounts are often undocumented and incomplete.

Willis family historian George B. Loeffler, now deceased, discounted any connection between John Willis Sr. of Richmond County and either Col. Henry Willis or Col. Francis Willis. When Mr. Loeffler was researching the family, he apparently did not have a complete copy of Francis Willis's will or King George County Will Book A-1. Based upon personal conversations and correspondence with Mr. Loeffler, I also do not believe that was he aware of the other Willis families discussed in Chapters X and XI. I have the greatest respect for Mr. Loeffler's work, but the myriad of clues I found in various sources prompt me not to discount the possibility of a relationship between those families. While no conclusions were reached, the information will be included here because it may be useful to other family researchers.

After working in the early Northumberland and Westmoreland County records, my curiosity about Francis Willis was heightened when I found a complete copy of his will in *Genealogical Gleanings in England*.[1] Because there has been so much speculation regarding this gentleman, I have elected to include it here in its entirety.

Francis Willis of the parish of Ware River, in the County of Gloucester, in Virginia, but now resident in the parish of East Greenwich in the County of Kent, Gentleman, written 6 July 1689, proved 25 April 1691.

My body to be decently buried, my executor not exceeding one hundred pounds sterling at my funeral, in costs & charges. To my loving sister Grace Feilder one hundred & twenty pounds per annum during her life, or until the sum of one hundred & twenty pounds be fully paid, which first shall happen. To Charles Feilder, the son of my sister Grace aforesaid, one hundred pounds sterling (in payments of twenty pounds per annum until the sum of one hundred pounds be fully paid). To my cousin Elizabeth Butler and her daughter Sarah Butts ten pounds sterling apiece. To my cousins Frances and Elizabeth Willis, sisters to Hugh Willis, clerk, deceased, the sum of ten pounds sterling apiece. To Francis & Christopher Willis, the sons of the said Hugh Willis, the sum of twenty pounds sterling apiece. To the widow of Hugh Willis ten pounds sterling. To Susanna Willis, the daughter of my brother

---

[1] Henry Fitz–Gilbert Waters, *Genealogical Gleanings In England*, vol. I (Baltimore: Genealogical Publishing Co., 1969), pp. 239–240. In his notes Waters did not mention John Willis's 1669 patent in Westmoreland (actually Old Rappahannock), his 1690/91 grant in Old Rappahannock, or his 1696/97 grant in Richmond.

Henry Willis, ten pounds sterling. To my cousins John & Joane Lipton one hundred pounds sterling and to her two children, Henry & Mary, one hundred and thirty pounds sterling apiece. To my cousin Mary Herren, the daughter of my brother Henry Willis deceased, the sum of three hundred and fifty pounds sterling. To Alice Willis, daughter of said brother Henry, three hundred & fifty pounds sterling. To my loving cousin Elizabeth Ironmonger one hundred pounds sterling and to her two sons Charles & Matthew Ironmonger one ;hundred pounds sterling apiece. To William Willis, the son of my brother William Willis deceased, one hundred and & fifty pounds sterling. To the poor of the parish of St. Fowles als St. Algate in the city of Oxford, the place of my birth, one hundred pounds sterling. And all my legacies I desire may be paid within eighteen months after my decease.

To my dear & loving wife Jane Willis, the sum of one thousand pounds sterling, to be paid her in the first place, within one year after my decease, and all the household vessels of plate, linen & bedding which she brought over with her from Virginia to England (& other personal estate).

I give unto the said William Willis, the son of my brother William Willis deceased, all that land & plantation which his father formerly lived upon & held of me, with the appurtenances, situate on the south side of Crany Creek, containing one hundred acres or thereabouts, to him & the heirs of his body lawfully begotten or to be begotten, and for want of such heirs then to the right heirs of me the said Francis Willis.

I give & devise unto the said Francis Willis, the son of my brother Henry Willis, all the rest & residue of all my other estate & estates whatsoever in lands, goods, moneys, cattle & chattells that I now at this time stand seized or possessed in Virginia and not herein already devised, also one thousand pounds, to be paid him within eighteen months after my decease.

I ordain & make William Willis, the son of my brother Henry Willis deceased, sole executor of this my will & testament. I give unto Mr. Edward Polter, of the Parish of St. Peters in the East in Oxford city, milliner, and Mr. George Richards of London, merchant, whom I desire & appoint to be overseers etc., the sum of ten pounds sterling apiece.

Wit. Richard Jones, Margaret Nicholson, Joseph Busfield
Vere, 201.

My review will focus on the facts in this will and information whi[.] ^h can be verified in the records. Francis was born in Oxford, England, and maintained ties there as evidenced by his naming of Polter, a milliner living in Oxford, as one of the trustees of his estate.

The date of Francis's birth is unknown, but if he was Clerk of Charles River County, Virginia, in 1640, he must have about the same age as John Willis who died in 1682 in Westmoreland County. To place Francis within the same time frame as other Willises in the Northern Neck who have been discussed above, it is known that James Willis was probably born by 1620 and lived on Yeocomoco Neck in that part of Northumberland which later became Westmoreland County where he died in 1655. John Willis who died in 1682 in Westmoreland County was born *circa* 1617. John Willis Sr. of Rappahannock and Richmond counties was born by 1648, received his first patent in 1669, and died in Richmond County in 1715.

Genealogies of Virginia Families gives some other information about the Willis family, but it might be used with caution because there may have been more than one man named Francis Willis in that area.[2] In 1648 Francis was one of the magistrates of York County. In 1652 he was one of the first two representatives of Gloucester County, and from then until he returned to England, he held a leading position in the colony, being a representative from Gloucester County to the House of Burgesses in 1658–59, as chairman of a committee which revised the laws in 1659–60, and councillor from 1658 to 1675 with the title of "Colonel." The article is in error, however, when it states that Francis left all of his estates in Gloucester County to his nephew Francis Willis (son of Henry), because Francis left 100 acres to his nephew William Willis (son of William).

Many "coincidences" were found in the records. On 11 July 1657 Capt. Francis Willis was present at Quarterly Court in James City regarding orders to counties pertaining to marriages. Others in the group were Samuel Matthews, Esq., and Governor, Col. Wm. Claiborne, Col. Thos. Pettus, Lt. Col. Walker, Mr. Bacon, Col. George Read, and Col. Abraham Wood. Again in 1665 Col. Francis Willis is listed as a member of the Court. As shown in Chapter XI, George Read received a patent in 1648 in Northumberland County, and his headrights included a John Willis. In 1650 Read received a patent for 500 acres on Herring Creek, and in 1664 Daniel Hutt (whose widow married John Crabbe, who was the executor of John Willis's estate in 1682) received a patent of 250 acres on Nomony and Cos Cos Creek which was part of Read's 500 acre patent and very close to this John Willis's land.

One account states that Francis Willis and Walter Gwin were the first delegates from Gloucester County to the House of Burgesses in 1652.[3] In 1694/95 (after Francis's death) there was a suit in Richmond County between David Gwin (who named a William Willis of London as his agent) and John Scott (see below).

According to *William and Mary Quarterly*, Francis Willis, Augustine Warner, and Nicholas Martiau were Justices of York County in 1647.[4] On 25 March 1666 the Governor (with eleven esquires present, including Col. Francis Willis and Col. George

---

[2] Compiled from *William and Mary Quarterly Historical Magazine*, vol. 5 (Baltimore: Genealogical Publishing Co., 1982).

[3] Louise Pequet du Bellet, *Some Prominent Virginia Families* (Baltimore: Genealogical Publishing Co., 1976), p. 269.

[4] 1st series, vol. 24, p. 46.

Reade) ordered that officers be continually assistant to Ned, the Indian.[5] Three years later John Willis Sr. received his patent of 261 acres, and Ned, the Indian (Edmund Gunstocker), was his neighbor for many years (see Chapters III and IV). Ned the Indian received a patent for 150 acres on the north side of the Rappahannock River in 1664, and it was later purchased by Nathaniel Pope from Gunstocker's heirs.[6]

The impact of the Servants' Plot of 1663 against the property of Francis Willis, "one of His Majesty's Councillors of State for the country of Virginia," and Mrs. Catherine Cooke is discussed in *The Virginia Magazine*.[7] The records imply that Francis was a Royalist and a supporter of Gov. William Berkeley. If true, that could have been a major reason for Francis's immigrating when Cromwell came into power.

Returning to Francis Willis's will, no children were mentioned although he may have had children who predeceased him and who did not leave heirs. The maiden name of his present wife, Jane, is unknown, although an earlier (1647) record suggests that either Jane or a prior wife may have been a Simons/Symons (see below).

Although the term *cousin* was commonly used to denote relatives other than brothers and sisters, including nieces and nephews, the will itself contains inconsistencies. Francis mentions several cousins without identifying the cousins' parents. He also named his *cousin* Mary Herren, daughter of his deceased brother Henry, which actually made Mary his (Francis's) niece.

Frequently half-sibling relationships and in-law relationships by marriage were not specified in wills. Many examples were found in the early wills when a half-brother or half-sister, a step-sibling, or a brother-in-law or sister-in-law was called "brother" or "sister." Another anomaly seen in early wills is that testators might refer to married women by their maiden names. Some of the people named in Francis's will may have been related through his wife's family.

His will directly identifies the following people:
1. Wife Jane
2. Sister Grace Feilder and her son Charles Feilder
3. Hugh Willis, clerk (clergyman), deceased (relationship not given)
4. Hugh Willis's sisters Frances and Elizabeth Willis (called cousins)
5. Hugh Willis's widow (unnamed)
6. Hugh Willis's sons Francis and Christopher Willis
7. Brother Henry Willis, deceased
8. Henry Willis's daughter Susannah Willis
9. Henry Willis's daughter Mary Herren (but called cousin)
10. Henry Willis's daughter Alice Willis
11. Henry Willis's son Francis Willis (who received the bulk of Francis's estate in

---

[5] 2nd series, vol. 16, p. 590.

[6] See Chapters II –IV.

[7] Vol. 15, pp. 38–40.

Virginia)[8]
12. Henry Willis's son William Willis (named as sole executor, so probably living in England)
13. Brother William Willis, deceased
14. Brother William's son William Willis (who received a tract of 100 acres on Crany Creek in Virginia, where Francis's deceased brother William had lived)
15. Edward Polter, milliner, living in Oxford (overseer of estate)
16. George Richards, merchant, living in London (overseer of estate)

Added to the above are the following people whose relationships are not clearly established:
17. Cousin Elizabeth Butler and her daughter Sarah Butts
18. Cousins John and Joane Lipton and their children Henry and Mary
19. Cousin Elizabeth Ironmonger and her sons Charles and Matthew Ironmonger

A few previous histories state that Francis's wife may have been Jane Simons [Simmons, Symonds] based upon entries in the early York County records. In March 1646 a suit between Francis Willis, administrator of the estate of Thomas Symonds deceased vs. Thomas Kerby was cited. In 1647 Richard Simons of York County made his will which named his brother Thomas Simons (then deceased), Richard's eldest son Richard (who was living in England), his friend Thomas Curtis of the New Poquoson Parish (York County), and his *brother* Francis Willis. Witnesses were Francis Willis, David Lewis, and John Barwick.[9] The term *brother* could have referred to Richard's wife's brother, another brother-in-law, or a half or step brother. It is noted that in Chapter XI a Francis Symons entered land in 1653 adjoining land surveyed for John Earle. Those records have not been thoroughly reviewed.

An old article on the Willis family in *Genealogies of Virginia Families* states that the above Thomas Curtis had a daughter named Averilla who married Major Robert Bristow of Gloucester County, Virginia, who later became a wealthy merchant in England and member of Parliament (see will of Robert Bristow below).

The records for Grace Feilder and her son Charles Feilder were not searched. The name Feilder, like Feild and Peirce, may have become Fielder.

Previous Willis histories suggest that Hugh Willis (1625–1683) was the son of John Willis, Gentleman, of New College, Oxford. As Francis stated he was born in Oxford, those records might be enlightening. An aside is that Washington family histories claim that Rev. Lawrence Washington (1602–1652), father of the immigrant John Washington, attended Oxford.

---

[8] It is noted that according to this transcription of his will Francis entailed the tract which he left to his nephew William Willis on Crany Creek, but left the rest of his Virginia estate to his nephew Francis Willis in fee simple.

[9] Virginia Meyer and John F. Dorman, *The Virginia Settlers and English Adventurers (Greenville, SC: Southern Historical Press, 1987)*, pp. 1324, 1011; *William and Mary Quarterly*, 3rd series, I:26.

Nothing is known about Francis's brother Henry at this time beyond what is given in Francis's will. We do know that at least one other brother, William, had lived in York County on one of Francis's tracts before his death and that William's son, also named William, was living on the tract in 1689. That tract may be the same as the one described in the following 1666 patent.

Col. Francis Willis, Esq., 100 ac. Gloster Co., 11 July 1666, p. 533 (654). S.W. side of Ware Riv., beg. at Tho. Tracyes corner, by sd. Terryes [sic] trees &c. up the same to Snare Cr. & up the same to the head. Trans. of 2 pers: Jno. Bryant, Wm. Bush.[10]

The 1751 Fry-Jefferson map of Virginia, which was reprinted in *Here Lies Virginia*, shows the Willis holdings in Gloucester County between the Severn and Ware rivers west of Mockjack Bay. Gloucester was created from York County in 1651.[11]

Both Nugent and *Records of Colonial Gloucester County, Virginia* by Polly Cary Mason indicate that an Edward Wills (or Willis) was granted 200 acres on Deep Creek of Ware River in Mockjack Bay in 1652 and that Edward Willis assigned it to Tobias Hansford who renewed the patent in 1662. It is not known if there was a relationship between this Edward Willis and Col. Francis Willis, but the fact that they both owned land on the Ware River suggests a connection.

An earlier patent, first granted to Francis Willis on 3 July 1642, is shown in Patent Book 2:199 (Nugent I:188):

Francis Willis, 450 acs., 29 Jan. 1649 (1650), p. 199. Beg. towards the head of the Eastermost br. of Severne at a point where the br. divides itself into two branches & measuring from the poynt unto marked trees that divides this from land of Richard Burt. Trans. of 9 pers. (names not given).

In 1664 Henry Freeman received a patent for 274 acres which may have been part of Tho. Symmon's estate.

Henry Freeman, 274 acs. at the New Poquoson, 24 Sept. 1664, p. 393 (450). 200 A. beg. at a rownd headed pine on a poynt between two creeks, running S.W. Sly. &c. to a pond in Bryce's nec(k), the E.most bounds being the main Cr. that goeth to Giles Tavenors; 74 ac. the residue bounded Nly. with a Cr. & the S.most bounds is the land patented by Tho. Symmons & 50 ac. granted Robt. Freeman 8 May 1638, both of which parcels are now due by purchase of sd. Freeman from Col. Francis Willis, and 24 ac. for trans. of 1 per. (name not given).

In 1653 a Gyles (Giles) Tavernor sued Hercules Bridges in Northumberland County Court for 950 pounds of tobacco, and the Court ordered that if "Phillip Silvester who

---

[10]Virginia Patent Book 5:553 and Nugent, I:565.

[11]Iver Noel Hume, p. 5.

is security for the said Bridges doe not bring forth the said Bridges to the next term then ordered to pass against the said baile for payment of the debt unto Richard Holden, Attorney of the said Tavernor, with forbearance and Charges of Court, etc."[12] On the same day James Willis served on a jury to hear the Barnes-Ashton case, and again there are references to a man named Phillip Silvester (see Chapter XI).

Old histories of the Willis family in *Some Prominent Virginia Families* and *Genealogies of Virginia Families* claimed that "although direct evidence is missing, Col. Francis Willis's nephew Francis (son of Henry) had two sons—Francis of Gloucester County and Col. Henry Willis of Fredericksburg." However, no proofs were given, and I believe that more research is needed to support this claim.

One source, *English Duplicates of Lost Virginia Records*, identifies a later Francis Willis as Burgess and Justice in Gloucester County in 1717, a Francis Willis as Sheriff and Justice in Gloucester in 1726, and a Henry Willis who was Coroner, Justice, and Burgess in Gloucester County in 1726. However, this same source says that (Col.) Henry Willis was Burgess in Spotsylvania County in 1714, but Spotsylvania was not created until 1720. Deeds which were found in Spotsylvania County suggest that (Col.) Henry Willis was residing in King and Queen County until 1729 when his place of residence was first given as Spotsylvania County.[13] There are so many inconsistencies that some conclusions which were previously accepted as fact may be open to closer scrutiny.

Francis (d. 1691) left 100 acres entailed to his nephew William on Crany Creek. As many of the early Gloucester records are missing, it may be difficult to trace that parcel through the land records even though it was entailed. Some researchers have claimed that Francis's nephew William was the man who married Bridgett Robinson in 1685 at Christ Church in Middlesex County and that he was the son of William (who they say died in 1663). William and Bridgett's marriage is found in the *Christ Church Register*, but I did not find any documentation of his father's death or proof that the William who married Bridgett was in fact his son. However, if it was true, it provides another connection to Westmoreland County because it appears that William and Bridgett moved to Westmoreland County where they both died (see Chapter X).

References to the Robinson family are particularly interesting because of information given in Maximilian Robinson's will in England abstracted below, especially as he names Robert Bristow and mentions a ship called *Avarelia*. The following wills were found in *Virginia Gleanings in England*[14] and *Genealogical Gleanings in England*.[15] They have been abstracted here for brevity with some additional notes found in various records. There seems to have been a link between some of these men and Francis Willis through Mr. George Richards of London, merchant, whom Francis named as

---

[12] Northumberland County Order Book 2:13.

[13] Crozier, op. cit., pp. 103, 106, 108.

[14] Lothrop Withington, *Virginia Gleanings in England* (Baltimore: Genealogical Publishing Co., 1980).

[15] Waters, op. cit.

one of the overseers of his estate.

George Richards of London, weaver, will 1690–1694 (who had previously worked at the custom house in London dealing in tobacco shipments); to be buried by wife in Aldgate Church; to brother Edward Richard's eldest son now at Oxford; to Edward's eldest daughter and her sister Elizabeth and his three other children; to brother-in-law Mr. John Neveyes' two eldest sons John and Edward; to niece Barbara Witall, my sister Barbara Phillpott's daughter, and her children; to the poor of St. Buttolphs, Aldgate; to Capt. Phillip Foster who was my master (at the custom house?); to daughter Sarah Richard when married; to son Phillip.[16]

Edward Creffield Jr., now of London, merchant, will 1694–1694; to friend Mr. Francis Willis now of London, mercer (i.e., one who dealt in merchandise, wares, or textiles); to friend and correspondent Mr. Phillip Richards of London, merchant, he to pay legacies to my daughter-in-law Mrs. Lucy now or late wife of Mr. Thomas Read of Gloucester County, Virginia, a diamond ring which my late wife, mother of said Lucy, used to wear, etc.; to friend Benjamin Clements of Ware, Gloucester County, Virginia, paying legacies to Mr. Phillip Richard(s), etc.[17] According to the notes in this source, Thomas Read of Gloucester County married Lucy, daughter of Edmund Gwyn/Gwin of Gloucester. The author states that therefore Mrs. Gwyn-Creffield [sic] was Lucy Bernard, daughter of William Bernard, Esq., of the Virginia Council who was a younger brother of Sir William Bernard, Bart. This Francis Willis could not, of course, have been Col. Francis Willis who died in 1691, but it may have been his nephew who, like Creffield, had returned from Virginia to London. Middlesex County, Virginia, Order Book 2:90 gives a long list of names in the inventory and appraisal of the estates of Christopher Robinson and Maj. Robert Beverley including Richard Willis, Mr. Edward Creffield, Henry Bray, and others.

Max(imilian) Robinson, late of Rederiffe, mariner, bound for sea, will 1694–1695; mentions part ownership in ship Jeffery and in ship Avarilia; brothers Hennage Robinson and James Robinson; niece Ann Robinson, daughter of James; goddaughter Margaret Bridger, money left in Alderman (Robert?) Bristow's hands until her marriage; to brother James Robinson, Tho. Creeston, Ann Robinson, and Elizabeth Haney, daughters of my late wife and son of my brother John Robinson by his first wife; to Maximilian Haney, son of my wife's daughter, land in King and Queen County which I bought from Mr. Breeding; to nephews William Robinson and James Robinson, tract in Rappahannock River called Southings (Southers) Ferry provided they or he that live to 19 actually go and live on the land; Mr. Henry Awbrey and Mr. John Dean to have custody of estate and ship crops yearly to Mr. Robert Bristow Jr., if living, otherways to Mr. Phillip Richards;

---

[16] Withington, op. cit., pp. 176–177.

[17] Ibid., pp. 310–311.

to Mr. Robert Bristow Jr.; executors Mr. Robert Bristow Jr., and brother Hen. Robinson.[18] Probate Act Book describes the testator as late of ship Avarelia dying on high seas, and the will was allowed in Richmond County, Virginia, by his attorney, Arthur Spicer. Maximilian's nephew William Robinson came to Virginia circa 1695 and settled in Richmond County. The Maximilian Robinson whose name was on the 1737 deeds from John Willis to the Church Wardens of Hanover Parish may have been William Robinson's son. Foxhall-Underwood's Mill was eight miles above Southern's (Southings, Southers) Ferry on the Rappahannock River.

Robert Bristow *(i.e., Sr.) of Gabriel Fenchurch Parish, London, will 1700–1707; mentions his wife, but not by name, and a marriage agreement which she signed on 24 November 1680; lengthy will and many legatees with the primary heirs being his daughter-in-law Catherine Bristow, widow of his son Robert Bristow "lately deceased," and their children (daughters Katherine, Avarilla, Elizabeth, Anne, Frances, Rebecca, and sons William, John, and Robert with Robert to receive his lands and assets in Virginia), all under the age of 21; also mentions a granddaughter Avarilla Madgwick, wife of William Madgwick of London, merchant, and her children; granddaughter Katherine Baily, daughter of Arthur Baily, Esq.*[19] The author notes that the testator was born in 1643 and settled in Virginia about 1669 where he married Avarilla, daughter of Major Thomas Curtis of Gloucester, and purchased several tracts in Lancaster, Gloucester, and Stafford (later Prince William) counties. Two of his patents were in Gloucester County, one on the North River on Mockjack Bay and the other on the Ware River. Bristow returned to England about 1680 and became a merchant. Robert Bristow Jr. was his only son. The notes do not give the maiden name of Catherine (or Katherine, widow of Robert Jr., but she was later involved in litigation in Westmoreland County with a Francis Willis against Lawrence Butler and his wife Margaret over John Bernard's estate. The Bernard family was related to the Ironmongers, but I have not been able to determine if there was a direct connection between them and the Corderoy Ironmonger who married the widow of Abram Field and died in 1675 in Westmoreland County or to the Elizabeth Ironmonger and her sons Charles and Matthew Ironmonger of Francis Willis's will.

Richard Bray, *late of Rappahannock River in Virginia; administration of his estate granted on 20 November 1691 in England to his sister Elianor Danniell,*[20] *for Bray's noncupative will dated 9 April 1690 and proved in Lancaster County, Virginia, that month; to wife Ann (in Virginia); to boy Ned (i.e.,* Edward Bray of Richmond County, nephew and heir of Richard Bray,

[18]Ibid., pp. 358–360. See Robert K. Headley, *Wills of Richmond County, Virginia 1699–1800* (Baltimore: Genealogical Publishing Co., 1983), p. 2. Hennidge Robinson was granted probate in Richmond County in 1695/96..

[19]Withington, op cit., pp. 114–117.

[20]Ibid., p. 15.

deceased, who deeded to John King of Bristol, England, mariner, on 5 June 1699. John King and Company were involved in the iron furnace near present Bristol Mines Run). Old Rappahannock County Orders on 6 August 1691 state that Mr. Richard Willis had married the executrix of Mr. Richard Bray, deceased. Middlesex County Orders of 6 August 1691 also state that Mr. Richard Willis married the executrix of Mr. Richard Bray, deceased, and Middlesex County Orders of 7 July 1690 give "Richard Willis and his wife Elizabeth Willis, exr. of Mr. Richard Bray." So it appears that Richard Bray's widow Ann was not the executor of Bray's estate and that Richard Willis did not marry Bray's widow, but Bray's executor, Elizabeth, whose maiden name is unknown. Also this Elizabeth could not have been Betty Landon, daughter of Thomas Landon, who married first Richard Willis and second Robert Carter in 1700 if, as Carter histories claim, Betty was only 17 years old when she married Carter.)

John Foxhall (i.e., Jr.) of Washington Parish, Westmoreland County, Virginia; will dated 10 February 1697/98, proved 13 August 1704; probated both in Westmoreland County and England as he owned land in England; to Robert Volkes Vaulx] and Sarah Elliott, estate in Warwickshire; to James Volkes [Vaulx] and John Elliot Jr., water mill [Underwood's-Foxhall's Mill]; to Susan Cornock [Cammock] plantation at head of Pope's Creek; to Elizabeth Volkes [Vaulx], plantation in Essex County; to James Volkes [Vaulx], horse and furniture; to Mary Elliott a mare; to Martha Elliott a colt; executor, loving brother [brother-in-law] Caleb Butler.[21] The will of John Foxhall Jr.'s grandfather, William Foxall, [sic] of the borough of Stafford in England (1653–1655) is also given in *Virginia Gleanings in England.*[22] As discussed in Chapter IV, John Foxhall Sr. died testate in Westmoreland County, Virginia, and his will is among the missing wills as is that of John Willis who died in 1682. Robert Valux, Augustine Washington, and John Elliott appraised the estate of Nathaniel Pope (alias Bridges) in Westmoreland County, Virginia, in March 1719/20. The mill which Foxhall left to James Vaulx and John Elliott Jr. was part of a 99-year lease from William Underwood to John Foxhall Sr. in 1670. After John Foxhall Sr.'s death the lease became the property of John Foxhall Jr. In 1721 the balance of the 99-year lease and the mill tract were sold by James Tutt and Richard Tutt (then the leaseholders) and John Underwood (who inherited the land) to John King and Company, Merchants in Bristol and sellers of the Iron Works.

Robert Terrell of London, merchant, will 1677; to cousin William Terrell, etc.; to friend Mr. Robert Vaulx, merchant; to brother Richmond Terrell, etc.; Mr. Robert Vaulx, merchant, to be overseer to assist executor in settling Virginia accounts.[23] The editor's notes state that Robert Vaulx was a

---

[21] Ibid., pp. 170–171.

[22] Ibid., pp. 601–602.

[23] Ibid., pp. 228–230.

prominent merchant of London and Virginia. It is claimed, but not proven as yet, that descendants of this Terrell family married into the Garnett and Willis families in Orange and Culpeper counties in Virginia.

John Pope *of Bristol, mariner, about to go to sea; will 1700/01–1702 [son of Thomas Pope and grandson of Nathaniel Pope Sr.]; to mother Joane Pope of city of Bristol, widow, all that plantation commonly called the Clifts in Westmoreland County, Virginia, etc.*[24] This John Pope was a first cousin to Nathaniel Pope alias Bridges. In 1710/11 Johanna Pope (John's mother) gave her Power of Attorney to Thomas Wills (or Willis) of Bristol, merchant, and Nathaniel Pope of Pope's Creek in Westmoreland County to sell the Clifts tract.

John Pope's father, Thomas Pope, died in 1684–1685. His will, as given by Waters, is found in *Genealogical Gleanings in England.*[25] *Thomas Pope of St. Philip and Jacob Parish, Bristol, merchant, bound on voyage, will 1684–1685; to wife Joanna (who was living in England), sons Charles, Nathaniel, Thomas, Richard, and John Pope who was to have his tract called "Clifts" in Westmoreland County, Virginia; kinsmen William Hardridge, Mr. Lawrence Washington, and Mr. John Washington to be guardians of sons until 21; to daughters Mary, Elizabeth, and Margaret, all under 21; executors Richard Gotley [or Gatley] and Charles Jones the younger, merchants in Bristol.* This Thomas Pope was an uncle to both Nathaniel Pope alias Bridges who witnessed John Willis Sr.'s deeds in Richmond County and to Ann Washington Wright whose son and husband deeded to Francis Thornton. Joanne (or Jane) Pope, wife of Thomas Pope, was Jane Dowle alias Gatly or Gotley.[26] In 1671 Richard Gotley and John Gotley of Bristol witnessed a Power of Attorney from Richard Betterton of Bristol, merchant, to "my well beloved friend Thomas Pope of the same city, merchant," to receive tobacco due from John Watts of Westmoreland County. The following year Pope, as Betterton's attorney, recorded his receipt of 3,225 pounds of tobacco from John Watts for full payment of Watts' account with Betterton. It is noted in Chapter IV that in 1679 John Willis (Sr.) was also paid 450 pounds of tobacco from the estate of John Watts.

Osmond Crabbe, Brislington als Busselton, Somerset, Gent., will 1684–1695; to brother John Crabb now in Virginia, merchant; to sister Adlam, wife of Joseph Adlam, and their daughter Ann Adlam; to brother John all houses in city of Bristol and Parish of Bedminster, Somerset; to sister Alice Vaughan, etc.[27] Osmond's brother, John Crabb(e) was executor of the will of John Willis who died in 1682 in Westmoreland County. John Crabb was living when his brother Osmond wrote his will in 1684, but was deceased

---

[24] Ibid., p. 272.

[25] Waters, op. cit., pp. 392–393.

[26] See Chapter IV and *George H. S. King, Marriages of Richmond County*, p. 166.

[27] Withington, op. cit., pp. 332–333.

in 1691 when John's will was produced in Westmoreland County Court by Capt. Wm. Hardidge—probably the same William Hardidge who presented Thomas Pope's will in Court in 1685. John Crabb married Temperance Gerrard as the widow of Daniel Hutt, another merchant (and the man to whom George Reed sold half of his patent). Temperance Gerrard Hutt Crabb then married Benjamin Blanchflower. Osman Crabb, son of John and nephew of the above Osmond who died in 1695, was one of the appraisers of the estate of Bridgett Willis in Westmoreland County in 1717/18. Osman, son of John and nephew of Osmond, died in Westmoreland County in 1719 (see Chapter X).

These wills exemplify just a few of the records which show vague, undefined, but persistent connections between these families in England and Virginia. There are far too many clues to ignore, and one solid piece of evidence might give researchers enough information to fit the pieces together.

One of the most compelling documents is found in the Westmoreland County Order Book on 25 May 1687 when Lewis Markham, attorney for Richard Gotley, sued John Crabb for 6,000 pounds of tobacco due by bond. Crabb produced a letter from Gotley showing that Gotley had ordered the tobacco to [be sent to] John Willis, and the Court dismissed the case. Based upon preliminary research of the Crabb(e) family, I suspect that he and John Willis who died in 1682 may have been business partners. Another record was found in the Richmond County Orders and suggests that the London based traders, including some of the Willises, were involved in a suit, David Gwin/Gwyn vs. John Scott, on 7 February 1694/95—the same day that John Willis Sr. and Francis Thornton Sr. were ordered to participate in a survey in another suit, Thomas Tippett v. Robert Vincent. Briefly, Gwin was part owner of the ship *Catherine* which sailed from the colonies in 1693 for London at which time Gwin had ordered merchandise from his agent, Mr. William Willis (in London?). Gwin never received his merchandise although William Willis had provided him with a Bill of Lading showing that it had been shipped on Scott's vessel. It seems likely that this William Willis may have been the son of Henry Willis, deceased brother of Col. Francis Willis, and the executor of Francis's will.

On August 1706 in Richmond County John Loyd of Chester, Esq., signed a deed of lease for several large tracts to Micajah Perry of London, merchant, and Francis Willis of London. It was presented at General Court on 18 October 1710 by Mr. John Clayton in behalf of Perry and Willis. John Taliaferro, attorney of John Loyd, acknowledged the deed of lease, and on motion of Daniel McCarty on behalf of Perry and Willis it was recorded.[28] If this Francis was the nephew of Col. Francis Willis who died in 1691, he must have returned to England and may be the same Francis Willis who was mentioned in Edward Creffield Jr.'s will in 1694.

On 27 August 1706 John Loyd sold the above land to Micajah Perry of London, Francis Willis of London, Thomas Meriwether, and John Taliaferro of Rappahannock

---

[28]Richmond County Deed Book 5:289–290.

River in Virginia for 2,000 pounds sterling. For an additional five shillings, Loyd assigned 100 slaves who were being used on the land plus all the livestock, wagons, grains, etc., on the property. Loyd appointed Thomas Meriwether and John Taliaferro his attorneys to acknowledge the deed in Richmond County. An affidavit of witnesses in London was sworn to before A. Spotswood, Chas. Chiswell, and Henry Bowcock, and the deed was recorded on 18 October 1710.[29] This was probably Alexander Spotswood who became Governor of Virginia. Charles Chiswell was active in mining interest in Virginia.

On 3 May 1711 the Richmond County Court took up an action of detinue which was brought by Micajah Perry and Francis Willis of London vs. Griffin Fauntleroy who was in possession of the estate of John Lloyd [*sic*]. Judgment was granted in favor of Perry and Willis, and the Court ordered that Fauntleroy deliver the estate "as well as cattle, slaves, and household furnishings in his custody to the said Perry and Willis and cost was added to the same."[30]

An entry in the Westmoreland County Orders shows that in August of 1713 an action of debt was brought by Francis Willis of London, merchant, and Katherine Bristow, widow of Robert Bristow, Esq., as executor and executrix of the last will and testament of Robert Bristow Jr., late of London, Esq., against Lawrence Butler and his wife Margaret, executrix of the last will and testament of John Bernard late of Westmoreland County. The Court ordered that Andrew Munroe, Joseph Bayly, Richard Watts, and Joseph Weeks meet at Butler's house and inspect, settle, and adjust accounts of the defendants relating to Bernard's estate. In September 1713 Francis Willis and Katherine Bristow were awarded £21.13.0 from Lawrence Butler and wife Margaret from the estate of John Bernard.

On 28 February 1710/11 Johanna (Dowle Gotley) Pope of Bristol, England, widow (*i.e.*, of Thomas Pope Sr. who died in 1685), appointed Thomas Wills (Willis?) of Bristol, merchant, and Nathaniel Pope of Pope's Creek in Westmoreland County as her attorneys to "recover debts and sell the plantation called the Clifts in Westmoreland County with all my lands, stock, etc."[31]

While the above documents do not prove a relationship between John Willis (d. 1682), Francis Willis (d. 1691), and John Willis Sr. (d. 1715), they provide several clues. First, the references in Francis's will to Elizabeth Ironmonger and Elizabeth Butler and their children should be explored to determine if there was any connection between them and Corderoy Ironmonger or the Butler family whose names appear in the records with the Willises on the Northern Neck.

Second, there may be a connection between William Willis and wife Bridgett, Col. Francis Willis, and John Willis who died in 1682 through John Crabb(e), John's executor. If this William was the nephew of Francis Willis, the likelihood of some

[29]Richmond County Deed Book 5:292–296.

[30]Richmond County Order Book 5:268.

[31]Essex County Deed Book 13:425; see Chapter IV.

relationship to this John Willis of Westmoreland County is greatly increased because both William and Bridgett died in Westmoreland. Also the fact that Francis entailed the tract which he willed to William might be helpful in establishing a connection between these men.

Third, I was surprised at the number of merchants or traders whose names overlap in the documents, and the wills in England suggest a business connection between Francis Willis, George Richards, Edward Creffield, and Maximilian Robinson. The records imply that James Willis who died in Westmoreland in 1655 was a merchant. John Willis of Westmoreland may also have been a merchant or employed by Crabb. And the inventory of John Willis Sr. who died in 1715 in Richmond contains numerous items which could have been held for trading.[32]

Although many questions remain, researchers should be aware of these possible connections. Family historians thrive on the possibility that there are documents not previously reported in the literature. Some of the old books are not indexed or are in poor condition. Others, like King George County Will Book A-1, can be missing for many years and then resurface. Because of the loss of early record books in York and Westmoreland counties, the answers to many of these questions may be found only in England.

---

[32]Richmond County Will Book 3:219–222.

Chapter XIII

Col. Henry Willis of Fredericksburg

W illis family historian George B. Loeffler dismissed the probability of a relationship between John Willis Sr. of Richmond County and Col. Henry Willis of Fredericksburg.[1] However, when I began researching the records for John and his family, I quickly became aware of the proximity of the two groups. Although descendants of both men lived in Orange County, the two lines are distinguished from each other there as "the other Willises."

A review of early articles on Henry Willis's family (which are often undocumented) increased by curiosity. As of this writing, I have not found records to either prove or disprove a relationship between Henry Willis and John Willis Sr. Nevertheless, I decided to include some of my notes for researchers who want to pursue this topic. My findings should be prefaced with the fact that I am no authority on the family of Henry Willis. There are many documents which I did not examine. However, I found inconsistencies in the sources I read and, in the end, more questions than answers.

I did not find any verification of Henry Willis's birthdate, but he was probably younger than John Willis Jr., William Willis, and Charles Willis (known sons of John Willis Sr.). Information given below suggests that he was probably born around 1690 (give or take a couple of years). John Willis Sr.'s descendants migrated from King George County to Orange County shortly after Henry's name began appearing in the Spotsylvania County records.

Several factors made analyzing records for these families difficult. John and Henry (and their descendants) owned land in Orange and Culpeper counties at approximately the same time. Both families used the Christian names John and William. (John Willis Sr. and his grandson John Willis, son of William and Sarah, had sons by those names, and Col. Henry Willis reportedly had two sons named John and at least one grandson named William.) Both John Willis (d. 1762) and Henry Willis had sons named Lewis; these two sons named Lewis Willis were involved in the same deed in 1783 in Orange County. Col. Henry Willis married three times with his second and third wives being named Mildred. Descendants of both men later moved to Kentucky, to Wilkes County, Georgia, and to Howard County, Missouri. Finally, there was an identifiable connection between both families and the Washingtons. John Willis Sr's 1669 patent joined John Washington, the President's great-grandfather, and Henry Willis married John Washington's granddaughter as his third wife. Another problem in tracing these families in early Orange County is that very little is known about William Willis (son of William and Sarah, and grandson of John Willis Sr.) or his descendants.

---

[1] Loeffler, George B. "Ancestry of the Willises of Locust Grove," *Journal* of the Willis—Gordon—Garnett & Allied Families, vol. 1, no. 10, 1982 (published privately by the family association).

The complexity of these lines and the problems involved in sorting the several men by the name "John Willis" can be seen in the following known facts:

John Willis Sr. was born *circa* 1648 and died in 1715 in Richmond County.

John Willis Jr., son of John Sr., was born by 1683 and died in 1728 in King George County.

John Willis, son of William and Sarah, was born *circa* 1705 in Richmond/King George County and died in 1762 in Orange County.

John Willis, son of Charles Willis, was born *circa* 1710 in Richmond/King George County and died in 1753 in King George County.

John Willis, the elder son of that name of Henry Willis and his first wife Ann (Alexander Smith?) was born in 1724 and died in 1750 in Orange County.

John Willis, the younger son of that name of Henry Willis and second wife Mildred (Lewis Brown?), was born in 1728 and was living in Culpeper County in 1749, with his date and place of death unknown.

John Willis, son of John who died in 1762 in Orange County, was born *circa* 1743 and died *circa* 1796/97 in Kentucky.

John W. Willis, grandson of Henry and son of Lewis Willis and first wife Mary Champe, was born *circa* 1758 and living in Spotsylvania County in 1789.

An early historian of Henry Willis's family was his grandson Byrd C. (Charles) Willis (1781–1846) who was the son of Lewis Willis (1734–1812) and his second wife. The name "Byrd" is found in both Willis lines, my grandfather being Joseph Byrd Willis, my great-great-grandfather being Byrd Thomas Willis of Kentucky (who was the great-grandson of John who died in 1762), and my first cousin being Keith Byrd Willis of Mineral, Virginia.

Byrd C. Willis's history was primarily about his own immediate family (his parents and siblings). He said very little about his grandfather's ancestry except that Henry was married three times and "courted his three wives when maids and married them all when widows."[2] This statement implies that the families lived near each other when they were growing up. Byrd's information on his grandmother Mildred Washington's family and his mother's Carter family was more lengthy, but it was undocumented (as histories written during that period often were) and contained discrepancies. This is not surprising as Byrd was probably reporting from recollections and family tradition rather than records.

Byrd said that his grandmother was Mildred Washington Gregory. Mildred was the sister of Augustine Washington (1694–1743), the father of the President. Mildred, Augustine, and brother John were the children of Lawrence Washington (1659–1698) and the grandchildren of John Washington the immigrant whose 1664 patent adjoined John Willis Sr.'s 1669 patent.[3] The fact that their patents were contiguous and that

---

[2] du Bellet, *op. cit.,* p. 281.

[3] See Chapters I–III and sketch on the Washington family in Chapter IV.

Henry Willis married a descendant of John Washington prompted me to take another look at the Washington wills which are discussed in Chapter IV and will be briefly summarized below.

Lawrence Washington (c. 1602–1652?) of Oxford, England, and All Saints, Purleigh Parish in Essex, is believed to have been the father of immigrants John Washington (1632–1677) and Lawrence Washington (1635–1677). Washington family historians have reported that Lawrence Sr.'s parents were the Reverend Lawrence Washington (d. 1616 in England) and Margaret Butler.

Washington histories and charts give slightly different data on John Washington's wives, but it appears fairly certain that the three children mentioned in his will (and who were all under twenty-one in 1675) were the issue of John and his wife Ann Pope, daughter of Nathaniel Pope Sr. Some accounts state that Ann was his second wife. Others give John's second wife as Anne Gerrard (daughter of Thomas Gerrard and the widow of Walter Broadhurst and Henry Brett), and his third wife as Frances Gerrard (sister of Anne and the widow of Speke, Peyton, and Appleton). This could be important because Temperance Gerrard (apparently a sister of Anne and Frances) married secondly John Crabb(e) who was the executor of the estate of John Willis in Westmoreland County in 1682 (see Chapter X).

John Washington, the immigrant, of Westmoreland County wrote his will on 21 August 1675 at which time he was married to Anne (Gerrard), and it was proved on 10 January 1677/78 at which time he was married to her sister Frances. His will, as given in *Genealogical Gleanings in England*[4] and by Dorman,[5] is summarized as follows:

> To eldest son Lawrence, seat of land where Henry Flagg lives which I bought of John Watts and Robert Hedges, being by patent 700 acres it being by my father Pope made over to me and my heirs, etc.; water mill and land at head of Rosier's Creek; about 250 acres I bought of Mr. Lewis Marcum [Markham] at the mouth of Rozier's Creek; about 900 acres on upper Machotock which I bought of Anthony Bridges and John Rosier; my ½ share of 5,000 acres taken up by me and Col. Nicholas Spencer, etc.;
>
> To son John, plantation where I now live which I bought of Robert Anderson; and plantation next to Mr. John Foxhall which was Richard Hill's; about 400 acres at head of Rappahannock Creek adjoining David Norway's orphans, the land being formerly John Whetsons and sold to me (by) him and his heirs; about 300 acres where Robert Foster lives; 1,350 acres where Robert Richards lives which I had [bought] of my brother Lawrence, etc.;
>
> To daughter Ann Washington [later the wife of Maj. Francis Wright], about 1,200 acres where Thomas Jordan lives; also about 1,400 acres where John

---

[4] Withington, op. cit., pp. 525–526.

[5] Dorman, *Westmoreland County, Virginia, Deeds, Patents, etc. 1665–1677*, Part four, p. 32.

175

Frier [Fryer] *lives after Mr. Fricke* [William Freake] *has his quantity out of it* [my note—the tract which joined John Willis], *cash, mother's ring, quilt, and curtains, etc., according to her mother's desire;*

One-fourth of personal estate to each child and wife; money I have in England to son Lawrence; to lower church of Washington Parish; to brother Lawrence 4,000 pounds tobacco; to nephew John Washington, my godson and eldest son of my brother Lawrence, a mare, etc.; wife to be guardian of daughter Ann until son Lawrence is of age, then he as guardian. Brother [in-law] Thomas Pope to be guardian of son John Washington until he is twenty-one; brother Thomas Pope to have 10 pounds out of money I have in England; to my sister Martha Washington 10 pounds out of money I have in England and whatsoever else she shall be owing me for transporting her to this country and a years accommodation after her coming in and 4,000 pounds of tobacco, etc.

Executors: brother Lawrence [who also died in 1677], *son Lawrence, and wife Ann*
Witnesses: Capt. John Lord and John Appleton
Proved 11 January 1677 [1678] by Capt. Jno. Lord, Capt. John Appleton being deceased.

John's son Lawrence (1659–1698) married Mildred Warner, daughter of Augustine Warner and Mildred Reade. After Lawrence's death, Mildred Warner Washington married secondly George Gayle and moved to England where she died in 1701. The Washington family contested Gayle's guardianship of Lawrence's children after Mildred's death, and the children were returned to Virginia where accounts suggest they lived with their paternal relatives.

John's son Lawrence Washington wrote his will on 11 March 1697/98 and it was proved on 30 March 1698 in Westmoreland County. Lawrence's will is summarized as follows:[6]

To be buried in Westmoreland County by the side of my father, mother, brothers, sisters, and my children;

To friends Mr. William Thompson, clerk [clergyman] *and Mr. Samuel Thompson; to godson Lawrence Butler 1 mare and 2 cows; to sister Anne Wirtts* [given in italics in sources, i.e., Wright's] *children who are underage age one man servant of 4 or 5 years (of age) or 3,000 pounds of tobacco to purchase same when they are twenty; to sister Lewis* [unidentified and unclear, but may be sister-in-law Isabella Warner, wife of John Lewis, and perhaps parents of Mildred Lewis Brown, second wife of Col. Henry Willis];

---

[6]Withington, op. cit., pp. 529–531; Dorman, *Westmoreland County Deeds & Wills No. 2, 1691–1699*, pp. 58–59.

To cousin John Washington Sr. of Stafford Co., wearing apparel; to cousin John Washington, eldest son of Lawrence Washington, my godson, 1 man servant or 3,000 pounds tobacco when he is twenty-one; to godsons Lawrence Butler and Lewis Nicholas [i.e., half-brother of Nathaniel Pope alias Bridges], *about 275 acres adjoining Meridah Edwards & Daniel White to be equally divided between them; to upper and lower churches of Washington Parish;*

Wife Mildred, son John, son Augustine, and daughter Mildred to have equal shares of personal estate (all surviving children underage);

To son John land where I now live and tract lying at mouth of Machodock to place called round hills with the addition "I have hereunto made of [purchased from] *William Webb & William Rush;"*

To son Augustine about 400 acres which I bought of Mr. Robert Lesson's [Lisson's, Robert being the brother and heir-at-law of Daniel Lisson] *children in England lying on Mattox between my brother and Mr. Baldridge's land where Mr. Daniel Lesson [Lisson] formerly lived by estimation 400 acres; likewise that land that was Mr. Richard Hill's; as likewise about 700 acres where Mr. Lewis Markham now lives after the said Markham's and his wife's decease;*

To daughter Mildred 2,500 acres on Hunting Creek in Stafford Co. where Mrs. Elizabeth Minton & Mrs. Williams live;

If any child dies, the land to be divided among his or her surviving heirs; if any child dies without issue, land to be divided between my surviving heirs; if all children died without issue, the land to go to my brother's children except land I bought from Mr. Robert Lessons' [Lisson] *children which is to go to my loving wife and her heirs;*

To son John, water mill and 200 acres near Storkes Quarter which I bought of my brother [in-law] *Francis Wright, etc.*

Executors: cousin John Washington of Stafford, friend Mr. Samuel Thompson, wife Mildred
Witnesses: Robert Redman, George Weedon, Thomas Howes, John Rosier

At a Court held for (Westmoreland) County 30 March 1698, the last will and testament of Lawrence Washington, Gentleman, deceased, within written was proved by the oaths of George Weedon, Thomas Howes, and John Rosier, three of the witnesses thereto subscribed, and a probate thereof granted to Samuel Thompson, Gentleman, one of the Executors therein named, and ordered recorded.

177

The above Lawrence's *brother*, Capt. John Washington, also died in 1698 and his will was recorded in Washington County.[7]

Washington histories state that Lawrence's *son*, John Washington, married Catherine Whiting and had at least five children (Warner, Henry, Mildred, Elizabeth, and Catherine who married Col. Fielding Lewis as his first wife).

Lawrence's son, Augustine Washington (1694–1743), married first Jane (or Jenny) Butler, daughter of Caleb Butler and Mary Foxhall. Augustine and Jane had two surviving children (Lawrence and Augustine) and lost two daughters in infancy (Butler and Jane). Augustine married secondly Mary Ball, and they had six children—George (the President), Betty (who married Fielding Lewis as his second wife), Samuel, John Augustine, Charles, and Mildred.

Lawrence's daughter, Mildred, was underage when her father wrote his will in 1697/98. She married first Roger Gregory by whom she had three daughters (Frances, Mildred, and Elizabeth Gregory). Mildred Washington Gregory married secondly Col. Henry Willis as his third wife.

On 17 May 1726 Roger Gregory of Stratton–Major Parish, King and Queen County, Gentleman, and his wife Mildred (nee Washington) sold the 2,500 acres on Hunting Creek which she inherited from her father to her brother Augustine of Washington Parish, Westmoreland County, Gentleman. Witnesses were Wm. Aylett Jr., John Washington, and Lawz (Lawrence) Butler.[8] Augustine willed this tract to his son Lawrence who did not have any surviving children. In 1755 Lawrence's widow leased this tract to her brother-in-law George Washington.

Augustine Washington died in 1743 at Ferry Farm which was then in King George County and which he had purchased from the executors of William Strother who married Margaret Thornton, daughter of Francis Thornton Sr. Augustine Washington's will is found in King George County Will Book A-1. It serves no purpose here to give the details of Augustine's lengthy will except to note that in his codicil he left his son George three lots in Fredericksburg—lot #40 which he bought from Col. John Waller, and lots #33 and #34 which he bought from the executors of Col. Henry Willis. On 31 October 1750 John Champe, Hancock Lee, and Enoch Innis met at the plantation (Ferry Farm) of the widow of Capt. Augustine Washington and divided the slaves according to his will.[9]

Mildred Washington Gregory was one of George Washington's godparents at his christening in 1732. She married Henry Willis in January 1733/34.

Augustine Washington's daughter Betty (1733–1797) married Fielding Lewis (1725–1781) of Fredericksburg as his second wife. Betty and Fielding Lewis had a

[7]Ibid., pp. 51–53.

[8]Withington, op. cit., pp. 531–533.

[9]King George County Deed Book 3:373 and King George County Will Book A-1.

son Maj. George Lewis who married Catherine Daingerfield, daughter of William Daingerfield Jr. and Mary Willis. This Mary Willis was identified as the daughter of John Willis (the elder son of that name of Col. Henry Willis and his first wife Anne) and his wife Elizabeth Madison. George Lewis and wife Catherine Daingerfield had a daughter Mary Willis Lewis who in 1800 married Byrd C. Willis (1781–1846), the grandson of Henry Willis. By this connection, according to Byrd C. Willis, he and his wife were related through both mother and father.

The Lewis family may be important because of a later King George County deed (Book 20:567). In 1872 Fielding Lewis and wife Mary Imogen (*i.e.*, Green, his second wife) sold 49.45 acres and part of a tract conveyed to the said Fielding Lewis by Edward T. Tayloe, executor of Charles Tayloe, deceased, originally known as "Bald Eagle" and in 1872 as "Como." Bald Eagle was one of the creeks named in early deeds involving our John Willis's land. This Fielding Lewis (1808–1877) was nephew to Mary Willis Lewis, wife of Byrd C. Willis.

According to Washington histories, Augustine's son, Charles Washington (1738–1799), was the last of his children to be born at Wakefield in Westmoreland County. If this is correct, the Washington family was still in the area when John Willis, grandson of John Willis Sr., sold his grandfather's 1669 patent to the Church Wardens of Hanover Parish in King George in 1737. It also means that the Washingtons were living in the locale when Charles Willis, son of John Willis Sr., deeded land on Roziers or Rosiers Creek (part of the Alexander, Alexander, and Lund patent) to William Duff in 1714/5 and 1719, and his son John deeded to Duff there in 1732/33. Because of missing records, it is not known how Charles Willis received this land, but it may have been his wife's inheritance. In addition, no records were found for Charles Willis's estate although he owned at least two tracts when he died. The name "Charles" was never used by the other descendants of John Willis Sr. (d. 1715) which may imply that Charles Willis was a half-sibling to John Willis Jr. and William Willis. These and related documents in Westmoreland County present several possible connections which potentially spanned perhaps three generations, but definitive answers were not found.

Charles Washington (son of Lawrence) married Mildred Thornton, daughter of Col. Francis Thornton and wife Frances Gregory who was the daughter of Roger and Mildred (Washington) Gregory. Augustine Washington's son Samuel (1734–1781 or 1787) married five times with his first wife being Jane Champe, the daughter of Col. John Champe. Samuel's second wife was Mildred Thornton, daughter of Col. John Thornton.

Before returning to the records of Henry Willis's family, these facts will be reviewed chronologically.

John Willis Sr. and John Washington Sr. owned adjoining patents in 1669. Washington married Ann Pope, daughter of Nathaniel Pope Sr. and aunt of Nathaniel Pope alias Bridges. Ann Pope Washington predeceased her husband. In 1674 John Washington deeded 300 acres of his 1664 patent to William Freake, and in 1675 he willed the balance of the tract to his daughter Ann (later the wife of Francis Wright) who was underage. John Washington also willed his tract near the head of Rosier's Creek at Mattox to his son Lawrence.

In 1694 John Willis Sr. deeded 100 acres of his 1669 patent to his son John Jr. and gave Nathaniel Pope (nephew of Ann Pope Washington) his Power of Attorney to acknowledge it in Court.

In 1697/98 Lawrence Washington named the underage children of his sister Ann Wright in his will and left his Rosiers/Mattox grant to his son Augustine. (In 1743 Augustine left the tract to his son John.)

In 1701 John Willis Sr. deeded the remaining 161 acres of his patent to his son William. Christopher Butler and Nathaniel Pope witnessed the deed, and John Willis Sr. gave Pope his Power of Attorney to acknowledge it in Court.

In 1705 Ann Washington Wright's son John Wright and her husband Francis Wright sold 1,000 acres to Francis Thornton Sr. out of one of the tracts which she inherited from her father. The land adjoined William Willis (son of John Sr.) and John Hauxford (who was living on that part of Washington's patent which had been sold to William Freake).

In 1709 John Hauxford and William Willis exchanged twelve acres. Hauxford's was part of Washington's 1664 patent (*i.e.*, part of the 300 acres which Washington sold to Freake in 1675) and William Willis's was part of his father's 261 acre patent which his father deeded to him in 1701.

In 1714/15 Charles Willis (son of John Sr.) and wife Matilda deeded 170 acres to William Duff, it being part of a patent to Alexander, Alexander, and Lund lying partly in Richmond and partly in Westmoreland adjoining Edward Tayler near Rosiers (Roziers) Dam. In 1719 Charles again deeded to Duff and the land was part of the same patent, and in 1732/33 Charles' son John released the tract to Duff (see Chapter VII).

John Willis Sr. died in 1715 leaving two tracts in Richmond County to his son Charles (except for portions given to Mary Willis James and Mary Cullins). These tracts were not part of the land which Charles sold to William Duff. Also in 1715 Mildred Washington Gregory's brother Augustine Washington married Jane Butler, daughter of Caleb Butler and Mary Foxhall who was the sister of John Foxhall Jr.

In 1716 William Willis, son of John Sr., died intestate, and his eldest son, John, became his heir-at-law.

In 1719 Charles Willis (son of John Sr.) deeded 78 acres which was part of the Alexander-Lund patent and near Rosiers Dam to William Duff.

In 1728 John Willis Jr. (son of John Sr.) died without issue, and 100 acres of his father's 1669 patent which was entailed to him became the property of his nephew John (son of William).

In 1732 Mildred Washington Gregory was godmother at George Washington's christening in Westmoreland County. In January 1733/34 Mildred married Henry Willis as his third wife.

In 1737 John Willis (son of William) and wife Elizabeth (Plunkett) sold his grandfather's 1669 patent to the Church Wardens of Hanover Parish to be used as a glebe.

Bible records of some descendants of Hancock Lee and his wife Mary Willis—said to be the daughter of Henry Willis and his first wife, Ann (Alexander Smith?)—are found in *Genealogies of Virginia Families*.[10] Portions of those records which seem to be important to this manuscript are given below.

2 November 1714 Henry Willis married Ann Smith
30 October 1726 Henry Willis married Mildred Brown
5 January 1733/34 Henry Willis married Mildred Gregory
23 January 1733/34 Hancock Lee married Mary Willis
30 April 1742 Henry Willis married Elizabeth Gregory

14 September 1740 Henry Willis died
5 September 1747 Mildred Willis, wife of Henry Willis, died
5 March 1750 John Willis the Elder died
  October 1752 Hancock Lee died, age 53 years
4 December 1766 Mary Lee, wife of Hancock Lee, died, age 50.

Although prior researchers claim that Henry was the brother of Francis Willis of Gloucester County, Byrd C. Willis did not discuss his grandfather's parents or siblings and did not mention any relationship to the Willises of Gloucester County. The executors of Henry Willis's estate were Francis Willis of Gloucester and John Grymes of Middlesex.

Quoting from published, but undocumented, sources, Henry Willis's first wife Ann (Alexander Smith?) was said to be the widow of John Smith of Purton whom she married in 1711 and who died prior to November 1714. Ann and John Smith reportedly had one son, John Smith of Gloucester, who was born 17 December 1712 and who made a will in 1735 naming his *grandmother* Ann Alexander, brother (half-brother) Henry Willis, and brother (half-brother) John Willis.[11]

[10] *Genealogies of Virginia Families*, taken from *William and Mary Quarterly Historical Magazine*, vol. 5 (Baltimore: Genealogical Publishing Co., 1982), pp. 509–511.

[11] See Spotsylvania County Deed Book G and Crozier, p. 259, which seems to be the basis of this information. This is confusing because the deed implies that Henry Willis Jr. predeceased his brother John Willis (the Elder) who died in 1750 according to the bible records.

Based on the bible records, Henry Willis and his first wife, Ann, may have had five children, although the records are problematic:

1. Mary Willis (1716–1766) who married Hancock Lee (1709–1762) on 23 January 1733/34. Crozier gives the date of their marriage license in Spotsylvania County as 5 January 1734.[12] The Lee family will not be discussed in this manuscript, but data suggests a possible connection to a Kendall family.

2. Francis Willis, born 12 October 1718 (given only in the bible records and not specifically identified as Henry's son). I believe that this Francis may have been the Francis Willis of Gloucester who was co-executor of Henry's estate. If the bible records are correct, Francis was twenty-two years old when Henry died and, as the eldest son, would have been the logical person to be Henry's executor. Crozier's records show that John Grymes had a son named Benjamin who later sold assets relating to mining operations, and Henry Willis is known to have been involved in mining in Spotsylvania County. As the weakest link in earlier Willis histories is the connection between Henry Willis of Spotsylvania County and Francis Willis of Gloucester County, efforts should be made to find a copy of Henry's will or estate papers in General Court. Those documents might be appended to later land records.

3. David Willis, born 17 December 1720 (given only in the bible records and not specifically identified as Henry's son). No other records were found for David, and the name is not carried through this family in later generations.

4. Henry Willis, born 22 September 1722 and died sometime before 1758. No guardian bond is shown in Crozier for Henry Jr. following his father's death, but he was over sixteen and could have chosen his own guardian in which case the data might be found in the Court Orders. Henry married his stepsister Elizabeth Gregory in 1743 and was the administrator of his stepmother's (Mildred Washington Gregory) estate in 1747 with Anthony Strother as his security.[13] Henry's estate does not appear in Crozier's transcription of the Spotsylvania County records, and his widow, Elizabeth Gregory Willis, married secondly Reuben Thornton.

5. John Willis (called John the Elder), born 17 August 1724 and died intestate on 5 March 1750 (1751?).[14] No guardian bond is given for this John in Crozier's records although he was sixteen at the time. John married Elizabeth Madison (1725–1773), daughter of Ambrose Madison. Elizabeth married secondly Richard Beale. John and Elizabeth had one daughter, Mary Willis (1746–1818?), who married William Daingerfield Jr. of Spotsylvania County. Elizabeth's daughter Ann by Richard Beale married John W. Willis of Spotsylvania County, son of Lewis and grandson of Henry. John Willis's estate papers, Elizabeth Madison Willis Beale's will and that of her second husband, Richard Beale, are all found in Orange County Will Book 2.

In 1730 a Thomas Smith and his wife Ann (Faulks or Foulk) Smith (who, according to the lease, was the widow of Thomas Fitzhugh) leased land and a mill in King

---

[12] Crozier, op. cit., p. 84.

[13] Crozier, op. cit., pp. 57 and 85.

[14] Orange County Will Book 2:146 and 2:183.

George County to Henry Willis of Spotsylvania County, Gentleman.[15] That tract has not been thoroughly traced and may be important because Henry Willis's first wife was said to be Ann (Alexander?) Smith.

According to the bible records, Henry Willis married secondly on 30 October 1726 Mildred Brown, said to have been the widow of Dr. John Brown, but with no documentation. Willis histories are inconsistent regarding her maiden name with some claiming that she was a Howell and others, Lewis. The latter appears to be the most correct from a 1730 deed from Henry Willis to John Lewis of Gloucester County and Charles Lewis of New Kent County as this land was later deeded by John Willis (the younger), son of Henry and Mildred.[16] Henry and Mildred (Lewis? Brown) are reported to have had four children, although this may be incorrect (see below):

1. John Willis, born 16 July 1728 and called "John Willis, the younger son of that name of Henry and Mildred Willis" in later deeds. This is very confusing as it means that Henry had two sons named "John" who were only four years apart in age, but the deeds confirm the existence of two sons named John. This John Willis was named as the primary legatee in Robert Spotswood's 1733 will which is given below.[17] According to Crozier, John Thornton was named guardian of John Willis Jr. in 1743 with Francis Taliaferro as his security. This John Willis married a woman named Nanny, was living in Culpeper County in 1749, and moved to Prince William County by 19 April 1750.[18]

2. Elizabeth Willis, born 12 January 1729/30 (given only in bible records with an undocumented source claiming that she married John Clayton).[19] No appointment of a guardian was found for Elizabeth in Spotsylvania County after Henry's death.

3. Ann Willis, born 14 September 1731. In 1744 Hancock Lee was named her guardian with Anthony Strother as security according to Crozier. Ann married (as his second wife) Duff Green who died in 1766 in Fauquier County, and she died by 18 October 1804. Duff Green may have been the nephew of William Duff who bought land from Charles Willis (son of John Willis Sr.) in 1714/15 and 1719.

4. Isabel Willis, born 10 June 1733 (given in bible records only).

The bible records show that Henry married Mildred (Washington) Gregory on 5 January 1733/34. Byrd C. Willis reported that they had one known son who survived them:[20]

---

[15] King George County Deed Book A1:105.

[16] Spotsylvania County Deed Book B:133.

[17] Spotsylvania County Will Book A; see Chapter VII.

[18] Dorman, Culpeper County Deed Book A:65–68.

[19] du Bellet, op. cit., p. 282; someone made a notation in the margin of Byrd C. Willis's manuscript that one of Henry Willis's daughter married a Clayton.

[20] Ibid.

1. Lewis Willis, born 11 November 1734 and died in 1812. Lewis married first Mary Champe, daughter of John Champe of King George County, and second Anne Carter Champe, daughter of Charles and Ann (Byrd) Carter and the widow of his brother-in-law John Champe.

It should be emphasized that the above names were taken from bible records and that those records may have contained information for more than one family. Information on Lewis Willis's children given below was not recorded in the bible, but is taken from Byrd C. Willis's history.

In 1733 an unidentified Robert Spotswood wrote his will leaving most of his estate to John Willis, Henry's younger son of that name. Spotswood's will is given as transcribed from microfilm with original spelling and punctuation retained:

> *Will of Robert Spotswood, Spotsylvania County, Virginia, written 5 May 1733, proved 3 July 1733.*
> *In the name of God Amen I Robert Spotswood of the County of Spotsylvania being sick in body but of perfect memory do make this my Last will and Testament in manner following comitting my body to the () and my soul to Allmighty God—trusting in () through the merits and intercession of my () Lord and Savior () for a joyfull resurrection—*
> *Item I give to my good friend Mr. Edmund Bagge my horse and sadle as a small acknowledgement of his kindness to me (1)*
> *Item I give to Henry Willis my watch—*
> *Item I give to Mary James twenty shillings—*
> *Item I give to Thomas Barnett all my wareing aparell (etc.)—*
> *Item my will and desire is that Mr. Elliot Benger be paid the money I owe him as soon as possible— (2)*
> *After all my just debts is paid I give and bequeath all my estate both real & personal unto John Willis forever, the son of Henry and Mildred Willis to him and his heirs forever. (3)*
> *I do appoint Col. Henry Willis Executor of my Will. May 5th 1733*
> *Robert Spotswood*
> *Signed sealed and delivered in the presence of us—*
> *Anth. Rhodes Junr.   William Booth*
> *John Gordon   Elizabeth Gordon*
> *At a Court held for Spotsylvania County on Tuesday July 3 1733 this Will being sworn to by Henry Willis, Gent., executor therein named was produced by the oaths of Anthony Rhodes Jr., John Gordon, Wm. Booth, and Elizabeth Gordon and admitted to record—Teste John Waller Clk Ct*
> *Bond given by Henry Willis (executor), John Waller, and John Mercer, Gentlemen, in the amount of 200 pounds sterling on 3 July 1733.*

According to Orange County historian Ann L. Miller of Madison, Virginia, the identity of Robert Spotswood and any relationship to Gov. Alexander Spotswood are unknowns.[21] However, the reference to Elliot Benger suggests that a relationship may have existed because Benger married Dorothy Brayne, sister of Ann Butler Brayne who was the wife of Gov. Spotswood. In 1734 Alexander Spotswood leased several tracts in his Spotsylvania grant on the Rapidan River to various people (see Chapter IX). As one of Gov. Spotswood's executors, Benger leased part of Spotswood's tract on the Rapidan to Anthony Garnett in 1741.[22] Spotswood's heirs deeded tracts to William Willis (son of John who died in 1762 and grandson of William and Sarah), Edmund Terrill, Joshua Hudson, Benjamin Hawkins, and others on the Rapidan in 1767.[23]

Both Gov. Spotswood and Henry Willis were involved in mining. As shown in Chapter XII, A. Spotswood witnessed a deed from John Loyd to Micajah Perry, Francis Willis, Thomas Meriwether, and John Taliaferro in London in 1706.

Robert Spotswood's will raises several questions. Was the above Mary James the daughter of John Willis Sr.? Her son William James was living in Spotsylvania County in 1742 when he deeded land to Jeremiah Murdock who was also involved in mining. The tract was in King George County and had been bequeathed in 1715 by his grandfather, John Willis Sr., to William James' father, mother, and elder brother David, all of who were deceased in 1742.[24]

Was Edmund Bagge the man to whom Alexander Spotswood deeded the following tract in 1732?[25]

> *Alexander Spotswood to Edmund Bagge of Essex County, planter ... for and in consideration of friendship and regard and for past services rendered, etc., 2,284 acres in St. Mark's Parish, Spotsylvania County, and part of a patent granted to Thomas Jones, John Clayton, and Richard Hickman on 22 June 1722 and renewed by patent 11 April 1732 ... and now actually belonging to said Spotswood ... known as Indian Field, etc.; witnesses John Grame, Elliott Benger, James McCullough; dated 6 November 1732.*

Eugene M. Scheel states that Jones, Clayton, and Hickman entered a large tract (later called the Spotswood tract) on behalf of Spotswood. Six years later the three men had died or withdrawn from their claim which allowed Spotswood to buy the entire patent for 200 pounds "in recognition of his seating in Spotsylvania County."[26]

When Orange County was created in 1734, St. Mark's Parish included all the land

---

[21] Personal correspondence.

[22] Orange County Deed Book 5:57–63. Anthony Garnett's daughter Elizabeth married William Willis, son of John Willis (d. 1762), and they became the parents of Isaac Willis whose descendants founded the Willis–Gordon–Garnett and Allied Families Association.

[23] Culpeper County Deed Book E.

[24] King George County Deed Book 2:398.

[25] Spotsylvania County Deed Book A; Crozier, op. cit., p. 123.

[26] Eugene M. Sheel, *Culpeper: A Virginia County's History Through 1920*, p. 20.

which is now Orange, Madison, Culpeper, and Rappahannock counties. While the boundaries of Spotswood's patent were vague (perhaps on purpose), it extended on both sides of the Rapidan River as far north as Cedar Mountain and as far west as the Robinson River in present Culpeper County.

Hurst stated that Spotswood's Tract was bounded on the south (in present Orange County) by four other patents—(1) Lawrence Taliaferro and John Taliaferro Jr., (2) Francis Conway, (3) Thomas Teylor/Taylor, and (4) Benjamin Porter.[27] This may be significant because the first three men are known to have been related to the Thornton family in some way, two of Henry Willis's stepdaughters married Thorntons, and John Willis Sr. lived next to the Thorntons in King George County. John Willis's 1669 patent was eventually purchased by a William Thornton in 1767 (see Chapter I).

The name "Bagge" may be important because Mary Foxhall, sister of John Foxhall Jr., married (as her fifth husband) the Rev. John Bagge and died in 1717. John Bagge died in 1724–1726 in Essex County, his will naming his cousin (perhaps nephew) Edmund Bagge who died testate in Essex County in 1734. John Bagge's legatees were his wife Katherine and his son Robert Bagge.

In 1715/16 a Thomas Willis of Bristol, England, gave his Power of Attorney to John Blagge (Bagge), clerk (clergyman) of Essex County, to conduct some business for him; witnesses were Jno. Elliott and Thos. Connery.[28] This may have been the Thomas Willis/Wills of Bristol, England, merchant, who received Power of Attorney from Johanna Pope, widow of Thomas, in 1710/11.[29]

In his will Robert Spotswood refers to John Willis as the son of Henry and Mildred. According to the bible records, in July 1733 Henry Willis was married to his second wife, Mildred (Lewis? Brown) and this John Willis would have been nine years old. Mildred died before January 1734 when Henry married Mildred Washington Gregory. After Henry's death, John Thornton was named as John's guardian with Francis Taliaferro as his security.

In 1749 Robert Spotswood's legatee John Willis and his wife Nanny of St. Mark's Parish, Culpeper County, sold 520 acres on both sides of Black Walnut River in Orange County to William Johnson. The tract, which adjoined Jonathan Gibson, was granted by patent to Robert Spotswood, deceased, and "by his last will and testament given unto the said Willis."[30] The deed was signed by John Willis Junr. and Nanny Willis. The appellation "Jr." was commonly used to identify the younger of two (usually related) men of the same name living in the area and did not necessarily mean that he was the son of a "Sr." Whether this William Johnson was related to the grandson of Elizabeth Willis's will in 1767 in King George County is unknown.[31]

---

[27] Patricia J. Hurst, *The History and People of Clark Mountain*, p. 5.

[28] Beverly Fleet, Miscellaneous Records, p. 59.

[29] See Chapter XII and Essex County Deed Book 13:425.

[30] Orange County Deed Book 11:170.

[31] See Chapter VII.

Also in 1749 John Willis Junr. of Culpeper County, son of Henry and Mildred Willis, deceased, and Nanny his wife sold four lots (#11, #12, #47, and #48) in Fredericksburg to Henry Willis, Gentleman. The deeds were signed by John Willis Junr. and Nanny Willis and were witnessed by Will. Lynn, John Willis (the Elder?), George Livingston, and Humphrey Wallis.[32] These lots had been deeded in 1740 by the Trustees in Fredericksburg to Henry Willis and John, the son of Henry and Mildred Willis, with Mildred to have a life interest.[33] Again, this is very confusing because it implies that John was the son of Mildred Washington Gregory Willis who was Henry's wife at the time. She may have been given a life interest in 1740 when Henry bought the lots because John was only twelve years old. If the John Willis who witnessed the deed was the elder son of Henry as given in the records, he was only twenty-four years old. Henry Willis Sr. was deceased before 1749, so the "Henry Willis, Gentleman" must have referred to Henry Jr. who would have been twenty-seven. John the younger would have been just twenty-one. While this is all possible, I find it problematic. The bible records state that John the Elder died on 5 March 1750.

John Willis of Culpeper County, "the younger son of that name of Col. Henry Willis, deceased," and his wife Nanny Willis sold two tracts (200 acres and 1,465 acres) on Massaponax Run in Spotsylvania County to Joseph Stevens of Caroline County in 1749. The deed stated that it was "made by Col. Henry Willis, deceased, as by deed of gift to the said John Willis."[34] The acreage of one of the tracts (1,465) was the same as the acreage in a 1730 deed from Henry Willis to John and Charles Lewis with Henry Willis to retain a lifetime interest, then his wife Mildred (who was Mildred Lewis Brown) for her life. Consequently, John and Charles Lewis may have been holding it in trust for John the younger although the record is unclear.[35]

John and Nanny Willis sold an additional tract of 400 acres in Culpeper County to Joseph Stephens of Caroline County in 1749, the land being formerly granted to Robert Spotswood, deceased, and willed by him to the said John Willis. It was on both sides of Mountain Run adjoining lands of Col. John Spotswood, Philip Clayton, James Pendleton, and in a line of a tract formerly held by Geo. Hoome known as Fox Mountain Tract.[36] There were two streams named Mountain Run. One was on the south side of Chestnut (Clark) Mountain in present Orange County, and the other was in Culpeper County. As this deed was dated 1749, it must have referred to the one in present Culpeper County. Fox Mountain is west of the town of Culpeper and should not be confused with Fox Neck which was on the Rapidan. Although John and Nanny were given as residents of Culpeper County in August 1749 when the deed was executed, they had moved to Prince William County by 19 April 1750 before her acknowledgment was obtained. Joseph Stephens and his wife Ann of Caroline County

---

[32]Spotsylvania County Deed Book 5:414 ff. and Crozier, op. cit., pp. 179–180.

[33]Crozier, op. cit., pp. 152 and 153.

[34]Ibid., p. 181.

[35]Ibid., p. 116.

[36]Culpeper County Deed Book A:65–68.

sold this tract to Ambrose Kemp of Culpeper County in 1761.[37]

Consequently, John Willis the younger sold at least 2,585 acres in Orange and Culpeper counties in 1749 plus four lots in Fredericksburg. No record of his death was found, but he may have died in Prince William County. By that time the descendants of William Willis (son of John Willis Sr.) were well established in Culpeper and Orange counties, and William's son John (who died in 1762 in Orange County) was married and had several children, but documents for the two families do not appear to contain any common threads.

Henry's third wife, Mildred Washington, and her first husband, Roger Gregory, had three daughters. According to the records in Crozier and du Bellet, they were (1) Frances Gregory who married Col. Francis Thornton Jr. of Spotsylvania County on 3 September 1736, (2) Mildred Gregory who married Col. John Thornton of Spotsylvania County on 28 August 1740, and (3) Elizabeth Gregory who appears to have first married Henry Willis Jr. (her stepbrother) and second Reuben Thornton although the records are confusing.[38] I suspect that this Thornton family was related to Francis Thornton Sr. who died in 1726 in King George and who was a neighbor to John Willis Sr.

In 1739 deed of gift Mildred Willis, "late Mildred Gregory and now wife of Henry Willis of Spotsylvania County, Gentleman," cited a pre-nuptial agreement dated 5 January 1733 [1734] between Henry, Mildred, and John Washington of Gloucester County, Gentleman. Pursuant to the terms of the 1733/34 agreement which gave Mildred a life interest in certain property which she owned when she married Henry Willis, in 1739 Mildred left certain slaves and property after her death to her son Lewis Willis with the stipulation that if Lewis died before Henry and Mildred, she could convey the property to her three daughters—Frances, the wife of Francis Thornton, Mildred Gregory, and Elizabeth Gregory. Witnesses were Augustine Washington and John Taliaferro.[39] Mildred may have been protecting her property due to Henry's over-leveraged position in land. As Byrd C. Willis described his grandfather, "He was a careless and extravagant man. The property was brought in after his death, as it was offered for public sale by my grandmother (*i.e.*, Mildred Washington), who by dint of industry and economy had amassed enough to save the property adjoining the town of Fredericksburg, afterwards called Willis Hill."[40]

Col. Henry Willis died on 14 September 1740 according to the bible records. Mildred Washington Gregory Willis died on 5 September 1747. Henry Willis Jr. was appointed administrator of her estate with Anthony Strother his security in the amount of 1,000 pounds.[41]

[37] Culpeper County Deed Book B:528–532.

[38] Crozier, op. cit., p. 85.

[39] Spotsylvania County Deed Book C:361 and Crozier, op. cit., p. 150.

[40] du Bellet, op. cit., p. 282.

[41] Spotsylvania County Administrative Bonds, Will Book *A*, and Crozier, op. cit., p. 57.

John Willis the Elder, who had married Elizabeth Madison, died intestate on 5 March 1750 in Orange County where his estate records can be found in Will Book 2. James Madison was the guardian of John's daughter Mary. Elizabeth Madison Willis then married Richard Beale.

I found it interesting that Zachary Lewis and George Taylor were James Madison's securities for Madison's guardianship bond for Mary Willis (daughter of John and Elizabeth) in Orange County in 1761, and that a Zachary Lewis was the attorney of Sarah and Edward Turberville during the settlement of Rush Hudson's estate in King George County in 1737. I also noted that although Byrd C. Willis spoke of his relationship to the Washingtons, he never mentioned the fact that his father's half-brother John married Elizabeth Madison.

Henry Willis Jr., who had married Elizabeth Gregory, died intestate before 1758 at which time his widow was married to Reuben Thornton.[42] Francis Thornton, husband of Frances Gregory, died in 1749.[43] In 1758 Mildred Washington Gregory Willis's daughters by her first marriage (Frances Thornton, widow, John Thornton and wife Mildred, and Reuben Thornton and wife Elizabeth) released their interest in Mildred's lifetime estate to their half-brother, Lewis Willis, and referred to the above 1739 deed. Witnesses were Charles Yates, Edward Carter, and William Champe.[44]

Although I have not researched the Champe family, I did find that in 1736 Edward Turberville of Hanover Parish sold 150 acres in Brunswick Parish to John Champe, Gent. Turberville was married to Sarah (—) Willis Wood Hudson at the time, and they may have been disposing of their land in King George County in anticipation of their move to Orange County.[45] I also found deeds in Westmoreland County in 1697 which involved John Champe, Capt. John Washington (and wife Ann), and Thomas James, but I do not know if this was the same Thomas James who married Mary Willis, daughter of John Sr.[46]

Henry and Mildred (Washington Gregory) Willis are reported as having only one surviving child—Lewis Willis, who was born 11 November 1734. Charles Dick was named his guardian in 1749. Lewis's will is dated 2 March 1812. He and his first wife, Mary Champe, had six children whom I have not verified: (1) Mildred Willis who married Landon Carter; (2) John W. Willis who married Ann Beale, (3) Henry Willis who married three times and moved to Wilkes County, Georgia, (4) Jane Willis who married Phillip Thornton Alexander of Chotank; (5) Mary Willis who married a Battaile; and (6) William C. (Champe) Willis of Orange County who married Lucy Taliaferro. Lewis Willis married second Ann Carter Champe, widow of his brother-in-law, John Champ Jr. Lewis and his second wife had at least two children (although one record says three): (1) Charles Willis who died at age three and (2) Byrd C. Willis

---

[42] Crozier, op. cit., pp. 263, 282, and 325.

[43] Ibid., p. 10, and Spotsylvania County Will Book B:1.

[44] Ibid., p. 206, and Spotsylvania County Deed Book E:418.

[45] Sparacio, *King George County Deeds 1735–1752* (Book 2), p. 13.

[46] Dorman, *Westmoreland County Deeds & Wills No. 2, 1691-1699*.

who married Mary Willis Lewis in 1800 in King George County according to his account.

During his lifetime, Col. Henry Willis was one of the Trustees in Fredericksburg and apparently was involved in land speculation and mining interests. Crozier's abstracts show that Henry purchased at least seventeen lots in Fredericksburg in 1740 and seven lots prior to that time besides the land he held by patent and purchase. Neither his will nor his estate administration is found in Crozier and may have been recorded in General Court.

Beginning in 1741, Henry's executors sold several lots which Henry had purchased, undoubtedly to pay debts and settle his estate, including lots #33 and #34 which they sold to Augustine Washington. In 1755 George Washington deeded (gifted) lot #40 (one of the lots which he inherited from his father) to John Thornton whom Washington called his *cousin* and the infant son of Francis Thornton late of Spotsylvania County, deceased, and his wife Frances (Gregory) Thornton, his widow and relict.[47]

In 1753 George Washington deeded lots #33 and #34 in Fredericksburg to Andrew Cochrane, John Murdock, William Crawford Jr., Allan Dreghorn, and Robert Bagle Jr., of Glasgow, Great Britain, merchants and partners, for 280 pounds.[48]

I believe that more research should be done to determine if Col. Henry Willis of Fredericksburg may have been related to our Willis line because the documents which I have found suggest a relationship extending back into Westmoreland and King George counties. I also believe that the Henry Willis of early Gloucester County records may not be the same man who was in Spotsylvania County in 1729 as claimed by some previous writers.

Several deeds which have been found may or may not relate to our research, but they show that some of Henry Willis's descendants lived in the same area as our Willis family in the 1700s. Byrd C. Willis said that he lived in Orange County near the Court House for a short time following his marriage in 1800.[49] I do not know whether or not his father, Lewis Willis, ever lived in Orange. However, Orange County deeds of particular interest include (by deed book and page number) 12:21, 12:513, 15:514, 17:126, 18:151, 18:401, and 18:410, a few of which will be summarized below.

In 1759 Lewis Willis, Gent., petitioned the Orange County Court for Alexander Waugh to erect a water mill on the Rapidan adjoining Waugh's land in Culpeper (on the opposite side of the river). Benjamin Porter was one of the subscribers who viewed the one-acre tract and appraised its value at 40 shillings.[50] According to Hurst, this and the following deed described an early mill which was called Rapidan Mill near the

---

[47] Crozier, op. cit., p. 198.

[48] Ibid., p. 193.

[49] du Bellet, op. cit., p. 289.

[50] Orange County Deed Book 12:513.

present village of Rapidan.[51] John and William Willis (sons of William and Sarah, and grandsons of John Willis Sr.) were living in this area in 1751.

In 1773 an acre of land belonging to Lewis Willis, Gent., in Orange County on the Rapidan was surveyed for the use of Lawrence Taliaferro, Gent., for a water grist mill, and the subscribers who signed included Robert Terrill, Joseph Boston, and Hay Taliaferro.[52] Hurst says that this mill was purchased by John Waugh in 1792 and was later owned by Thomas Richards and at various times called Taliaferro's Mill, Waugh's Mill, Richard's Mill, Rapidan Mill, Central Mill, and Orange Mill.

In 1805, just prior to migrating to Kentucky, William Willis (son of John Willis who died in 1762 in Orange County) and his wife Elizabeth (nee Garnett) sold 1,408 acres on the Rapidan River to Robert Patton of Fredericksburg. Locators in the deed included Thomas Richards' (now William Mortons') corner, Waugh's road, and Taliaferro's line.[53] In 1790 Elizabeth Willis (nee Plunkett, widow of John who died in 1762) discharged part of a debt to John Glassell with bonds from Lawrence Taliaferro, John Waugh, and her son Reuben Willis. Hurst states that Lewis Willis conveyed property to Thomas Richards in 1804, and that Richards insured his mill for $6,500 in 1805.[54] While these deeds do not prove a relationship between the two Willis families, they show that the families owned land in the same neighborhood.

Charles Porter and his wife Sarah of Orange County deeded his interest in several tracts to Lewis Willis of Fredericksburg in 1779.[55] The land included a patent to his father Benjamin Porter who devised it to Charles, plus a mill and ten acres which had been conveyed to Benjamin Porter by John Taliaferro Jr. and Francis Taliaferro on 4 November 1729. Hurst says that this early Porter's Mill was just downstream from the village of Rapidan and near Dr. Campbell's and Petty's Mill which places it directly in the area where our Willis family lived.[56]

Finally, in 1783 Lewis Willis of Orange County, planter, mortgaged the tract where he lived and five slaves to Francis Taliaferro of Orange County, Gent., as security for a bond which Taliaferro had co-signed for Lewis (of Orange) and which was payable to Lewis Willis of Spotsylvania County, Gent.[57] Benjamin Willis was one of the witnesses. Lewis and Benjamin were the sons of John Willis who died in 1762 in Orange County, Lewis being born *circa* 1755 and Benjamin *circa* 1745. Lewis Willis, son of John, later moved to Wilkes County, Georgia, where he died testate in 1817. Henry Willis, son of Lewis Willis of Spotsylvania, also moved to Wilkes County, Georgia.

---

[51] Hurst, op. cit., p. 39.

[52] Ibid.; also seeOrange County Deed Book 15:514.

[53] Culpeper County Deed Book AA:265; also see S:397, X:98, and X100.

[54] Hurst, op. cit., p. 39.

[55] Orange County Deed Book 17:126.

[56] Hurst, op. cit., pp. 38–46.

[57] Orange County Deed Book 18:151.

The above Benjamin Willis, son of John Willis and Elizabeth Plunkett, owned land on both sides of the Rapidan including a tract which he purchased from John and Milly Lee in 1798.[58] Benjamin died a single person in 1810 leaving legacies to several of his siblings and nephews, but bequeathing his lands to his nephew Capt. Isaac Willis who lived and died at "Locust Grove" on the north side of the Rapidan and with whom Benjamin lived before his death.[59] Two slaves which Benjamin willed were named Henry and Milly. Benjamin's will was challenged by a sister and brother, and the suit was finally settled in 1816.[60]

By 1813, at which time William Willis (brother to the above Benjamin, Lewis, and others) and his wife, Elizabeth (Garnett) Willis, were living in Boone County, Kentucky, they sold their last tract of 308 acres on the Rapidan to their son Isaac.[61] Locators in the deed stated that the land joined tracts belonging to Peter Hansbrough, Head, and George Morton.

In 1810 William Willis and Rowland Botts (who was the son-in-law of Margaret "Peggy" Terrill, then deceased) sold their interest in 100 acres on the Rapidan as heirs of William's brother, Benjamin Willis.[62] All of these tracts can be traced back in the documents to the Spotswood heirs.

In summary, I believe that there are too many inconsistencies in the old histories and too many clues in the records to rule out the possibility that Col. Henry Willis of Fredericksburg and John Willis of King George and Orange counties (grandson of John Willis Sr. who died in 1715) had an unknown, common ancestor. Whether or not the proving or disproving of a relationship between the two families will be valuable in identifying the parents or wife/wives of John Willis Sr. is another issue.

---

[58]Orange County Deed Book 21:225.

[59]Orange County Will Book 4:372–373.

[60]George H. S. King, "A Digest of the Suit Papers *Willis vs. Willis*," unpublished manuscript taken from loose papers in the defunct Fredericksburg District Court. Also see George B. Loeffler, *Journal*, op. cit.

[61]Culpeper County Deed Book FF::464 and Boone County, Kentucky, Deed Book C:92.

[62]Culpeper County Deed Book HH:423; also P:100, T:14, U:68, and AA:247.

Memorabilia

This journey is over and the weary traveler has returned home. As I sit at my PC on a bright March morning, I consider the massive changes which have taken place in the last three hundred and twenty-eight years since John Willis Sr. received his patent. A 747 passes over, bound perhaps for Seattle or Tokyo. Sirens echo from the interstate, signaling an emergency for some stranger who enters my thoughts for a few seconds and then is forgotten. The telephone rings, but I decide to let my answering machine take the call. Then silence as I watch the winter snow melting and the first cardinal of spring exploring the bird feeder. Life is a chain of happenings. Ebb and flow. A marvelous symphony in counterpoint. What has been, what is, and what will be.

For more than a decade I have been living something akin to a double life by immersing myself in the past for a few hours each day. In many ways I have come to think of it as a retreat into reality—away from what often seems transient and mundane compared to those qualities which remind us that we are beings of substance and purpose.

And I think of Wallace Stegner's premise that history is not truly remembered until it is vividly imagined. My mind wanders back to the rivers and forests of the early Northern Neck. I visualize John's land and family and neighbors—not as nameless faces and meaningless dates, but as real, living people whose unique gifts helped to compose this symphony to which our lives are choreographed today. It is a humbling experience. I marvel at their tenaciousness and endurance, and I wonder how we would cope under similar conditions.

John and I walk around the garden, carefully lifting the leaves to see if the squash and beans have set on. He shows me his new foal which he has named Bright Star who at the moment is all legs and stays close to its mother. Then we thread our way through the hilly stubble and inspect his tobacco plants. With the help of a little more rain, the crop will provide for things which the family needs and cannot grow, and the rest will be used to buy more ground or livestock. A neighbor rides up and tells us the latest rumors about a road which will be cut through the fields this summer. John has mixed feelings about the road. He needs it to roll his tobacco crop to the warehouse, but it will divide his land and destroy some of his timber. John knows the value of his virgin forest and has admonished his sons not to waste the trees. In spite of their hard work and occasional setbacks, the land has been good to them. His philosophy was straight and simple. Take care of the land, and it will take care of you.

Moving slowly now, John reminisces about the "old days" and how things were in '69 when he was a young man. Soon, he says, it will be up to his sons and grandsons to continue alone. He hopes that he has taught them well.

Like a reluctant guest, I do not want to leave yet because I have more questions, but the shadows were lengthening and I yearn for my own fireplace. We will talk again.

But when I return, the years have passed as if in a moment. John and two of his sons are gone. His grandson and namesake has sold his land to the church, and the family is preparing to move to another farm on another river many miles away. Sarah is packing, deciding what is to be taken and what is to be sold or given away. The books and her trunk are placed under the seat of the first wagon. Neighbors help with the loading and say their farewells. Promises to remain in touch are made knowing that most will be unkept. But, thinks Sarah, the tears of leaving her garden and her home will be dried by the promise of fertile land for her sons and her daughter. As the caravan disappears in the distance, I say a little prayer for their safe journey and new beginnings.

My sense of history has grown through the process of writing this story. I appreciate where we have been and where we are now. I also wonder where we are going as a people and what future generations will remember about our time. What will our symphony be?

This history is my small gift to my grandchildren. I want them to know something about the intricate tapestry from which their own lives emerged. I hope that it will give them a sense of continuity and wonder and the courage to look beyond the moment when they are faced by new challenges. But, most of all, I hope that it will remind them that families and communities, like gardens and groves, need to be tended and cherished because they carry the seeds of tomorrow.

Bibliography

Cocke, Charles Francis. *Parish Lines, Diocese of Virginia.* Richmond: Virginia State Library, 1967, Repr. 1978.

Crozier, William Armstrong, ed. *Virginia County Records,* vol. I, Spotsylvania County 1721–1800. Baltimore: Genealogical Publishing Co., 1990.

Dorman, John Frederick. "Colonial Laws of Primogeniture." Paper read at the World Conference on Records and Genealogical Seminar at Salt Lake City, Utah, in August, 1969.

Dorman, John Frederick. Westmoreland and Culpeper County record books, deed, will, deed and patent books, and court orders as given in footnotes above. Washington, D. C.: author, various dates.

du Bellet, Louise Pequet. *Some Prominent Virginia Families.* Baltimore: Genealogical Publishing Co., (1907) 1976.

Eaton, David W. *Historical Atlas of Westmoreland County, Virginia.* Richmond: Dietz Press, 1942. Available on LDS microfilm, roll #0032377.

Fleet, Beverley. *Virginia Colonial Abstracts,* vol. II: Northumberland County Records 1652–1655; vol. VIII, Essex County Wills & Deeds 1711–1714; and vol. XX, Northumbria Collectanea 1645–1720. Baltimore: Genealogical Publishing Co., 1971.

Fothergill, Augusta B. "Underwood Family of Virginia," *Virginia Historical Magazine,* vols. 38–40.

Fothergill, Augusta B. *Wills of Westmoreland County, Virginia 1654-1800.* Baltimore: Clearfield Publishing Co, 1990.

Freeman, Douglas Southall. *George Washington: A Biography,* vols. 1 & 2. New York: Charles Scribner's Sons, 1948.

— *Genealogies of Virginia Families* from *William and Mary Quarterly Historical Magazine,* vol. V. Baltimore: Genealogical Publishing Co., 1982.

Gray, Gertrude E. *Virginia Northern Neck Land Grants 1694–1742.* Baltimore: Genealogical Publishing Co., 1988. Available on LDS microfilm, roll #0029509 and #0029510.

Groves, Mrs. Norris. Unpublished transcriptions from Richmond County, Virginia, Order Books 6–8 and King George County, Order Books 1–3 and Inventory Book 1. Rochelle, IL, 1977.

Hall, Newman A. "The Family of Sarah, wife of Rush Hudson," *Hudson Family Association (South) Bulletin* #81, January, 1993, and personal correspondence.

Headley, Robert K. *Wills of Richmond County, Virginia 1699–1800.* Baltimore: Genealogical Publishing Co., 1983.

Hurst, Patricia J. *The History and People of Clark Mountain, Orange County, Virginia.* Rapidan, VA: author, 1989; and personal correspondence.

Jones, Mary Stevens, ed. *An 18th Century Perspective: Culpeper County.* Culpeper: Culpeper Historical Society, 1976.

Joyner, Peggy Shomo. *Abstracts of Virginia's Northern Neck Warrants and Surveys,* vol. IV.

King, George H. S. *King George County, Virginia, Will Book A-1, 1721–1752 and Miscellaneous Notes.* Easley, SC: Southern Historical Press, 1978 (1985).

King, George H. S. *Marriages of Richmond County, Virginia 1668–1853.* Easley, SC: Southern Historical Press, 1964 (1985).

King, George H. S. *The Register of Saint Paul's Parish 1715–1798.* Easley, SC: Southern Historical Press, 1960 (1985).

Loeffler, George B. "Ancestry of the Willises of Locust Grove, Culpeper County, Virginia," *Willis-Gordon-Garnett & Allied Families Journal,* vol. I, no. 10, 1982, and personal correspondence.

Loeffler, George B. and Elizabeth L. Loeffler. "William Willis (1739–1833) of Virginia and Kentucky," *Willis-Gordon-Garnett & Allied Families Journal,* vol. I, no. 6, 1974.

— Map, Rollins Fork (King George County), Virginia. United States Department of the Interior, Geological Survey, 1968.

— *The Papers of George Mason,* vol. I. University of North Caroline Press, 1970.

Meyer, Virginia M. and John Frederick Dorman, eds. *The Adventures of Purse and Person, Virginia, 1607–1624/5.* Greenville, SC: Southern Historical Press, 1987.

— Microfilmed records reviewed at the Family History Center, LDS Branch Library, Minneapolis,

Minnesota, including selected original patents and grants in Virginia and various records for Northumberland, Westmoreland, Old Rappahannock, Richmond, King George, Spotsylvania, Orange, and Culpeper counties.

Miller, Ann. Madison, VA. Personal correspondence.

Miller, Mary R. *Place Names of the Northern Neck of Virginia*. Richmond: Virginia State Library, 1983.

Mosher, Merrill Hill, C. G. "Corrections to Published Maps of County Boundaries of the Northern Neck," *Virginia Genealogist*, vol. 37, no. 4, 1994, and personal correspondence.

Norris, Walter Biscoe, Jr., ed. *Westmoreland County, Virginia 1653–1983*. Montross, VA: Westmoreland County Board of Supervisors, 1983.

Nugent, Nell Marion. *Cavaliers and Pioneers. Abstracts of Virginia Land Patents and Grants*, vol. I. 1623–1666. Baltimore: Genealogical Publishing Co., 1934 (1991); Greenville, SC: Southern Historical Press, 1934 (1992).

— *Cavaliers and Pioneers. Abstracts of Virginia Land Patents and Grants*, vol. II, 1666–1695. Greenville, SC: Southern Historical Press, 1986 (1992)

— *Cavaliers and Pioneers. Abstracts of Virginia Land Patents and Grants*, vol. III, 1695–1732. Greenville, SC: Southern Historical Press, 1986 (1992).

— *The Parish Register of Christ Church, Middlesex County, Virginia, from 1653 to 1812*. National Society of the Colonial Dames of America in the State of Virginia. Southern Historical Press, 1988.

Scheel, Eugene M. *Culpeper: A Virginia County's History Through 1920*. Orange, VA: Green Publishing, 1982.

Sparacio, Ruth, and Sam Sparacio. Northumberland, Lancaster, Middlesex, Old Rappahannock, Essex, Stafford, Richmond, King George, and Orange County deed, will, inventory, and order book abstracts as given in footnotes above. McLean, VA: The Antient Press, various dates.

Sweeney, William Montgomery. *Wills of Rappahannock County, Virginia 1656–1692*. Lynchburg, VA: J. P. Bell Co., 1947. Taken from LDS microfilm, roll #1421588.

Torrence, Clayton. *Virginia Wills and Administrations 1632–1800*. Baltimore: Genealogical Publishing Co., 1990.

Vogt, John and T. William Kethley Jr. *Orange County (Virginia) Marriages 1747–1850*. Athens, GA: Iberian Publishing Co., 1984.

Vogt, John and T. William Kethley Jr. *Culpeper County (Virginia) Marriages 1780–1858*. Athens, GA: Iberian Publishing Co., 1986.

Warner, Thomas Hoskins. *History of Old Rappahannock County, Virginia 1656–1692*. Tappahannock, VA, author, 1965.

Waters, Henry Fitz-Gilbert, ed. *Genealogical Gleanings in England*, vol. I. Baltimore: Genealogical Publishing Co., 1969.

Withington, Lothrop. *Virginia Gleanings in England*. Baltimore: Genealogical Publishing Co., 1980.

Index

Ducksberry (cont.), Mary (—?—)Coghill 78–79
Duddleston, Edward 139
Duff, Elizabeth (—?—) Rush 99, 108;
William vi, 97, 99, 105–108, 179–180, 183
Durrant, Henry 133
Dyne, Luke 146, 151
Dyos, Thomas 131, 156
Earle, John Sr. 21, 145–146, 148–150, 153–157,
163; John Jr. 154, 156; Mary 157; Mary Jr. 149,
156; Mary Sr. 149, 158; Samuel 154
Edmunds, Thomas 147
Edwards, Meridah 177
Edrington, Christopher 78, 93
Elliott, 51; John 48, 140, 186; John Jr. 29, 168;
Martha 168; Mary 168; Sarah 168
Eskridge, George 140, 153–154
Faulkner, David 142
Farguson, John Jr. 50; Joshua 50, 60,
Fauntleroy, Griffin 171
Fenley, Thomas 79
Feilder/Fielder, Charles 159, 162–163;
Grace 159, 162–163
Field/Feild, Abram 46, 134–135, 167
Abraham Jr. 109; Ellenor [Rosser] 103;
Mary 134
Fitzhugh, Alce (Thornton) 71; John 71
Flagg, Henry 175
Fleet, Elizabeth 37; Henry Jr. 36–37, 39, 52, 58,
60, 70; Henry Sr. 36, 60, 153; Sarah 60
Flint/Flynt, Richard 147, 152–153, 155–156
Foster, Phillip 166; Robert 175; Seth 152
Foxhall, John Jr. 29, 51, 59, 132–134, 139, 168,
180, 186; John Sr. v, 21, 25–27, 29–30, 38, 45,
49–50, 52, 58, 132–135, 138, 168, 175;
Mary 135, 178, 186; mill 29, 35–36, 39, 50–51,
56, 58, 138; William 168
Frank (slave) 78
Frank(e), Frances 48, 65, 98;
Robert 48–49, 65, 98
Freake, Ann [Hayberd] 31, 52, 154;
Martha x, xvi, 52, 61, 83, 109, 154;
William x, xvi, 20, 23–24, 28, 31–32, 38,
45–46, 49, 52, 61, 69, 83, 89, 109, 146,
154–155, 176, 179–180
Freeman, Henry 164; Robert 164
Fryer, John 21, 30–31, 33–34, 51, 130,
137–138, 176; Rosamond 34, 137
Fairfax, Thomas Lord 41–42
Gaines, Thomas 128
Gammon, John 140
Gardener, Mary 7, 16, 90
Garland, William 140
Garnett, Ann/Nancy [Willis] 116, 127;
Anne [Willis] 126; Anthony 125, 128,185;
Elizabeth [Willis] 116, 125–126, 128;
Reuben 128
Gayle, George 176
Gerrard, Anne 136, 175; Frances 136, 175;

Gerrard (cont.), Justinian 154; Temperance 137,
141, 155, 175;Thomas 136, 148, 155, 175
Gibbert, Anne 158
Gibble, Richard 22, 156
Gibbs, James 124; Robert 154
Gibson, Alice [Catlett] 70; Jonathan Jr. 70;
Jonathan Sr. 40, 70; Margaret (Catlett) 70;
Rachel [Taylor] 70; Sarah 70
Gilbert, John 58; Sarah (Underwood) 58
Gillett, John 21
Glassell, John 119
Goddard, Charles 139; Edmund 142
Goff(e), Ann 64–65; John 64–65, 121;
Margaret 16, 56, 64–65, 92, 107, 122;
Martha 63–64; Robert 64; Sarah 64;
Thomas x, 16–17, 36–38, 41–43, 52–54, 56,
62–64, 68, 78, 92, 97, 102, 107–109, 111;
William 68, 81, 92
Good, Richard 141
Gordon, Elizabeth 184; John 184
Gorge, Alexander 139
Gotley/Gatley, Jane/Joanna [Pope] 136, 139,
169, 171; John 169; Richard 136, 169–170
Gowers, Arthur 141
Grame, John 123–124, 185
Grant, William 110
Gray, George 101
Green, Abigail (Triplett) 63, 95; Duff 183;
George 41, 63, 68, 80–81, 83, 92, 94–97;
John 43, 53, 57, 63, 81, 85–86, 95–97, 107;
Richard 97; Robert 99
Gregory, Elizabeth 178, 181, 188–189;
Frances 178, 188–190; Mildred 178–189;
Roger 178–179, 188
Griffin, David 156; Elizabeth viii; Francis viii;
Oliver viii, 132
Grymes, Benjamin 182; John 181–182
Gunstocker, Edmund (Ned the Indian) i, 26, 30,
37–38, 41, 47–48, 52–54, 62, 64–65, 67;
heirs 48, 53, 162; Mary 36, 38, 41–43, 47,
53–54, 56
Gwin, David 161, 170; Edmund 166; Walter 161
Hailes, Thomas 150–151
Halbert, Michael 98
Hallowes, John 19–20, 27, 46, 146, 155
Haney/Hany, Elizabeth 166; John 146,155–156;
Maximilian 166
Hannah (slave) 77
Hansbrough, Peter 192
Hansford, Tobias 164
Harbin, Ann 125
Hardidge/Hardridge, William 137, 169–170
Hardwick, James 133–134, 137; Joseph 133
Harly, Elisha 76–77; Elizabeth 76, 82
Harper, George 28; Margaret (Reeds) 28;
Harper, Samuel 28; Thomas Jr. 28;
Thomas Sr. 28, 50
Harris, William 134

Lee (cont.), Mary 153, 157, 181; Milly 192
Lendrum, Thomas 71
Lenton, Anthony 152–153
Lewis, Catherine (Daingerfield) 179;
   Charles 183, 187; David 163;
   Fielding, 178–179; George 179; John 176, 183,
   187; Mary Imogen (Green) 179; Mary Willis
   190; Mr. 151; Thomas 123–124;
   Zachary 96, 189
Lightfoot, John 124
Linto(n), Jno. 53
Lipton, Henry 160, 163; Joane 160, 163;
   John 160, 163; Mary 160, 163
Lisson, 52; Daniel 47, 135, 149, 177;
   Jane Lisson Butler 135; Robert 177
Littlefield, Joseph 68
Livingston, George 187
Locker/Lohier, Charles 139–140
Lord (Loyd?), John 176
Loyd, John 185
Lowrey, Rebecca 10
Loyd, John 170–171
Loyden, Wm. 157
Lunn/Lund, Christopher 105, 107, 110, 179
Lynn, Will 187
Mackay, Wm. 12–14, 50, 71
Madgwick, Avarilla 167; William 167
Madison, Ambrose 121, 182; Elizabeth [Willis]
   70, 121, 189; James 70, 189
Man, (?), Christopher 79
Manwering, Stephen 134
Marders, Jane 112; William 110
Markham, Lewis 136, 170, 175, 177
Marks, John 92, 118, 120, 123, 125; Mary 123
Marshall, Ann (Hudson?) 98; George 34, 44,
   60, 98; Hudson 98; John 29, 50;
   Martha (Sherwood) 98, 103; Merryman 98;
   Rush 98; Thomas 28–29, 98, 102;
   William 95–96, 98
Martiau, Nicholas 161
Mase/Moss, Agnes 132
Mason, Ann 54; Indian 38; Joseph 38;
   Josiah/Josias 35–37, 52, 54, 59, 61, 66
Matthews, Samuel 161
McCarty, Daniel 170
McCormick, John 71, 77, 108; Neal 66, 68, 93,
   95, 107–108
McCullough, James 185
McDonald, Sarah 77
McPherson, Archibald 14
Mercer, John 184
Meriwether, Nicholas 37; Thomas 170–171, 185
Middleton, Robert 157
Miller, Simon 124; Susannah 77
Millie (slave) 118
Milly (slave) 192
Minthorne, Charles 9
Minton, Elizabeth 177

Moore, Ann (Harbin?) 125; Francis 100, 121,
   125; Harbin 120, 125; Harbin Jr. 125;
   John 71; Thomas 69
Mordaunt, Lestrange 132
Morgan, Evan 36–38, 66, 81, 98
Morton, Elijah 120, 124; George 192;
   Jeremiah 124; John 87; William 123–124, 191
Moseley, Henry 146; Mary [Underwood] 55–56;
   William 69
Mottrom, John 148, 153
Munroe, Andrew 171
Murdock, Jeremiah 29, 44, 96, 111, 114–115,
   185; John 190; Joseph 15, 64, 67–68, 71
Naylor, John 125
Netherton, Henry 140
Neveyes, Edward 166; John 166; John Jr. 166
Newman, Robert 21, 146, 156
Newton, Thomas 81, 140–141
Niccols, John 60
Nicholas, Lewis xi, 46, 177
Nicholson, Margaret 160
Noell, Cornelius 80
Nolan, John 131
Norway, David 175
Nurse, Robert 21, 25–26, 28, 51
Offile, Mary 48, 60, 138, 142; William 48, 60,
   138–139, 142
Overett, William 131, 132, 156
Oxford (Hauxford?), John 98
Paine(?), John 138
Pannell, Sarah 124; William 124
Parker, John 133; Tho. 8, 106
Parrott, Tho. 2–3
Parsons, family 129; George 126; Jonathan 148;
   John (Parso) 152; John Jr. 39, 59–61, 80, 139;
   John Sr. 3, 18, 30, 35–36, 39–40, 43–44, 50,
   56, 58–61, 80
Patton, Robert 126, 191
Payne, Richard 15
Peal(e), Mallachy 36–37, 43, 63–64
Pellow, John 79
Pendleton, James 187
Perry, Micajah 71, 170–171, 185
Pettus, Thos. 161
Petty, Christopher 123; George 122; Jemima 122;
   John 123–124; John Jr. 125; Katherine 123;
   Rebecca 123; Thomas 120, 123
Petty's Mill Pond/Run 121, 128, 192
Peynon, Elizabeth 77
Peyton/Payton, Col. 131
Philpot(t), Barbara (Richards) 166;
   Rachel [Willis] 145–158; Thomas 145, 148,
   152–154, 156–157
Pierce/Peirce, Sarah (Underwood) 130, 157;
   William 130, 155–157
Piper, David 49; John 98; John Jr. 28, 49–50;
   John Sr. 21, 25–30, 45, 49–50;
   Margaret (Reeds) 28, 49

201

Spiller, David 147
Spillman, Clement 58; Thomas T. 59
Spotswood, Gov. Alexander 115, 123, 171,
184–185, 191; John 121, 128, 187;
Robert 115, 121, 183–187
Spycer/Spicer, Will 152
Stapp, John 127–128
Steele, John 139
Stephens, Ann 187; Joseph 187
Stone, Roger 151, 153
Strother, Anthony 182, 188; Benjamin Sr. 77;
James 115; Joseph 11–15, 82, 93,95, 110, 115;
Margaret (Thornton) 178; Thomas 86;
William 36, 66, 86, 178; William Jr. 93
Sturman, Richard 131–132
Such, Robert 152
Sutten, Rich. 157
Symons/Simmons, Francis 155–157;(Jane?)163;
Richard 163; Thomas 163–164
Taliaferro, Francis 1893 186, 192; Hay 191;
John 71, 170–171, 185, 188; John Jr. 186, 192;
Lawrence 70, 119, 186, 191; Lucy [Willis] 189;
Sarah (Thornton) 70; William 101
Tankard 37, 41, 56
Tankersly, Richard 93
Tanner, Thomas 40
Tavenors, Giles 164
Tayler, James 10; John 92
Taylor/Tayloe, Charles 34, 179; Edward 98,
105–106, 179–180; George 70, 87, 119–120,
189; John 98; Mary 33; Mr. 135;
Reuben T. 33; Thomas 186
Tebbs, Daniel 141
Temple, John 2–3
Terrill/Terrell, Edmund 101, 116, 118–119,
125–128, 185; Margaret/Peggy (Willis) 101,
116, 126, 192; Mary [Hudson] 116, 128;
Richmond 170; Robert 126, 128, 168, 191;
William 168
Thacher/Thatcher, Thomas 68, 95
Thacker, Henry 9, 17, 106; Matilda 9, 17, 106
Thom (slave) 118
Thomas, Elizabeth [Willis] 116, 127;
Oliver 2–3; Wm. 156
Thompson, Alexander 98, 102;
Samuel 176–177; William 176
Thornley, Aaron 94
Thornton, Alice (Savage) 69;
Ann [Anderson] 60;
Ann (—?—) Riding 29, 70;Anthony 70–71;
Elizabeth 71; Elizabeth (Catlett) 33, 70–71;
Elizabeth [Conway Gibson] 37, 40, 60, 70–71;
Elizabeth (Gregory) Willis 182, 188–189;
family xvi, 33, 69–72; Frances (Gregory) 179,
188–190;Francis 60, 70–72, 77, 83, 89, 94,
108, 111–112, 122, 125, 127;
Francis Sr. xvi, 25, 28–29, 31–33, 36–37, 50,
60–61, 66, 69–71, 80, 88, 93, 97, 112, 125,

Thornton (cont.), Francis Sr., 169–170, 178,
180, 188; Francis 179, 188–190;
John 183, 186, 188, 190; Luke 124;
Margaret [Strother] 70, 178;
Mildred (Gregory) 188–189; Presley 71;
Reuben 182, 188–189; Rowland xvi, 32–33,
69–70, 86, 93, 94, 112, 124;
Sarah [Taliaferro] 70; Susannah (Smith) 60;
Thomas 60; William xvi, 2, 15–17, 33–34, 44,
55, 69–72, 81, 83, 85; Winifred (Presley) 71
Tippett, Abigail [Green] 53; Ann [Donahoe] 53;
Catherine 53; Thomas xvi, 31–33, 35, 53, 56,
61–62, 69–70, 89, 93, 95, 102, 107, 170;
William 53, 62, 94–95
Tom (slave) 78
Triplett, John 15
Trussell, John 152–153
Turberville, Edward 14–15, 62–63, 65, 68, 82,
90, 95–96, 99–101, 103, 116–120,
121–122, 189; Elizabeth [Shropshire] 100;
George 100; Sarah 14–15, 62–63, 68, 82,
116–128, 189; William 100
Turnbridge, George 48
Turner, Harry 12, 44, 111, 115; Thomas 12, 14,
69, 82, 95, 98, 100, 110; Wm. 77
Tutt, Ann 125; James 29, 168; Mary 125;
Richard 8, 16, 29, 55, 58, 107, 125, 168
Underwood, family 55–58;
John 29, 58, 82, 168;
Margaret (Slaughter) 58;
Mary (Moseley?) 55–56; Sarah [Pierce] 157;
William 29–30, 35, 37, 41, 47, 51–52, 54–58,
61, 82, 102, 125
Vaughan, Alice (Crabb) 169; John 49
Vaulx, Elizabeth 168; James 29, 168;
Robert 48, 139–140, 168
Vawter, Bartholomew 80
Veale, Morris 131–132
Viccars, Jno. 59
Vincent, Elizabeth 147; Henry 152–153;
Martha [Freake] 31–32, 53, 61, 69, 89;
Robert xvi, 31–32, 53, 61–62, 69, 83, 89, 109,
154, 170; William 146–147, 155
Waddy, John 146–147, 153, 155
Waight, John 102
Walker, Charles 120; John 37, 60; Lt. Col. 161;
Richard 146; Robert 67; Robert Jr. 67;
Sarah 37, 60, 70; William 156
Waller, John 178, 184
Walllis, Humphrey 187
Walton, John 150
Ward, Samuel 142
Ware, Henry 77
Waring, Ella (Tayloe) 34; Thos. R. 34
Warner, Augustine 22, 176; Isabella 176;
Warner, Mildred [Washington] 176
Washington, Ann 176, 198; Ann (Pope) 20,
46, 175, 179; Ann [Wright] xvi, 20, 25, 31, 34,

204

www.ingramcontent.com/pod-product-compliance
Lightning Source LLC
Chambersburg PA
CBHW070906270326
41927CB00011B/2481